WORLD OF WISDOM

Your Passport To Living with More Passion, Purpose, and Pleasure

LORI & WILLIAM SMALL

WISDOM

Your Passport To Living with More Passion, Purpose, and Pleasure

BY
Lori & **William Small**

Copyright © 2025 Best Day Every Day, LLC
World of Wisdom
Your Passport To Living with More Passion, Purpose, and Pleasure

Published by Pierucci Publishing, P.O. Box 2074, Carbondale, Colorado 81623, USA

www.pieruccipublishing.com

Edited by Stephanie Pierucci
Cover design by Alana Newman

World of Wisdom Workbook: 978-1-962578-68-4
Ebook: 978-1-962578-69-1
Hardcover: 978-1-962578-74-5
Paperback: 978-1-962578-68-4

Library of Congress Control Number: 2025918937

Scripture marked (NKJV) taken from the New King James Version®. Copyright © 1982 by Thomas Nelson. Used by permission. All rights reserved.

All rights reserved. Except as permitted under the U.S. Copyright Act of 1976, no part of this publication may be reproduced, distributed, or transmitted in any form or by any means, or stored in a database or retrieval system without the prior written permission of the copyright owner. The scanning, uploading, and distribution of this book via the Internet or via any other means without the consent of the author is illegal and punishable by law. Thank you for purchasing only authorized electronic editions and for withdrawing your consent or approval for electronic piracy of copyrighted materials. Your support of the author's rights, as well as your own integrity, is appreciated.

Pierucci Publishing books may be purchased in bulk at special discounts for sales promotions, fundraising, or educational purposes. Special editions can be created to specifications. For details, contact the Special Sales Department, Pierucci Publishing, PO Box 2074, Carbondale, CO 81623, or Publishing@pieruccipublishing.com, or toll-free telephone at 1-855-720-1111.

PRAISE FOR
World of Wisdom

Being part of this book is an honor and a joy. Lori and William have a gift for turning everyday moments into something magical. Through our "salotto" nights, we've shared meals, laughter, and beautiful traditions that remind us what truly matters: friendship, connection, and living fully. Their passion for discovering the soul of a place and the people who bring it to life is what makes this book so special. It's not just a passport to the world; it's a passport to the heart. Happiness is real only when shared with people you love.
— *Spartaco Donati, Master Sommelier & Curator of Italian Hospitality*

The first time I had the opportunity to see Bill and Lori together, it was like two puzzle pieces finding their match—an effortless fit, perfectly in sync, as if the world had been waiting for that moment. Their appreciation for life is reflected in this book; they never let a precious moment pass by. The philosophy of our "salotto" nights has always been an expression of joy and connection, opening our hearts to anyone who wished to join in. With true love at its center, I'm deeply honored to be part of it.
— *Cristiano Labia, Master Sommelier, Chef & Ambassador of La Dolce Vita*

Live every day as if it were your last, because tomorrow is never guaranteed. As we grow older, that truth becomes even more important to remember. I often think of 9/11—so many people went to bed on 9/10 never knowing it would be their last night. It's a powerful reminder to embrace every day we're given.
— *Maria Wing, Global Traveler*

A lifetime of friendship with Lori has meant a lifetime of laughter, adventures and more stories than we could ever count. She has a way of turning ordinary days into extraordinary days!
— *Marian Kilpatrick, Community Connector*

For me, hospitality has always been about more than luxurious hotels or exquisite meals. It is about creating moments where happiness becomes tangible. Seeing Lori and William embrace this philosophy, both at Le Sereno in St. Barths and Il Sereno on Lake Como, has been deeply rewarding. They understand that la dolce vita is not only found in breathtaking destinations but can also be carried into everyday life. I am honored to have shared such meaningful experiences with them and to see their book bring this spirit of joy, purpose, and connection to a wider world.
— *Samy Ghachem, General Manager of Orient Express and Managing Director of Sereno Hotels, Shaping Icons in Hospitality and Real Estate Development*

Bill and Lori have captured something truly rare in The Joy of Travel—a reminder that travel is not just about movement through places, but expansion of the self. Their writing doesn't simply describe destinations; it reveals perspectives, emotions, and human connections that stay with you long after the journey ends. Each chapter is an invitation to live more fully, to notice more deeply, and to celebrate the art of being present wherever you are. This book is both a passport to adventure and a guide to living beautifully. A must-read for anyone who believes that the greatest journeys are the ones that change how we see the world—and ourselves.
— *Shailen Majithia, Friend, World Traveller, Curator of the Highest Experiences, and Rose Wine Enthusiast*

I wanted to let you know how much I enjoyed your book! It was validating—to me as a 43-year-old woman who quit her career for "quality of life." many of the practices you spoke about I have learned through dialectical behavior therapy/emotional intelligence studies. I also found it beautifully written, informative, and inspiring. Well done! I'm excited to share with my friends and families, with whom I know will benefit—and better them hearing it from you than me.
— *Lauren Boyer, Publishing professional*

DEDICATION

We express our deepest gratitude to the dozens of guides and muses who made this book possible. Your wisdom, generosity, and insights have transformed our lives into the Best Day Every Day. Through your stories, teachings, and support, you've helped us - and our readers - see the world in new, profound ways. Thank you for sharing your unique perspectives and for lighting the way to a life of purpose, passion, and joy.

Your guidance has unlocked the doors to deeper confidence, greater resilience, and more fulfilling lives for everyone who takes this journey. This book is as much yours as it is ours, and we are forever grateful. Here's to you, our muses and mentors, for making every day the Best Day Ever.

YOUR GUIDES

Alberto Galassi, Saint Tropez, France
"A Mysterious Parisienne Woman," Paris, France
Arrigo Cipriani, Venice, Italy
Captain Sergey Tunikov, The Strait of Malacca, Malaysia
Charlie Monger, Omaha, Nebraska, USA
Cristiano Labia and Spartaco Donati, Rome, Italy
Dr. May Baselton, Bangkok, Thailand
Dr. Steven Gundry, Namale Resort, Savusavu, Fiji
Dominic Augustine, Mansfield, Ohio, USA
Geoffry Gertz, New York City, NY, USA
Giulio Marconi, Taormina, Sicily, Italy
Hattie Bickmore, Washington, D.C., USA
John Finamore, Ho Chi Minh City, Hanoi, and Hoi An, Vietnam
Julian Torres Rizo, Havana, Cuba
Kenn and Pamela Ricci, Santorini, Greece
Marc Rueckle, "La La La," Mykonos, Greece
Loren Lahav, Namale Resort, Savusavu, Fiji
Massimo Piccin, Bolgheri, Italy
Peter Farina, Molise, Italy
Peyman Umay, Istanbul, Turkey
President Ronald Reagan, Washington, D.C., USA
"The Islander," Toberua Island, Fiji
Ray Dalio, Davos, Switzerland
Samy Ghachem, St. Barths, F.W.I. & Lake Como, Italy
Satish Kapoor, New Delhi, India

Shailen Majithia, Monte Carlo, Monaco
Sister Maria Di Benedetto, Varanasi, India
Sofia Rossi, Florence, Italy
Stefan Heinen, Mykonos, Greece
"The Future William & Lori," Santorini, Greece
Tony Robbins, Gold Coast of Australia
Vivienne Bell, New York City, NY, USA
Warren Buffett, Omaha, Nebraska, USA
Weems Westfeldt, Aspen, Colorado, USA
William U. Small, Presque Isle, Maine, USA
Young Lori Augustine, Mansfield, Ohio, USA
Young William Small, Presque Isle, Maine, USA

PUBLISHER'S NOTE

The experiences and encounters described in this book are inspired by real events, though certain details, locations, and timelines have been adapted for storytelling purposes. Some names have been changed to protect privacy, while others remain true to the individuals who shaped our journey. The guides and people mentioned reflect real encounters, even when aspects of their identities have been respectfully obscured.

This work is presented as a personal narrative and should not be construed as medical, health, or professional advice. The authors and publisher expressly disclaim any responsibility for any adverse effects resulting from the reader's application or interpretation of information contained herein.

Readers are encouraged to consult qualified healthcare professionals before adopting any practices described in these pages. Our story is offered as inspiration rather than prescription.

TABLE OF CONTENTS

Praise For World of Wisdom	v
Dedication	vii
Your Guides	ix
Publisher's Note	xi
Prologue	1
Introduction: The Untold Truth Of Personal Development	5

Part One: Your Mission
Chapter 1: From Law Library to the White House	15
Chapter 2: Become The Writer, Producer, and Director of Your Life	25
Chapter 3: Remodeling Your Brain	41
Chapter 4: Leadership & Confidence	55

Part Two: Staging Happiness
Chapter 5: A Case For Beauty	73
Chapter 6: Happiness Is Your Birthright	85
Chapter 7: No Rearview Mirrors	107

Part Three: Micro Purpose
Chapter 8: Cultivating Your Community	119
Chapter 9: Health is Wealth	133
Chapter 10: Never Work A Day in Your Life	153
Chapter 11: Securing Your Financial Future	167

Part Four: Macro Purpose

Chapter 12: Will It Affect You Six Months From Now? — 193
Chapter 13: Your True Love is Out There Somewhere — 203
Chapter 14: Nobody Manifests Their Best Life In Crocs — 213

Part Five: Celebrating Your New Life

Chapter 15: Become A Magnet For Abundance — 233
Chapter 16: Enjoying Culture and Great Works of Mankind — 255
Chapter 17: The Joy of Travel — 263
Chapter 18: How To Live In A Beautiful State Every Day — 273
Chapter 19: Find Joy in the Journey, Not Just the Destination — 279
Chapter 20: Lessons From Our Fathers — 285
Conclusion — 291

A Poem For My Dad By Lori Small — 295
Appendix A: Resources For Confidence Training Further Study — 297
Lectures/ Webinars/ Talks — 300
Notes — 301

PROLOGUE

Welcome to *World of Wisdom: Your Passport to Living with More Passion, Purpose, and Pleasure.*

Let's ask you something—what if you could wake up every single day feeling alive, energized, and completely in love with your life? Not just when you're on vacation. Not just when things are going your way. But every single day—regardless of the circumstances.

That's what this book is about. Not just having "the best day ever" as a rare, lucky moment—but intentionally creating a life where every day holds the potential for passion, purpose, and joy. Because while this book is titled *World of Wisdom*, at its heart, it's about living your Best Day Every Day—not as a fleeting idea, but as a repeatable, sustainable way of life. No magic wands—just proven strategies that work

We know what you might be thinking: That sounds great, but what about real life? What about when responsibilities pile up, when the car breaks down, when stress takes over? What about when I'm not in Aspen sipping cocktails, but knee-deep in caregiving, deadlines, or daily chaos?

Here's the truth: those are the exact moments when the Best Day Every Day philosophy matters most. Life isn't about avoiding challenges—it's about mastering them.

Look, this book isn't going to gaslight you into thinking that just because you read it, everything will magically transform overnight. If you're hoping to manifest a life of effortless luxury while sitting in your pajamas, cutting pictures out of magazines, you're in for a wake-up call.

We think *The Secret* is inspiring, well-marketed, and yes—it gets some things right. But even one of its most famous authors said, "The law of attraction is nothing without action." The universe rewards action.

We've seen it firsthand. We've faced financial struggles, business challenges, and personal loss. We've broken down on an icy road in Aspen, navigated career pivots, and had moments where everything seemed to fall apart. But time and again, we've trained ourselves to reset, reframe, and reclaim our day—because we refuse to let life happen to us.

And that's precisely what this book delivers: a proven strategy for creating an extraordinary life, no matter where you are or what you're facing.

Best Day Every Day Is a Game Anyone Can Win

The *World of Wisdom* game isn't just for the lucky few who hit the jackpot, inherit wealth, or stumble into success. It's not about privilege, luck, or waiting for the stars to align. It's about perspective, strategy, and intentional action.

We've spent decades traveling, learning, and studying the world's most extraordinary minds, uncovering the secrets to living with passion, purpose, and pleasure—every single day. Inside these pages, you'll meet the guides and muses who have shaped our philosophy. Each one holds a key to unlocking more confidence, energy, financial freedom, and deeper relationships. They'll show you what's possible—not just in theory, but in practice.

But let's get one thing straight—this isn't about doing more. It's about choosing better.

The Truth About What Really Works

Too many books promise "the easy way" to a better life. Let's be real—we're not easily invested in easy. We're committed to efficacy. We know the *World of Wisdom* blueprint works because we've spent decades testing and refining it. It works for people who already have strong habits and for those who are brand new to personal development.

Instead of giving you a checklist of things to do, we'll show you exactly what we did—step by step, through a collection of powerful, real-life experiences. We'll introduce you to the people who embody these principles so you can see what's possible. Whether you're single, married, raising small children, or empty-nesting, there's something in these pages that will shift your mindset, rewire your approach to life, and get you playing the game at a higher level.

That said, Best Day Every Day isn't about saying yes to everything. That's a one-way ticket to burnout. Sometimes, the most powerful thing you can do is say no to the obligations, distractions, and energy drains that pull you away from your highest potential.

The Best Chapter of Your Life Is Just Beginning

If you'd have held up a crystal ball and told us 10, 15, or even 30 years ago that we'd find our greatest happiness and fulfillment in our forties and fifties, we probably would have laughed in disbelief.

And yet, here we are—not just deeply fulfilled in our relationship, but completely in love with life itself.

But the kind of love we're talking about isn't just about a romantic relationship. Over the coming pages, you'll learn how we became lovers of life. Like many of you, we weren't born with silver spoons. In fact, this book will detail the exact roadmap we used to MacGyver our way from humble beginnings to a life that literally everyone wants.

The good news? You don't need a trust fund, a lucky break, or the perfect circumstances to make this happen for yourself. You just need a willingness to step up and take control of your life. This book is an extensive, battle-tested guide designed to reshape your vision, unlock your potential, and give you the tools to create the life you've always wanted.

Translation? You can live your Best Day Every Day.

This mindset shift allows you to:

- ✓ Turn the ordinary into extraordinary
- ✓ Transcend the mundane
- ✓ Eliminate "boring" and "good" from your vocabulary
- ✓ Brim with purpose, passion, and profound fulfillment

So let us ask you this:

Do you dare to transcend the ordinary?

Once you answer this question affirmatively, allow your body to sit with the integration of that permission. You have given yourself the green light to peer into the depths of your aspirations and contemplate the possibilities that lie beyond the confines of conventionality.

For those who refuse to settle for mediocrity and yearn to dream beyond the boundaries of conventional living, *World of Wisdom* emerges as more than a guide—it becomes a steadfast companion on your journey toward creating extraordinary days. Within the pages that follow, anticipate a transformative odyssey that not only reveals the secrets to cultivating exceptional days but also ensures that you seize and cherish life's most fulfilling moments with intention and gratitude.

One of our best days, captured forever.
Scan the code to watch our wedding video on YouTube.

Introduction:
THE UNTOLD TRUTH OF PERSONAL DEVELOPMENT

It's actually pretty easy to write a book about personal improvement or self-development. We have invested thousands of hours jet-setting across the world to personal development conferences, even having sit-down meetings with some of the most renowned personal development "gurus" on the planet, including Tony Robbins, whose company we enjoyed on several occasions around the world.

As Platinum Partners in Tony Robbins' exclusive program for personal and professional growth, we were introduced to places unlike any we had ever seen and engaged with some of the greatest masters of emotion and fulfillment the world has to offer. Tony provided an entirely new perspective on our lives.

At "Unleash the Power Within," Tony Robbins' signature firewalk is the kickoff experience on day one, and it's electrifying. Picture thousands of participants gathered at dusk, ready to walk across a bed of hot coals—a vivid test of mental strength, where mindset shapes experience. Robbins and his team guide us through focused breathing techniques, calming any jitters, and fueling our confidence. The walk is more than just an adrenaline rush; it's a powerful breakthrough, an act of leaving fears behind to embrace new possibilities.

The atmosphere was electric. Surrounded by others facing their own doubts, you feel part of something extraordinary, and that energy shifts your own inner limitations. For me (Lori), it's a reminder of how much growth lies just beyond our comfort zones. Later that weekend, a fellow coach at the conference—a high-powered executive drained from endless demands—confided in me, "What's your secret, Lori? I feel stuck." Despite her success, she felt like she was on autopilot, with days filled with obligations but no personal fulfillment. It was a cycle of exhaustion and burnout, and she felt like she was barely keeping afloat.

Listening to her, I felt a deep sense of empathy; I've been there myself.

I shared my journey of rediscovery, how self-care and setting boundaries can reignite passion, even when you feel drained. She finally felt understood and ready to reclaim her life. That's the magic of the firewalk, not just the act itself but the inspiration it sparks in everyone there. We left with our hearts on fire, knowing we're capable of so much more.

"You know, Rachel, this is my secret. I approach each day as a balance of movement and exploration, both physically and mentally. Just as travel broadens the mind, training strengthens the body, and together, they create a life of vitality and discovery."

This book mirrors that journey, guiding you through life's lessons with stories that inspire both growth and adventure. We, Lori and William, are your captains. We will navigate your course, steering toward a myriad of exotic destinations where you'll taste, smell, hear, and see the events and guides who've impacted our lives from Washington D.C. to New York City and Paris to Milan, and even Udaipur, India.

Why have we structured the book in this manner? You see, there's a principle in science called "neuroplasticity;" it's the science of rewiring neural pathways in the mind. Our intention in this book is to help thrust you into a neuroplastic state of readiness. As we guide you through the exotic locations in this book and into the embrace of several dozen guides who've illuminated the Best Day Every Day lifestyle for us, you'll actually be training your brain in a sophisticated way! In some ways, you can absolutely change your life from your pajamas; that's maybe why you picked up this book.

However, the higher intention is to deliver you out of the ordinary, quotidian of your daily life, where you may be plagued with the unextraordinary. Before picking up this book, you may have found yourself trapped in "Groundhog Day," experiencing feelings of sadness or monotony. By embracing the principle of neuroplasticity, you can transform your unfulfilled life into something new.

When we first set out on the journey, William had visions of this book being as effective a tool as something by Louise Hay or Dr. David E. Hawkins, but with the wonder and excitement of the classic *Around The World In Eighty*

Days, one of William's favorite books as a child, where the protagonist travels from London east through Europe, Asia, and North America back to London in, as you might have guessed, eighty days. Mind you, in the late 1800s, there were no planes nor fast cars (or vehicles that weren't attached to horses, for that matter), and travel by boat could be slow. Certainly, there were no electronic ticket apps. That said, traveling around the world in eighty days wasn't merely a feat of logistics, but, at the time, nothing short of miraculous. And, too, the book is a blend of realistic stories with a touch of magic.

William remembers reading this imaginative tale of an otherwise boring man who lived a life that was predictable down to the minute. There wasn't a clock that was one second off, nor a fireplace that burned a moment past the second English gentleman Phileas Fogg chose for it to burn. When Fogg first embarks on the journey, his brand new assistant "Passepartout" was shocked that this ordinary, regimented, and almost cripplingly punctual new employer was making himself vulnerable to a thousand unreliable factors on the journey from departure times on trains, boats, and even elephants to his own physical capacity to travel (often on foot) from one location to the next.

Fogg's whimsical journey stuck with William. He determined that, one day, when he penned the "Best Day Every Day" blueprint, it would, too, be whimsical, exciting, exotic, and unforgettable. When authors such as Dr. Bruce Lipton and Dr. Joe Dispenza popularized neuroplasticity, Lori and William sat up many nights. They dreamed together of how they could at once entertain readers with the lessons in this book while progressively thrusting their audience into the advanced practice of neuroplastic rewiring of the mind. Lori used Rachel as an avatar for her readers and wondered how she could radically impact the life of just that one woman so that she could one day impact and inspire you, too.

Without getting too scientific, a core tenet of this book is rewiring your ordinary life into the extraordinary through brain science. Although our own publisher has published many books about the brain and personal development, she has never seen another author create such a unique self-help approach. *World of Wisdom* contains a yin and yang balance of travel and training. Each chapter allows you to travel to an exotic place with Lori and William as your captains and many other remarkable and fascinating people as your guides. To engage another critical component of this brain training, you'll then exercise your mind muscles with additional training in the form of worksheet-style challenges in the supplemental *World of Wisdom Workbook*. We highly recommend you purchase a copy for yourself, your partner, your children, and your friends. Remember, one of the most important tenets of your Best Day Every Day lifestyle is to cultivate a community of like-minded souls around you who transcend the bonds of normal friendship and become your partners in a spiritual mission to make each day truly, deeply satisfying. Part Three of this book will underscore the importance of a supportive, high-vibrational community.

Some of the core science of neuroplasticity is tied to the technique of changing your physical environment to rewire your brain, or your "mind environment." As children, we learn how to interact with our families or within a workplace. Mannerisms, language, and even feelings for survival are installed or "wired" into our subconscious minds. When we experience trauma, we also wire our minds to cope with or adapt to that trauma, such as an abusive parent or injury.

Many people who aspire to an extraordinary life often choose to read a hundred books and meditate for thousands of hours, yet they may never break free from negative or stuck patterns. Knowing this, we chose to guide you through this book to help you change your environment, making it easier to change your brain. That is why we have chosen to teach through travel. As you enter each room or city street around the world, you are transported to a fertile ground for neuroplasticity.

World travel isn't critical for rewiring the brain. In fact, you can begin shaking up subconscious patterns today. Let's take your daily commute. Pretend you drive eastbound out of your condominium complex and head north on a main highway. You notice a billboard or mural. Then you head West on another two-lane road for a defined set of miles. You see the same stores, you look at the same steering wheel. You may even subconsciously change lanes in the exact same spots, or take the same line or trajectory with your vehicle in the exact same places.

If you take a different route, you inevitably think different thoughts. You see new colors, signs, or trees. You made different turns or lane changes. You might drastically alter the time of arrival (hopefully not causing you to be too late).

World of Wisdom is your new route to your desired destination. The stories have been designed to help you think new thoughts or to take subjects such as "mindfulness" or "gratitude" and think about them with new stories and characters that will help cement the lessons. We've invested decades into decoding this Best Day Every Day blueprint, and we are now ready for you to experience the same delicious flow in your life, too. We don't just tell you what to do; we show you how it's done, regardless of your age, wealth, or location.

There are various ways we'll disrupt your patterns throughout these stories to help you shift out of your old ways of thinking (and doing) and embrace a more extraordinary life, replacing what may be ordinary, dull, mundane, or even depressing. Best of all, you don't have to delve into a scientific workbook to understand brain science or neuroplasticity to benefit from the Best Day Every Day blueprint.

1. **Exposure to new experiences,** which challenge the brain to adapt and learn, promotes the formation of new synaptic connections.

2. **Sensory stimulation** in a new environment, which can activate different neural pathways, enhancing synaptic plasticity (plasticity in the brain means mobility or the ability to change, in this case, improve).

3. **Cognitive Challenges** in new environments require learning new information or skills, stimulate the brain's learning and memory centers, and lead to structural changes in the brain.

4. **Engagement in Complex Activities:** This book challenges you to engage in a range of activities, from personal style choices to financial investments, to promote dendritic spine growth, synapse location, and enhanced connectivity, thereby solidifying or consecrating the new connections formed during the **Training** portion of each chapter.

5. **Stress.** That's right, moderate levels of stress (not chronic stress) are actually going to help you change your brain to change your life.

That's because adapting to a new environment releases cortisol. In controlled amounts, this can enhance learning and memory.

6. **Coping Mechanisms.** Although you may experience some stress from the changes in your environment that come with traveling and training with us throughout this book, we will gently guide you in developing coping mechanisms that strengthen the neural circuits involved in stress regulation and resilience.

7. **Physical Activity.** Lori is a fit and fabulous personal trainer in her fifties with a physique, stride, and a bounce in her step that every woman we meet longs for. New environments encourage exploration and physical activity, which has been shown to promote neurogenesis (the growth of new neurons). Not only will we guide you to move into new environments physically, but also to begin engaging in increased mindfulness and discipline in your bodily exploration; even if that means picking up your resume and walking door to door looking for new professional employment, or committing to a "burpees challenge" as you read the book.

8. **Social Interaction** in a new environment can stimulate cognitive functions and emotional regulation, contributing to neuroplasticity. It's been said that you are the sum of your five closest friends. That said, you might find that reading *World of Wisdom* compels you to spend a little less time with the people who are promoting an ordinary life or sabotaging your growth.

In short, by challenging the brain to adapt to new conditions, a change of environment can facilitate the development of new neural connections, strengthen existing ones, and improve overall cognitive function. The process of challenging your brain to think about living your Best Day Every Day won't be all work; the **Travels** portion of each chapter will be so enjoyable that even if you're consuming this book during the eve of your life from a comfortable armchair, you will be transported into a world of imagination, whim, beauty, culture, adventure, and provocation that will satisfy any itch to simply read a "good book." However, suppose you picked up this book as a lifeline because you don't want to remain stuck in an ordinary life that falls short of an intoxicating purpose. In that case, you'll find that the exhilarating **Travels** will be best paired with action through the **Training** sections in your *World of Wisdom Workbook*.

WHY TRAVEL?

Experiencing diverse places and cultures worldwide fuels joy through the satisfaction of intellectual and emotional refinement. Although we may cherish home, the perspective gained from exploring the globe goes beyond what can be achieved through watching TV, movies, or reading books, magazines, and newspapers. Stepping onto the plaza of the Taj Mahal in India, sipping rosé at "Club 55" in St. Tropez, sailing through the Fiji Islands, wandering amid the ruins of the Roman Empire, skiing the Vallée Blanche in Chamonix, France, strolling through the halls of the Louvre in Paris, or observing African wildlife on safari in South Africa are just glimpses of what awaits travelers. No substitutes exist for immersion in such situations.

In the years we've spent together, we've extensively traveled through Europe and embarked on significant journeys through Asia, Australia, the South Pacific, Central America, and South America. Our travels are meticulously documented on our website, https://bestdayeveryday.com/. The more we explore different corners of the world, the stronger our passion to discover new places grows. Sharing travel experiences with fellow enthusiasts is a comforting and enjoyable aspect of our journeys.

Beyond the physical act of traveling, another shared passion is the research and planning of remarkable trips. Having a curiosity about unfamiliar places and delving into those we've enjoyed in the past is essential. When planning trips to beloved destinations like Paris and Rome, we take pleasure in uncovering new areas and neighborhoods to explore. The joy of researching destinations and crafting fabulous itineraries, including finding exceptional places to stay, identifying noteworthy attractions, dining at extraordinary restaurants, enjoying cocktails at iconic bars, and immersing ourselves in the local culture, is truly gratifying. We relish leaving our own cultural perspectives at the door, forging understanding, compassion, and appreciation for people who have developed in different environments than the ones that shaped and molded us.

As we embark on this profound exploration, we invite you to join us on a quest to unlock the full potential of your life and turn your dreams into a vibrant, lived reality. Each chapter encourages you to celebrate every moment, embrace change, and see problems as opportunities for growth. Life is not a scripted play; instead, it's an improvisational act where you are the writer, producer, and director of your own extraordinary story.

Our exploration into the purpose of life takes us on a journey of happiness as a central theme. Chapters guide you on the path to making happiness your job, celebrating life as a continuous party, and becoming an achiever of enjoyment. Life is meant to be lived with boundless joy, and *World of Wisdom* provides insights and strategies to infuse your days with fulfillment and happiness - to live your Best Day Every Day.

All aboard!

Part One:

YOUR MISSION

Chapter One:
FROM LAW LIBRARY TO THE WHITE HOUSE

"William, the only limit to your achievement
is your own imagination and commitment.
Your ability to articulate your thoughts will open doors.
Stay true to your principles, and they will take you far."
President Ronald Reagan to William Small

*

"When you don't know where you're going,
any road will take you there."
Alice in Wonderland

WILLIAM'S STORY

On a picturesque spring afternoon in Washington, D.C., during late March, the cherry blossoms were in full bloom around the Tidal Basin, creating a breathtaking backdrop to the Jefferson Memorial. I was, that afternoon, a guest at the White House. Not just the White House, but a guest of the President himself.

On this Friday afternoon, I found myself standing on the White House South Portico, gazing over the Rose Garden with a glass of champagne in hand, accompanied by my good friend Gordan.

In the distance, the Presidential helicopter, Marine One, approached the landing pad on the South Lawn. A few minutes after it touched down, President Ronald Reagan and his wife, Nancy, emerged from beneath the South Portico, strolling towards the waiting helicopter. Midway across the lawn, President Reagan turned and waved to us on the South Portico, prompting a reciprocal toast with our glasses of champagne.

Gordan, the youngest member of the Republican National Committee, and I, the former Executive Director and current legal counsel of the Maine Republican Party, had just attended a two-hour reception hosted by President Reagan and the First Lady. This marked the first such gathering for the

Republican National Committee since Reagan's 1980 landslide victory over President Jimmy Carter.

During those two hours, we engaged in conversation with the President, the First Lady, Republican Party leaders, and various White House staff members. While I had previously met Ronald Reagan and his wife during the 1980 campaign and inauguration in my capacity as Executive Director of the Maine Republican Party, standing that afternoon on the South Portico, watching Marine One depart for Camp David, felt surreal. I had come a long way in a few short months.

Two Hours Earlier: Clinking Glasses at The White House

Hattie Bickmore, the Chairwoman of the Maine Republican State Committee, walked across the Main Entrance Hall of the White House with a sense of confidence and relaxation few can match. She was one of the most recognizable people in the Republican Party leadership, a large but attractive blonde with a big personality and stature; more of a Marilyn Monroe than a Melania Trump, to be sure. Her commanding demeanor, confidence, and magnetic personality made her known by everybody from the President to the remaining ranks in the White House simply as "Hattie." She was continually surrounded by people who wanted to talk to her. At this White House Republican National Committee reception, it was no different. She held court surrounded by committee members, senators, members of Congress, and members of the administration, all waiting for President and Nancy Reagan to arrive at the reception. Hattie Bickmore is our first "World of Wisdom Muse."

The reception took place on the White House State Floor. The State Floor is the main event floor at the White House, which includes the Main Entrance Hall, East Room, State Dining Room, the East Room, Red Room, Blue Room, and Green Room. The Floor has a jaw-dropping presence that few, if any, buildings can match.

The State Floor invites a sense of history, power, and understated elegance combined with a faint fragrance of authority and refinement. Everything is meticulously maintained, including the ceremonial guards stationed around the floor.

My friend Gordon and I couldn't believe we had access to so much square footage of the White House. Being our first time there, we moved from room to room, attempting to look as though we'd been there before with stoic faces masking our schoolboy grins that would have been more authentic. With no President yet in sight, we helped ourselves to a tray of delicate finger foods served by an army of impeccably dressed servers. As I grabbed one of the delicacies, I noticed that the small white napkin handed to me by a waiter was embroidered with the Presidential seal, a symbol of prestige and honor. I wanted to keep it forever, but chose to stuff it in my memory rather than my pocket.

I helped myself to another sip of the fruity and invigorating sparkling wine. The swig may have appeared as if it were meant to beg for courage, because just then, I felt the reassuring grip of Hattie's hand on my shoulder. The gesture of support and confidence illustrated to me that not only was she magnetic, but also empathetic. I remembered in that moment that she wasn't just an accomplished, high-profile GOP Chairwoman, but a mother, too.

Hattie was an inspiration for me. When she was in her late 20s, she witnessed her beloved husband, the father of her three infant children, drown in front of her in a tragic boating accident. She also experienced the loss of an infant child shortly after childbirth. Despite her personal tragedies, Hattie was upbeat and jovial with a good sense of humor. After her husband's death, she had to go to work to support her young family. She gravitated to the world of politics, working in the Congressman's office for the 1st district of Maine. She worked her way up through the Republican Party apparatus to become the Chairman of the Maine Republican Party and one of the leaders of the party nationally. Hattie was one of my mentors and showed me what was possible when you have a goal and are willing to work toward it. She told me on my first day on the job as the Executive Director of the Maine Republican State Committee, "I'm not sure where this will lead us, but you are about to experience something that will change your life and the trajectory of your career. You're going to meet people that you never thought were possible to meet." She was right on all counts. I realized at a young age that anything is possible if you have the right mindset. Hattie was a living example of what's possible.

The chatter of small talk, accompanied by the elegant background sound of music from the White House string quartet, filled the air. But suddenly, a hush came over the room as President and Nancy Reagan entered the East

CHAPTER ONE: FROM LAW LIBRARY TO THE WHITE HOUSE

Room. The entire audience erupted into applause. The President and Mrs. Reagan navigated the reception, greeting friends and party members in a slow parade. President Reagan stopped when he saw Hattie and me, and then slowly headed in our direction.

President Reagan exuded confidence and charisma that few can match. As he grew closer, he reached out to shake my hand and Hattie's as well. With a humble greeting, he said, "I want to thank you both for your help in the campaign. We couldn't have been successful without people like you." After a few minutes of chit-chat, the President turned to me and said, "William, the only limit to your achievement is your own imagination and commitment. Your ability to articulate your thoughts will open doors. Stay true to your principles, and they will take you far."

"Thank you, Mr. President," I replied. "It was a great honor to be part of your Presidential campaign, and I look forward to helping you, however possible, to make sure your administration is highly successful."

A member of the President's security personnel reminded him, "Mr. President, we need to keep to the schedule."

He kindly replied, "Of course. William, keep up the fantastic work. You're going places."

With a nod to the security personnel's reminder of his schedule, President Reagan bade farewell, leaving me with a renewed sense of purpose and gratitude for this unforgettable afternoon at the heart of American power and history.

Shortly thereafter, the President and First Lady left the reception to prepare to travel to Camp David for the weekend. My friend Gordan and I continued exploring the main floor of the White House and worked our way to the South Portico balcony. Marine and security guards littered the lawn as the President and First Lady made their way to Marine One, nodding at us and a few others on the balcony from the lawn as he saluted the Marine guard at the bottom of the stairway leading into Marine One.

"Can you believe we're here, William?" Gordon asked.

"It's not by accident, my friend." With a final clink of our glasses, we took one last gulp of the sparkling wine and one last run of the White House. That afternoon, as we exited the White House, I thought of a lifetime of outstanding possibilities before me.

The Road to Presidential Hobnobbing

So, how did I get invited by the President to the White House that March afternoon? My journey started twenty months earlier. It was late summer in 1979, and I had just spent three months studying for and passing the Maine bar exam. I decided one day to stop by our local congressman's office in Portland, Maine, to say hello to my friend and mentor Hattie Bickmore. Hattie had just become the Chairman of the Maine Republican Party. Hattie invited me to lunch, and after catching up, asked me if I had any plans after I passed the bar. I told her that I would likely look for a job with a law firm in the Portland area. She surprised me when she said, "How would you like to become the next Executive Director of the Republican Party?" I realized what a great opportunity that would be and accepted her offer.

In a few months from being a lowly law student, spending my days studying in the corner of the library at the Seattle University Law School, I was now thrust into the spotlight meeting and hanging out with high-ranking political celebrities from former Presidents like Gerald Ford to candidates running for President in 1980, such as the former Governor of California Ronald Reagan and Ambassador George Bush, Sr. At one point, I even met and gave Henry Kissinger a ride from the Portland Airport to a fundraising banquet where he was the keynote speaker.

During my two years as Executive Director of the Maine Republican Party, I was instrumental in organizing the party's 1980 campaigns for the President, Congress, and control of the Maine State Legislature.

During that time, I spent a lot of time in Washington, D.C., attending numerous national Republican National Committee meetings. In the summer of 1980, I attended the 1980 Republican National Convention in Detroit as the Maine delegation's aide on the floor of the Convention.

After a successful 1980 campaign, I resigned my post as the Executive Director of the Maine Republican State Committee. I joined a major law firm as a lobbyist in the Maine Legislature, quickly gaining a reputation for my sharp mind and persuasive arguments. As a lobbyist for key issues in the state legislature, I skillfully navigated the political landscape. I earned the respect of my peers, which led to my appointment as legal counsel to the Maine Republican State Committee.

As time went on, I caught the eye of influential figures in Washington, D.C., leading to invitations to attend events in D.C., including events at the White House, where I interacted with members of the administration and the President.

What if life could be exceptionally good, excellent, magnificent, fantastic, superlative, exceptional, first-rate, great, terrific, tremendous, amazing, sensational, fabulous, awesome, brilliant, remarkable, extraordinary, memorable, and out of this world? That's the definition of outstanding, and we're living proof that if it's possible for us, it's achievable for you, too. What if you didn't believe in making the impossible possible, because the word "impossible" didn't enter your vocabulary in the first place?

William at age 21 launching his campaign for the Maine Legislature.

As a college junior at the University of Maine, I attended a debate among three candidates running for Governor of Maine. The event inspired me, and that evening I had an epiphany that I should get involved in politics. I enjoyed history, leadership, and the challenge of solving complex social problems. This led to my decision to run for the Maine State Legislature at the young age of 21.

Although I lost that race for the legislature by twenty-one votes in a closely watched recount, I impressed several high-ranking officials in the Maine Republican Party. I was invited to join the Maine Republican State Committee, the party's governing council, as its youngest member at the time.

Since then, I've spent over three decades visualizing and pursuing what others call the impossible. However, with the power of my mind set to specific intentions through visualization, confidence, and proactive work, I decided at a young age that the word "impossible" would no longer be a part of my vocabulary.

Outstanding Life

What does it mean to live an outstanding life? The word "outstanding" is commonly used to describe something remarkable or exceptional in some way. It can refer to a variety of qualities or attributes, including excellence, talent, performance, or achievement. For example, an outstanding student is one who consistently excels in their academic pursuits, while an outstanding athlete is someone exceptional at their chosen sport. I decided to be outstanding as a law student when I spent my nights huddled in the corner of the law school library instead of partying and fraternizing like many of my peers.

The term "outstanding" can also be used to describe something outstanding in terms of its uniqueness or importance, such as an outstanding piece of art or an outstanding contribution to a field of study. In short, it is often used to describe something that stands out from the ordinary or average and is recognized for its exceptional qualities.

Many of us seek to be outstanding in our careers, sports, or other endeavors. We'll attend college to get educated and get a degree in the field we think we want to pursue as a career. We'll attend graduate school to further enhance our knowledge of a particular subject or acquire the skills necessary to be outstanding in our careers. After our formal education, we continue

CHAPTER ONE: FROM LAW LIBRARY TO THE WHITE HOUSE

to learn and gain experience in our chosen profession, in hopes of becoming outstanding in what we do.

How often do we think of applying those same principles to creating an outstanding life?

Outstanding can mean different things to different people. Everyone has different passions and ideas about what makes them happy and feel like their life is special. An outstanding life also consists of developing skills that all have to work together in concert to produce the outstanding results we're trying to achieve. Each of us must determine what our outstanding life looks like and develop the skills that will create our personal vision of an outstanding life. So, what are those skills, and how do we create them? Reflecting on my journey to the White House that day, I remembered being a twenty-five-year-old law student just twelve months earlier, spending most of my days in the corner of the Seattle University Law School library. Two years earlier, in the spring of 1979, my aspirations were significant. Still, the idea of attending White House receptions and discussing politics with the President seemed beyond the realm of possibility, until I chose to take "impossible" out of my vocabulary. As I stood there that afternoon overlooking the South Lawn of the White House, I recalled all the events that took me from law student to guest at the White House.

> *A summer studying for the bar exam;*
> *A pivotal lunch with a mentor who was Chairman of the Maine Republican State Committee;*
> *My appointment as the youngest Executive Director of the Maine Republican Party.*
> *Encounters with luminaries like Henry Kissinger, George H.W. Bush, and Barbara Bush;*
> *Sharing a speaking platform with future President George W. Bush;*
> *Mingling with political heavyweights like Senator George Mitchell;*
> *Participating in the 1980 Republican National Convention in Detroit;*
> *Attending my first Presidential Inauguration—*
> *all before my twenty-sixth birthday.*

That afternoon, standing with my friend Gordan on the South Portico, I knew that I was going to have an outstanding life, and what I've experienced in my life goes well beyond anything I could have imagined on that spring day.

In the following chapters, you'll travel with me and my wife, Lori, through several events and countries in the light of what it means to believe in what's possible. You will learn about our incredible journey from very modest beginnings and all the wonderful experiences and life lessons we learned along the way. Instead of making the impossible possible, let's make every day outstanding; there is no such thing as impossible, as our following story illustrates.

Chapter Two:

BECOME THE WRITER, PRODUCER, AND DIRECTOR OF YOUR LIFE

YOUR PASSPORT TO:
New York City, Capri, Italy & Fiji

YOUR GUIDES:
Geoffry Gertz & Peter Farina, & "The Islander"

*"Your story is yours to write.
Don't let your surroundings limit your dreams.
Lord knows I didn't."
Geoffry Gertz*

Fashion by Geoffry Gertz[1]

LORI'S STORY

The buzz of New York City's fashion district engulfed me as I stepped out of the subway, a stark contrast to the quiet parks of my Mansfield childhood. The air buzzed with the electricity of dreams in the making, punctuated by the rhythmic clacking of sample racks being wheeled down the sidewalk and the staccato clicks of stilettos on concrete.

Geoffry Gertz's showroom was a feast for the senses. The moment I pushed open the heavy glass door, I was enveloped by the familiar scent of charcoal pencils and freshly pressed fabric. Bolts of luxurious silks and wools lined the walls in a kaleidoscope of colors, their textures begging to be touched. The faint hum of sewing machines provided a soothing counterpoint to the city's chaos just beyond the windows.

As Geoffry spoke, his hands danced through the air, punctuating each word with graceful movements that seemed to sketch his ideas into existence.

---

1   https://Geoffrygertz.com/portfolio/fashion-design/

His voice, rich and dynamic, filled the room with an infectious enthusiasm that made my heart race with possibility.

"Lori, your story is yours to write," he said, his eyes twinkling. "Don't let your surroundings limit your dreams. Lord knows I didn't." For a man barely older than me, Geoffry had gained immense wisdom, and not all of it was learned in a classroom, but rather, in the school of hard knocks.

Geoffry was, like me, unwilling to settle for the confines of Ohio, from where he, too, hailed. He broke the mold and became a top young fashion designer during a time when there was uncertainty about sexuality in this country. Geoffry was extremely flamboyant, and his full expression would have been frowned upon in Ohio. He, too, was liberated in the big city both personally and creatively.

Outside, a raucousness of city sounds filtered through – car horns honking, sirens wailing, the rumble of the subway underfoot. Yet within the showroom, these sounds seemed to fade into a distant hum, overwhelmed by the rustle of fabric and the scratch of pencil on paper as ideas took shape.

As I ran my fingers over a bolt of sumptuous velvet, I could almost feel the weight of my aspirations materializing. The texture was vastly different from the simple cottons of my childhood picnic dresses, yet it filled me with the same sense of simple joy. In this moment, surrounded by the electric chaos of New York's fashion world, I felt the first stirrings of becoming the writer, producer, and director of my own life story.

The city beyond the windows offered a medley of possibilities from the enticing smell of street vendor pretzels or bagels and cream cheese to the distant laughter of tourists. Every sensation in Manhattan reminded me that I was far from home, yet, in the encouraging smile of Geoffry and the endless possibilities stretched out before me, I found a new kind of home – one where life held more possibility than resigning myself to becoming a nurse or secretary – one sketched in charcoal, infused with the scents of fresh sketch pads and stitched with threads of ambition.

Lori with her parents at home in Mansfield, Ohio.

In the heart of Ohio, nestled between rolling hills and a sky that seems to stretch endlessly, lies the modest city of Mansfield with a population of nearly 50,000 residents, but far fewer opportunities. This is my hometown, where life unfolded at a gentle pace. The fertile soil blanketed the rich farmland, which supports the cultivation of corn crops, strawberries, and apple trees. The city's parks and wooded areas offer a haven of green, where families gather for picnics and friends meet beneath the shade of ancient oak trees.

On many a summer afternoon, my large family would gather in these parks. The adults would sit around picnic tables playing cards and sharing stories while the children played games and laughed out loud without a care in the world. These picnics were impressive, featuring homemade potato salads, taco salads, Bing cherry salads, and plenty of Kentucky Fried Chicken. The family recipes of sugar cookies, chocolate cakes, apple, butterscotch, and lemon meringue pies were always on the menu, meticulously and lovingly prepared by each of my aunts.

Easter Sunday in Mansfield — Lori on the hunt for Easter eggs.

In Mansfield, there was no hustle, no bustle, and no crowds. There was no emphasis on or even an idea of what the rat race is really like. It was a peaceful community where children played freely amid the soothing sounds of crickets on warm summer nights. The tranquil environment was ideal for anyone seeking respite from the stresses of urban life and those with a deep appreciation for the simple pleasures life has to offer.

Lori and her sister, Karen, shooting hoops in their Ohio driveway.

But I wanted more. I had a vision for my life that was bigger than Mansfield, Ohio. As a young girl, I wondered what my life might be like. What exciting worlds existed out there for me to discover? I had an urge to explore the world and see it all.

What kind of career could I have? What exciting places could I live in?

I loved the idea of traveling and visiting other places around the world that I had heard about growing up.

The minimal traveling I did as a teenager whetted my appetite for exploration. Before I ever set foot out of Mansfield, I had visions of an exciting life and career, a fabulous relationship, and an extraordinary life. This is where my small-town living story ends, and my journey to Geoffry's showroom in New York City begins.

After completing a college degree at Kent State University in fashion design and merchandising, I knew that my talents and training wouldn't be of any use in Mansfield, so I headed to New York City. I left sleepy Mansfield en route to the concrete jungle that never sleeps. I packed my bags and said farewell to my family, friends, and familiar streets. New York's towering skyscrapers would replace Ohio's tranquil hills. The subway's rumble would replace the crickets' symphony. The city's bright lights would replace the gentle glow of lightning bugs back home—trading nature's quiet charm for the electric pulse of boundless possibility. And the endless throngs of strangers would replace the friendly faces of my neighborhood.

I knew that nothing happened by chance even then, barely out of my teenage years. Although Geoffry went out of business when a flood in his showroom caused irreparable damage, I clung to Geoffry's words as I, too, started over following the flood. With resourcefulness that has punctuated my entire successful life, I secured an internship with another prominent womenswear designer quickly. I was a fast learner: by twenty-two years old, I became the writer, producer, and director of my life.

I chose to play a bigger game, and ultimately, worked with some of the top names in high-end fashion, including Hugo Boss, Joseph Abboud, Donna Karan, and Tommy Hilfiger, even collaborating with the band Outkast. Dressing celebrities became an everyday activity. I became responsible for managing sales to the most influential specialty stores and largest department stores in North America, and for outfitting some of the greatest professional athletes of all time. I never anticipated having the luxury of attending major sporting events, sitting as a VIP guest, or socializing and pondering life with Michael Jordan, Scottie Pippen, Mariano Rivera, Charles Barkley, Emmitt Smith, Evander Holyfield, and more.

Moving to New York to pursue a life nobody told me I could obtain was a combination of lessons from many of the guides you'll meet throughout this book. There was no place more unlike Mansfield than New York City, but even that fast-paced pandemonium became home.

My experience of moving to New York and subsequently living my life of world travel and adventures with my future husband and soulmate, William, was beyond my wildest imagination as a young girl. Mansfield was a great place to grow up, but the cultural diversity of New York City is a testament to the human spirit's boundless potential. I left a simple town to reside in a sprawling metropolis of ambition, culture, and complexity. It was upon leaving my comfort zone that life began happening for me. As style knows no bounds, nor did the future I began to visualize once I escaped the small town environment.

Life before you picked up this book was a small town.

You may have thus far been able to muffle your dreams under a pillow while you binge on Netflix and Häagen-Dazs. Perhaps you used your spouse, children, dependent parents, or job as an excuse to avoid taking steps towards your Best Day Every Day life. Geoffry recognized that I had taken a big step, but also that I was a fish out of water. When he told me that my story was mine to write, it wasn't to coddle me, but to infuse me with a sense of personal responsibility for becoming the writer, producer, and director of my life.

BECOME THE WRITER, PRODUCER, AND DIRECTOR OF YOUR TRIBE

The book *Bowling Alone* by Robert Putnam, a study of sociology and anthropology, unveiled statistics nearly thirty years ago when it was published that shook the world, but with bad news. The book asserts that each generation becomes increasingly lonelier and, thus, more miserable.

In a study of over 200,000 people, Nick Seneca Jenkel learned that the unequivocal key to both happiness and longevity in life is not wealth, but social relationships. If you want to live an outstanding life, you're not going to get there alone.

As the writer, producer, and director of your life, you critically include friendships and romantic relationships, which we'll dive deeper into in Part Three. I always visualized a tribe of soulmate friends and, one day, my romantic soulmate, too. When I connected with Geoffry, I found not only a mentor, but I also unlocked the key to both sanity and success: a tribe of friends who support and believe in me.

I made the goal of having wonderful friends and eventually meeting my soulmate central to my life's vision. The latter took time, but in the urban jungle, I discovered the true meaning of friendship. What started as laughter-filled brunches, late-night conversations, and shared dreams has evolved, at the time of writing this book, into a thirty-year bond between four women that transcends time and distance. I was an original "Sex and the City" character with these friends.

Christmas lunch in New York City with Maria and Marian
— friendships that last a lifetime.

My female tribe has endured intimate closeness for over thirty years because the relationships among us are built on a foundation of mutual support, trust, and unwavering loyalty. We have celebrated each other's triumphs and consoled each other through life's many trials, creating a circle of strength that remains unbroken.

Lori and her dear friend Christine making memories in New York City.

In our early years, as my friend tribe navigated the challenges of careers, love, and personal growth, these friends were my confidants, sounding board, and partners in adventure. Whether it was conquering the corporate world, experiencing the ups and downs of relationships, or simply sharing stories over cosmopolitans, we were there for each other, offering advice, encouragement, and a shoulder to lean on.

New York City shenanigans — laughter, mischief, and the joy of being together.

As time has passed, and the city's skyline has changed, our friendships remain constant. Even as life's paths led us in different directions, the bond remains unshaken. We've witnessed each other's milestones while providing a support system that only true friends can offer. The shared experiences have created a treasure trove of memories. Our friendship stands the test of time because it was nurtured with love, kindness, and understanding. These friends are keepers of my history, my partners in crime, and the family I chose.

My story was at a pinnacle when my career went full circle at my Aspen wedding to William. I was styled by renowned fashion designer Donna Karan, years after having the privilege of working with her in her couture fashion house in New York.

Did I ever return home? In more ways than one, absolutely yes.

BLOOM WHERE YOU'RE PLANTED

April 1991, Toberua Private Island Resort, Fiji

Becoming the writer, producer, and director of your life isn't just active; sometimes it has more passive qualities, too.

Although cultivating a career and a community are critical to materializing your ideal life, sometimes the best moments of manifestation are in the silence. Children learn how to interact with the world through nurture. Unlike *nature*, which encompasses your factory-installed, innate gifts and characteristics, *nurture* refers to the aftermarket installations. If you had parents who yelled, you might have hidden in your room to escape their fighting. However, as an adult, not knowing how to interact with your own family, you may become a "yeller."

Emotional regulation isn't something all children grow up seeing. You might identify that yelling or reacting with anxiety are not ideal ways to respond to a crisis, but your family unit conditioned you to respond in such a way. That's where meditation, priming, affirmations, and a strong morning and evening practice from your *World of Wisdom* guide will be critical to helping you interact with the world in an abundant, sociable, peaceful, and regulated way.

I learned my greatest lesson about emotional regulation during a life-threatening crisis on the island of Fiji. After years of saving spare change in our "Fiji fund," my first husband and I finally made it to our dream honeymoon on Toberua Island. The resort was a secluded paradise with one unforgettable twist—a nine-hole golf course that only emerged when the tide was low. Twice a day, we'd tee off from the island and play on the ocean floor with two friendly guests from New Zealand and a local islander who guided us through this unique game.

The course was charmingly primitive. The flags and pins were planted in the sand, and if your ball landed in a circle drawn around the pin, you were considered 'in the hole'. It was unlike anything we'd ever experienced, and the mood was light-hearted—until the eighth hole, where things took a dramatic turn.

One of the guests, the husband from New Zealand, was teeing off ahead of us. With one swing, his club snapped in half mid-air. Before I could react, the broken shaft flew through the air and harpooned me just above my collarbone, piercing the soft triangle of tissue that protects vital arteries leading to the heart. I spun around, feeling the shock but no immediate pain. "I'm okay! I'm okay!" I insisted. But I wasn't. Blood gushed from the wound like a whale's blowhole.

The islander acted fast. He pressed his massive thumb into the wound to stop the bleeding and calmly walked me back to the island. My husband, pale and frantic, was sent running for help. It hit me then—here we were, stranded on a tiny island in the middle of nowhere, with no real medical help nearby.

The hotel staff scrambled, calling the mainland for an emergency boat. As we sped toward the mainland, the New Zealand couple joined us, trying to comfort my terrified husband. After a wild ride across the ocean and a bumpy hour-long journey down a dirt road, we reached a basic cement clinic where a doctor, who seemed to have limited resources, stitched me up with what looked like chicken wire. My husband, determined not to faint, kept dousing his head with water while watching every move so he could explain it all to doctors back in the U.S.

After receiving a tetanus shot from a used, blunt needle—which later caused an abscess in my arm—we were sent off with regular-strength Tylenol, which the doctor was thrilled about because it was "new" to them. I couldn't help but feel a bit underwhelmed by this so-called "pain management." Back at the resort, they gave me a local remedy—kava—to help numb the pain. An ice cream cone also helped lift my spirits.

My husband was nearly widowed that day, but somehow, I made it through. I'm lucky to be alive, and I'll never forget how close I came to losing everything in what was supposed to be the most magical time of our lives.

The lesson from this story is one of resilience and adaptability in the face of unexpected challenges. It shows how, even during a dream experience like a honeymoon, life can throw curveballs, and it's our ability to remain calm, seek help, and trust in others that can turn a crisis into a survivable event. The experience also highlights the importance of gratitude for life, health, and the people who step up in moments of need.

In terms of encountering someone who taught the lesson, it could be the islander who saved my life with his quick thinking and calm demeanor. His resourcefulness and steady presence under pressure serve as a reminder that when faced with unexpected adversity, it's essential to stay grounded and act swiftly. His quiet heroism taught me that even in remote, unfamiliar places, you can rely on the kindness and strength of others to get you through life's most unexpected trials.

The islander became an unexpected guide, showing me that resilience isn't about fighting against what happens, but about accepting the moment and adapting to it with grace.

Recently, my car broke down in the winter on a highway in Aspen. My editor called and asked me for a deliverable. I responded that I hadn't been on email because I was hitchhiking my way out of a pickle.

"Lori, I'm so sorry. Just call me on Monday, and we'll take it from there."

"Oh, don't worry!" I responded through chattering teeth.

"William and I are going to enjoy the greatest hot chocolate of our lives tonight as we thaw out. I'm still going to make this the Best Day Ever.

In times of crisis, whether you're trying to locate the quickest rescue you can get off the side of a freezing mountain at dusk or making your way across an island with a gaping hole in your chest, emotional regulation and equanimity can be a life-or-death quality to cultivate.

Even if the situation is not life-threatening, consider the last time you were faced with a bully. Perhaps it was your boss, a colleague, a difficult client or customer, or even a vindictive former employee threatening to sue after being terminated, despite repeated warnings that their chronic lateness was jeopardizing company operations. Handling yourself with grace in the face of adversity can give you control over a situation. In a courtroom, it is he with the most emotional regulation who has the upper hand. In poker or card gaming, it's your "poker face." In a relationship, it's the emotional regulation of one partner that often helps the angry partner to calm down and communicate. Yelling, screaming, or waving your fists in response to stress impairs critical thinking skills and causes undue stress on the body and life.

PICK UP YOUR PASSPORT AND MAKE LIFE HAPPEN

July 2023, Molise, Italy

My journey that summer unfolded across two very different corners of Italy, one rooted in my past, the other awakening something entirely new. Days earlier, I had been in Molise, standing in the quiet mountain village of San Pietro Avellana where my grandmother was born. The air there carried the scent of pine and fresh bread from the local forno, a reminder of the simple rhythms that shaped generations before me. It was in Molise, walking those narrow lanes, that the reality of my newly reclaimed Italian citizenship finally settled into my bones.

Capri came next, or perhaps because of Molise, Capri felt different this time. The sun-drenched island isn't part of my ancestral region, but it became the place where everything crystallized. After tracing my grandmother's footsteps, Capri became the setting where I could absorb the meaning of what I had just reclaimed. It was the contrast, the quiet mountains of Molise followed by the radiant energy of Capri, that allowed me to feel the full span of what it means to come home to yourself.

The terrace of my hillside hotel on Capri opened to a scene so vivid it felt cinematic: lemon trees tumbling down the cliffs, bougainvillea draped like silk over stone walls, and the Tyrrhenian Sea shimmering below like a sheet of blue glass. Yet woven through all that beauty was something deeper. It was an overwhelming new sense of belonging that had followed me from Molise.

As I stood there, I traced the edges of my deep burgundy Italian passport, still so new it barely opened on its own. The embossed coat of arms beneath my fingers was more than a symbol; it was the bridge between two worlds. It connected the woman I had become with the girl from San Pietro Avellana who left Italy more than a century ago, never imagining her granddaughter would one day return with citizenship restored.

Walking toward Capri's town center, my footsteps echoed against sun-warmed stone, a rhythm that somehow carried the same music as the cobblestones in Molise. The lively chatter in the piazzetta mingled with the memory of church bells in my grandmother's village. Even the smell of espresso drifting from a café blended with the scent of bread from Molise's mountain ovens. The two places, so geographically distant, felt unexpectedly intertwined, each awakening a different part of my heritage.

Capri, in that moment, became the canvas where my rediscovery took shape. Molise had given me roots; Capri gave me wings. One reminded me where I came from; the other reminded me how far I could go. Together, they formed the beginning of a story I was ready to write with intention.

Under the brilliant Capri sky, I felt, perhaps for the first time, like the writer, producer, and director of my own life. The chapters ahead would carry the imprint of both places, the timeless authenticity of Molise and the radiant, expansive energy of Capri. My passport was no longer just a document; it was a promise that every step I took from here on would honor the journey of those who came before me.

Since 2006, italyMONDO! has been the gold standard in Italian Citizenship services, Family Tree Research, and Heritage Tours. They successfully helped me reclaim my citizenship in 2023, guided by the expertise of founder Peter Farina. His own story, leaving New York in search of his roots, beautifully aligned with my own desire for expansion and a life lived fully.

If a small-town girl from Mansfield, Ohio can walk the cobblestones of her ancestral village, stand overlooking the cliffs of Capri, and hold an Italian passport in her hands, then anyone reading this can create a life that is extraordinary in its own way. Your story may unfold differently, but it can be just as remarkable, if not more.

Chapter Three:
REMODELING YOUR BRAIN

"Change your story, and you will change your life. The strongest force in the human personality is the need to stay consistent with how we define ourselves." – Tony Robbins

May 2016, The Gold Coast of Australia

Standing on the vast, golden sands of the Gold Coast of Australia as the sun is rising over the ocean to the east is an awe-inspiring experience. The first light of dawn spills over the horizon, casting a warm, golden hue that slowly transforms into a soft, peach glow across the sky. The waves gently lap at the shore, their tips glinting with the first touches of sunlight, creating a dazzling display of light dancing on the water's surface. The air is crisp and fresh, carrying the subtle scent of salt and seaweed, while the fine sand beneath our feet feels cool and smooth, imprinted only with the gentle footprints of early risers like ourselves.

As the sun rises higher, the intense blue of the sky deepens as we walk along the beach, blending seamlessly with the turquoise expanse of the ocean. The beach of the Gold Coast stretches out endlessly in both directions, bordered by the lush greenery of palm trees that sway gently in the soft morning breeze. Skyscrapers gleam in the distance, their reflective glass facades catching the sun's rays and casting shimmering patterns onto the sand below. To our left, the surf rolls in with rhythmic precision, surfers already paddling out to catch the first waves of the day, silhouetted against the golden backdrop.

The visual beauty of the Gold Coast is unparalleled; it's a blend of natural wonder and modern allure. The contrast between the deep, striking blues of the sea, the brilliant gold of the sand, and the emerald greens of the coastal foliage creates a vivid mix of colors. As we walk further, the beachfront curves gracefully, revealing hidden coves and rocky outcrops bathed in soft, warm light. The ocean stretches infinitely, its vastness meeting the sky at a distant, barely visible horizon, while behind us, the skyline of the city stands tall, a testament to human ambition framed by the serene and unchanging beauty of nature.

As we walked along the beach that beautiful morning, we mused about our weekend before and what we were experiencing this week. Just before arriving on the Gold Coast, we had spent an amazing weekend in Sydney, one of the world's great cities. Over three days, we attended a Josh Groban concert at the Sydney Opera House, hiked the famous Bridge Climb on the Sydney Harbour Bridge, spent an afternoon at the amazing Sydney Zoo, spent a couple of days relaxing at Manly and Bondi beaches, and explored the restaurant and nightlife scene in downtown Sydney. But here we were early in the morning walking the beautiful beach of the Gold Coast.

Two Days Later

We hear thousands of wrappers crinkle gently in the large conference room as attendees carefully open the complimentary Quest bars handed out to everyone by staff during the break. No one, including us, wanted to leave our seats in fear of missing what the speaker was saying. His massive hands are both rugged and wild, clapping together and dynamically illustrating his words as he lectures with no less enthusiasm than a preacher giving a sermon he feels might be his last. The speaker's voice is deep, powerful, and resonant, but not intimidating to the audience of men and women. Some of us have traveled thousands of miles to hear the iconic speaker in person.

Despite the speaker's towering presence, the room wafts gentle perfumes of essential oils and fresh flowers, invigorating the audience with a sense of life and potential. Above all, the atmosphere is one of hope.

We are attending a week-long program called "Date With Destiny" on the Gold Coast of Australia, where the speaker is none other than the famous Tony Robbins, our sixth *World of Wisdom* Guide. Throughout the week, we had been learning how to reprogram our minds to live an extraordinary quality of life—a life on our terms.

The program is about understanding why we feel and behave the way we do and what strategies and tools we can use to align with these forces to create the happiness, joy, love, passion, success, and fulfillment we desire and deserve.

Although every session during this program has been impactful, this particular day altered the course of our lives, becoming a part of our morning routine every day since we attended the Date With Destiny program.

On this particular morning, Tony had intentionally married the tastes, sights, sounds, and smells of the event to the lesson of that morning: the power of visualization using sensory triggers. In this book, we will call it somatic visualization, not to be confused with "vision boards."

Throughout this event, Tony emphasized the incredible potential of our brains to rewire themselves—a concept known as neuroplasticity. By using techniques like mantra, meditation, and visualization, he explained how we can reshape our mental landscape and set ourselves up for success.

Robbins explained that sensory triggers, particularly smell, evoke powerful emotions and memories from childhood. The method taps into the deep connections between our senses and emotions, helping to create a vivid and immersive experience. The audience listened to Tony lecture about the science behind this form of somatic visualization, followed by a guided practice. First, participants were asked to recall a cherished memory from their childhoods. They were then instructed to close their eyes and focus on the sensory details of that memory, particularly the smells associated with it.

My (William) sensory experience included an image from my childhood. I remembered the soothing sound of my mother's voice, ushering in a sense of peace and security. During my visualization, I recalled the rich, nostalgic scent of my grandmother's kitchen during the holidays, where there were freshly baked cookies and spices in the air. I felt both the comforting texture of my old, worn-out teddy bear as I clutched it tightly and basked in the warmth of my family being present. I tasted the cookies and other favorite childhood treats evoked by this memory.

Tony explained how these sensory details, especially smell, can create powerful anchors in our minds. By repeatedly visualizing these positive memories and associating them with our goals and intentions, we can harness the emotional strength they provide. Taste, touch, smell, and sound provide the backdrops that fuel future accomplishments. This technique not only makes our visualizations more vivid and realistic but also helps in reinforcing the positive emotions and beliefs we want to cultivate.

Now we practice sensory visualization every morning before we start our day, certainly before looking at our cell phones. When you begin the day with sensory visualization, you prime your brain for peak performance. This routine has helped us achieve far more than our childhood selves could have imagined. By focusing our minds on sensory visualization first thing each morning, we've been able to unlock new levels of potential and productivity.

Let's take a look 30,000 feet above the practices Tony Robbins teaches about visualization so that we can land the plane on a runway of real practices you can start using today to begin engineering an outstanding life where the word "impossible" no longer exists.

*Lori and William with Tony Robbins
at Date With Destiny on the Gold Coast of Australia.*

Tony Robbins & Neuroplasticity

Tony Robbins didn't get to where he is with fluffy practices that help people feel good for a short time, but by teaching people how to make lifelong changes. That change starts in the mind. Tony Robbins brilliantly integrates neuroscience into his teachings and practices through several key approaches, including:

1. **Neuro-Associative Conditioning:** This method involves reprogramming the brain's reward system by associating positive feelings with desired behaviors and negative feelings with undesired behaviors. This technique helps individuals break bad habits and form new, positive ones by leveraging the brain's plasticity—the ability to form new neural connections throughout life. The above section of this chapter about sensory visualization is an example of neuro-associative conditioning.

2. **NuCalm Technology:** Robbins advocates for the use of NuCalm, an FDA-approved clinical system designed to relax the brain and body naturally. Our friend is close with Jim Poole, the founder of NuCalm. Following her assault in 2019, Mr. Poole encouraged her to use NuCalm as part of her healing journey. She went from being in a high-anxiety and weakened state of mind and body, barely sleeping for nine months, to sleeping without disruption eight hours a night, no matter where she is or what is happening in her life. She initially doubted the power of NuCalm, but after being convinced by the CEO himself of its effectiveness, she brought scores of her loved ones to NuCalm to eliminate trauma from their brains, making them more receptive to the other neuroscientific practices listed in this book. NuCalm is used by trauma victims, including victims of human trafficking, as well as individuals suffering from financial distress, divorce, or even veterans who have PTSD. NuCalm uses biochemistry, physics, and neurophysiology to reduce stress by guiding brain waves from high alert states to relaxation states. It's used for various purposes, including improving sleep, reducing anxiety, and enhancing overall mental clarity. With skyrocketing use of pharmaceutical antidepressants, which are prescribed very easily, we, the authors, hope that if it's possible to try natural methods for healing trauma before going on antidepressants, NuCalm will be included in your vault of trauma healing tools.

3. **Mindfulness and Meditation:** Robbins emphasizes the importance of mindfulness and meditation for stress reduction, emotional regulation, and overall brain health. Meditation can be a practice of emptying one's mind. Still, we prefer meditation that focuses on listening to the breath while visualizing something you intend for your future or are grateful for in the present moment. Meditation and mindfulness enhance cognitive function and foster emotional well-being by promoting a state of present-moment awareness, which we will discuss in a later chapter. Present-moment awareness can seem a bit esoteric for some. Therefore, we've left it for later in the book. For

the time being, please focus today's efforts on somatic visualization, incantations, priming, and meditation.

4. **Diet and Nutrition:** In Chapter Nine, we'll discuss the importance of health in creating your Best Day Every Day life. The truth is that we cannot conceive of having the mental acuity and peace of mind we have without healthy habits. Tony Robbins highlights the role of a nutrient-rich plant-based diet in maintaining brain health. If you're worried about your health or plagued with pain or disease, it's hard to focus on visualizing your best life. Foods rich in omega-3 fatty acids, vitamins, and antioxidants support cognitive function and protect against neurodegenerative diseases. This holistic approach combines physical health with mental well-being to optimize brain performance.

5. **Brain Health Education:** Robbins collaborates with experts to disseminate knowledge about brain health. For example, his podcast with neurosurgeon Sanjay Gupta discusses the importance of neurogenesis and maintaining brain health through exercise, learning new skills, and meaningful social connections. Neurogenesis is the phenomenon we discussed in this book's introduction, wherein you form new neural pathways by exposing yourself to a new environment. The concept will be continually addressed in this book, and your practice of the Training Days will assist you in rewiring your brain for the Best Day Every Day.

In short, by integrating these neuroscience-based techniques and tools, Tony Robbins aims to enhance mental and emotional well-being, helping individuals achieve their personal and professional goals more effectively.

"Your brain is the most powerful tool you have.
Use incantations to charge your emotions, visualization to see your
success, and affirmations to believe in your potential. Prime your day
by setting your intentions first thing in the morning."
Tony Robbins

Priming

Priming is a psychological technique used to prepare your mind and body for a desired state or outcome by exposing yourself to specific stimuli that can positively influence your thoughts, emotions, and behaviors.

Priming is different from affirmations and incantations in several ways. While priming involves focused sessions, often as part of a morning routine, utilizing visualization, sensory experiences, or physical movements, affirmations are about rewiring the brain over time through consistent repetition of positive statements throughout the day. Affirmations aim for long-term neuroplastic changes without the need for passionate spoken performance. On the other hand, incantations are designed to create immediate emotional and physiological changes by chanting mantras or phrases with emotional intensity and physical movement, providing a quick boost of energy. Priming sets a mental and emotional foundation for achieving goals. Affirmations work on gradually changing thought patterns, and incantations focus on an immediate shift in energy and mindset. For example, a priming exercise might include visualizing your ideal day, expressing gratitude for three things, engaging in physical activity, and reciting positive affirmations, thereby preparing your mind and body for success in a holistic way.

Meditation

The majority of this chapter has thus far focused on what we refer to as "sensory visualization." Now we'll peel back another layer to show you a little bit about incantations and priming, the next steps to preparing your mind for a remodel!

You'll hear us remind you often that to live an extraordinary life, you must train for it every day without a break. That's right, creating the Best Day Every Day life doesn't take off on the weekends. Just as muscles need to be conditioned, your emotions and beliefs must also be trained to be in peak performance. You are in charge of your mind, body, and spirit. Conditioning your mind, body, and spirit is an ongoing process. If you build your internal muscle, the body responds immediately.

How will you make every day the Best Day Ever or the most productive day ever? Despite the lofty promises in books like *The Secret*, the truth is that nothing happens by chance. The Best Day Every Day method is nothing short of a training plan, not unlike what your personal trainer would provide for you. Our experience proves that the Best Day Every Day starts first thing in the morning. That's because when you take control of your day from the very beginning, you set yourself up for success and create a foundation for an outstanding life.

The first practice Robbins encourages from the above list is meditation and breathing. Meditation is a powerful tool that can help you quiet your mind, focus your thoughts, and set your intentions for the day ahead. By taking just a few minutes to sit in silence and breathe deeply, you can create a sense of calm and inner peace that will carry with you throughout the day. Now is the time to practice meditation. Deep breathing equals energy. Your mind can be directed through your breath. Inarguably, the most powerful breathwork practice is the "4-7-8" breathing technique, during which you inhale for four heartbeats, hold it for seven heartbeats, and exhale for eight heartbeats. If you think this practice is just for the New Agey "woo-woo" audience, think again.

This method of meditation and breathing has been practiced for centuries by various religions. We know Christians who use this technique paired with the phrase, "Lord Yeshua, (hold), have mercy on me, a sinner," as is described in the book *Stressed Out: Learn How an Ancient Christian Practice Can Relieve Stress and Overcome Anxiety*. Other variations include calling on the "Great Spirit," "Universe," or simply breathing and listening to one's heartbeat in silence. Those with busy minds may find that the former "mantra" attached to the 4-7-8 breath helps them calm down enough to eventually simply enjoy the melody of their own heartbeat. While this example uses a Christian phrase, this practice can be adapted to any belief system or personal preference. By using a mantra and rhythmic pattern, anyone can find a structured and effective way to meditate, promoting relaxation, mindfulness, and personal growth.

Notice that the mantra includes four syllables, followed by a 7-beat pause, and then eight syllables, so that instead of counting, the practitioner repeats a mantra.

Incantations

The word "incantations" might sound, again, rather witchy. However, we're going to unpack the use of incantations so that you can use them in your Best Day Every Day morning practice. Incantations are mantras or phrases we chant consistently with emotional intensity. They are an active, somatic, physiological event. Incantations are designed to manifest your Best Day Ever, whereas affirmations (explained below) are for long-term neuroplastic rewiring of the mind.

Some of our favorite incantations are, "I am the voice, I will lead, not follow, I will believe not doubt, I am a Force for Good, I am a leader!" and "This ends here and now: my new life begins today" and "I control my mind and use it to achieve my 100% personal best in everything I do" and "I am a powerhouse of vibrant energy and radiant health. Every cell in my body is thriving with strength and vitality" and "I am connected to my highest self, embracing peace, love, and joy" and "My mind, body, and spirit are in perfect harmony, attracting endless opportunities and abundance into my life."

Lori's favorite daily mantra is, "Every day in every way I am happy and healthy."

Try saying these out loud right now, while shrugging your shoulders and allowing your arms to dangle or dance as you sway. Can you feel the energy and vitality transmute from your words to your body?

Our friend chants, "I am healthy, wealthy, blessed, and highly favored! Effortless abundance and joy flow into my life." Another friend chants, "Everything always works out for me." Still another chants, "I gratefully receive the magnificent flow of abundance that is pouring into my life right now."

Words you speak with excitement and conviction can become the life that you live. The woman we know who chants, "Everything always works out for me," was homeless when she began her incantation, and is now living in a $10,000,000 home near Aspen with a thriving business and a healthy, loving relationship. Everything, indeed, worked out for her!

This friend, a hiker and trail runner, would often state her intention through incantations on the hill hundreds of times a day. You can also use these incantations while walking, cooking, showering, or biking. Scientists believe that it takes between 8 and 24 weeks to rewire a single thought. Once you develop an affirmation or incantation, focus on this one mantra for at least two months.

Happily, your incantations will evolve as you make your journey. Perhaps your first incantations will come from a place of survival, but as your life becomes more abundant, your incantations will shift towards spiritual matters; think of it as moving from survival to spiritual strength or even as moving up the chakras.

As your goals and aspirations evolve, your incantations can change and become affirmations.

Affirmations

Affirmations are similar to incantations, but said throughout your day without necessarily the chanting and passionate "spoken" performance.

Neuroscientists believe that it takes several months to rewire a single thought, which means that although you can call in positivity with a variety of daily incantations to set your mood, the real brain rewiring happens slowly, one thought at a time. Affirmations are "aftermarket" tweaks to your brain. You might not have grown up believing a particular positive thought. That's why affirmations are critical to eliminating the thoughts that have been "nurtured" into you. One thought you might have grown up with is, "once you're poor, you'll always remain poor. People in our family never create wealth. That's just the way the world works."

The Best Day Every Day affirmation might be, "I create wealth and prosperity in my life. I never worry about money."

Incantations are a daily "cheerleading" exercise to start your morning on a positive high. However, affirmations will give you strength and make you stable for the long-distance race of life. Both incantations and affirmations translate your thoughts into words and actions. The phrase, "what you think, you become," attributed to the Buddha, suggests that our thoughts shape our reality. When you articulate your desires and the experiences you wish to embrace, you begin to manifest them in your life.

Once you have meditated and designed your incantations, it's time to prime yourself for success. This means taking a few minutes to visualize your goals, envision yourself achieving them, and set your mindset for success.

Additional Visualization

Remember when we said that the law of attraction is nothing without action? Knowing your beliefs will not make you better. Acting on them will change your life.

Healing is also a crucial part of planning ahead each morning. Take time to reflect on emotional wounds or negative experiences that may be holding you back. By acknowledging and healing these wounds, you create space for growth and transformation, and you free yourself from the limitations of the past.

You have also heard the phrase, "You don't get what you don't ask for." Did you know that 90% of people are afraid to ask for things? We, as humans, are so scared to ask because we fear rejection. The simple magic to getting anything you want in life is just to ask. Let's take it a step further. Ask until you get what you want. But if you don't believe in what you are asking for, then "the ask" will never come to fruition. The way you ask yields quality results. We have to feed and strengthen your mind to build your confidence and become the best version of yourself that you can be. Most often, that means getting out of your comfort zone to create change and putting it all out there. It is your responsibility to make life happen. Decide the outcome of your life and take yourself and others there.

Don't steer your mind in the direction of destruction or desolation. Focusing on what you don't want drives your life in that direction; it's actually called the "Baader Meinhof phenomenon," often referred to as the "Red Honda Syndrome." The theory suggests that when you visualize a vehicle, such as a red Honda, you tend to see it everywhere. The Baader-Meinhof phenomenon, also known as the frequency illusion, is a cognitive bias whereby a person notices something and subsequently sees it more often because of that awareness. This is why it's so important not to look at what you don't want. Instead, concentrate on and visualize your desires, allowing them to become an integral part of who you are. Put your attention on your focus, and your focus will begin to evolve. Or, as it's been said, "Where your focus goes, your energy flows."

A vision board is a great tool to represent your goals and dreams. Placing your goals in a visual format can increase your confidence and motivation to become who you want to be. Select vivid and attractive images and words from glossy magazines for your board design, and place it in a visible location where you can refer to it daily.

Lori's 2017 vision board — a snapshot of dreams in motion.

Planning ahead each morning is a powerful way to take control of your life and create a foundation for an outstanding life. By meditating, using incantations and affirmations, and visualizing your Best Day Every Day, you will bring it closer to reality each day. What's more, with the practices in this chapter, the road to your Best Day life will become more hopeful, exciting, and happy.

Chapter Four:
LEADERSHIP & CONFIDENCE

"Confidence is built through preparation and perseverance. Face your fears head-on, and you'll emerge stronger."
Captain Sergey Tunikov

William, Lori & Captain Sergey Tunikov aboard the "Star Clipper"

Between the Malay Peninsula in Malaysia and the Indonesian island of Sumatra is one of the most important shipping lanes in the world. The narrow Strait of Malacca is a narrow stretch of water where approximately one-quarter of the world's traded goods travel, including oil, natural gas, and manufactured products. Despite its global economic importance, the narrow strait is riddled with pirates and armed robbery against ships, threats of maritime accidents caused by heavy maritime traffic, and turbulent weather.

CHAPTER FOUR: LEADERSHIP & CONFIDENCE

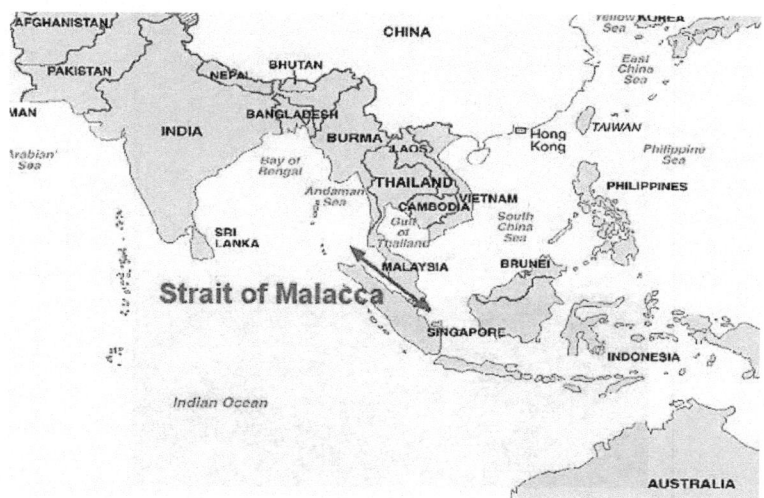

Location of the Strait of Malacca

As our sailing ship, the Star Clipper, glides smoothly through the turquoise waters of the Andaman Sea, the morning sun casts a warm golden light over the surroundings. The gentle breeze fills the sails, propelling the ship forward, while the rhythmic sound of waves lapping against the hull creates a soothing melody. To the east, the distant skyline of Singapore has faded into a faint silhouette, and ahead, the horizon stretches endlessly, painted in shades of blue and green. Small islands dotted with lush, emerald-green vegetation occasionally break the expanse of water, creating a picturesque contrast against the clear sky. Seabirds swoop gracefully above, occasionally diving into the water in search of a morning meal.

The "Star Clipper"

The Star Clipper is a 379-foot-long four-masted luxury modern sailing ship designed after the famous Clipper ships of the mid-19th century. The Star Clipper is one of three tall sailing ships of the Star Clipper fleet based in Norway. When fully loaded, the ship carries 170 passengers and crew. Standing on the Star Clipper under full sail, with its 36,000 square feet of white sails catching the wind, feels like being at the heart of a majestic dance with the wind and sea, a thrilling blend of freedom, power, and serene connection to the elements as the ship gracefully cuts through the water.

Our next muse, Captain Sergey Tunikov, is the distinguished Captain of the Star Clipper. Tunikov is a dashing silver fox from Russia who is a showman, has an eye for the ladies, and loves to tell stories of his seafaring adventures. His silver hair and strong Russian presence command authority when you're around him, while also making you feel safe in his hands.

Captain Sergey, as we like to call him, is a master of sailing at its highest level and one of the foremost experts in the world on sailing tall ships. As a kid growing up in Russia, he learned his sailing skills on various sailboats and on the lakes and seas surrounding Russia. He spent several years in the Russian Navy as a sailing and navigation instructor. Following his Naval career, he crewed and captained several tall sailing ships, setting records in months-long transatlantic sailing races, and has circumvented the globe several times. When he wasn't captaining the Star Clipper, he was a professor at Moscow State University.

This is not the first time we've sailed with Captain Sergey. The first time we traveled on the Star Clipper with Captain Sergey was through the Greek Islands from Athens to Turkey in 40-knot winds. During that journey, we watched in amazement as Captain Sergey navigated the intricacies of both the sea and the web of ropes and winches on the deck, commanding his crew authoritatively with "All sails up! Jibs! Staysails! Square sails out!" and other calls as we looked on in wonder.

The Star Clipper and crew under the leadership of Captain Sergey off the coast of Thailand.

In the foreign, non-European, more exotic Singaporean and Malaysian cultures, our second voyage with Captain Sergey felt measurably more exotic, exciting, and a bit unnerving and adventurous. However, knowing our Captain and the seventh World of Wisdom Muse was in charge of the ship put us at ease that we were in good hands.

It was our first morning on the ship, so we got up early and made our way to the top deck for coffee. As the ship sailed, we were serenaded by the rhythmic creaking of the ship's timbers and the flap of sails catching the wind. The distant, ominous whispers of pirate legends as we navigated the treacherous Malacca Strait, punctuated by the occasional shout of "land ho!" from the lookout, gave the day an anticipatory feel. The melodic calls of exotic birds harmonized with shouts and wailing wind. In some moments, we could hear the faint rustling of leaves in the lush forests we passed. In other quiet moments, we enjoyed the serene sound of waves lapping gently against the hull, a soothing, constant background noise of which we never tired.

At the beginning of the journey between Singapore and Phuket, we admired breathtaking landscapes featuring crystal-clear tropical waters, lush forests, and cascading waterfalls. In Singapore, we savored the colonial charm at the Raffles Hotel, the birthplace of the Singapore Sling, and strolled through the picturesque pre-war homes of Emerald Hill. We explored the Victorian Botanic Gardens and the verdant lawns of the Padang Cricket Club. We dove into some of the world's most spectacular swimming and diving spots. While on land, the enchanting paddy fields carved into limestone hillsides captivated nature lovers.

All is peaceful and serene that first morning until our friend and muse, Captain Sergey, comes through the galley door that opens onto the al fresco Tropical Bar to join us for coffee at our little, round high-top table next to the railing.

The Captain had remembered us from the voyage in Greece and Turkey. He approached us, helping himself to a seat at our table. We marveled at the sturdiness of his shoulders, the crispness of his jacket, and his thick, black, polished boots. Lori imagined she could use each of them as free weights for her morning workout— they looked heavy and served to illustrate how sturdy their Captain was. We three enjoyed our coffee with cordial conversation. Captain Sergey was casual, talkative, and unintimidating, despite his strength and stature.

CHAPTER FOUR: LEADERSHIP & CONFIDENCE

Lori and William at an invitation-only dinner at the Captain's Table aboard the Star Clipper.

"Captain Sergey, what should we be aware of on this trip?"

"We have to be on the lookout for pirates. These waters are infested with pirates."

Both Lori and William's eyes widened with a look that said, "Are you serious?" It was the first they'd heard of the pirates, a detail which they've now verified and can, they are embarrassed to admit, be found by a cursory Google Search. It appears that piracy in the Strait of Malacca has long been a threat to ship owners and mariners since the 14th century.

"Captain," we asked, "what kind of protection do we have against the pirates?"

Captain Sergey went on, "We have a cannon on the front of the ship to fight those pirates. Last time they bothered us, we shot women's panties out of it."

Lori and William laughed, grateful for the elegant way Captain Sergey diffused the anxiety he saw on their faces.

"No, really, Captain. What do you do if you see pirates?"

61

Turnikov replied calmly, "First, you rely on your sailing skills, then you call for help; other nations have ships on these straits. He then told us that a few months earlier, he'd sailed the Star Clipper off the pirate-infested East Coast of Somalia. "The ship was encased in razor wire and we had several armed security men patrolling the deck with machine guns while off in the distance, a US Naval Destroyer accompanied our passage". He had a great sense of humor, but it was clear he had a big job on his hands.

For the next thirty to forty-five minutes, the three chatted casually and laughed much more. Lori and William were honored to be in the good graces of this remarkable man, their Captain.

Later, we received a Special Invitation in the form of a formal, carefully written, and sealed note at the door of our cabin.

"You are cordially invited to join Captain Sergey Turnikov tonight at his Captain's Table for dinner at 20:00 hours."

The Captain rarely, if ever, attended dinner with the ship's guests, but this was the Captain's Dinner night, and his table only sat eight guests total. We were flattered and knew we'd gained some respect and admiration in the eyes of the Captain, who was at once a sort of super-heroic and courageous figure and also a man we were beginning to see as a genuine friend.

We changed into formal attire, thrilled to have started the voyage with this unique invitation and an experience money couldn't buy. As we traveled from our cabin to the dining room, the sharp tang of salty sea air mixed with the lingering flavors of fresh seafood grilled on deck kept our senses heightened.

On the way to dinner, we asked a bartender for two "Singapore Slings," a drink originating from the Raffles Hotel over a hundred years ago that's a blend of both herbs and sweet fruits due to the use of gin, cherry-flavored liqueur, Benedictine, Cointreau, pineapple, lime, Grenadine, and bitters. Despite the myriad of ingredients and complexity of the cocktail recipe, the drink, concocted originally at the famous Long Bar in the Raffles Hotel, is a favorite among locals who enjoy it in a tall "highball" glass garnished with pineapple and a maraschino cherry.

For us, the bright pink cocktail was a welcome feminine fusion amidst the otherwise masculine energy of the trip—the rough waves, deafening winds, and abrasive saltwater scent and feel on our skin. All said, the balance was an invigorating harmony, and we were careful to savor each drop mindfully.

As we walked along the deck towards dinner, we each ran a free hand admiringly over the ship's smooth, polished railings. The cool night air invigorated us after an afternoon of warming up our skin on the deck chairs of the boat. Finally, we entered the top level of the ship's main dining galley and descended the large central stairway leading to the dining level. At the base of the staircase, the ship's maître d' escorted us to the Captain's table.

The Captain's table was surrounded by a ceremonial rope that reminded us of the course ropes we handled earlier when we took a break to help the crew with the rigging. We had felt powerful and still small on the ship's crew for a brief few moments, feeling the resistance of those brash, tattered rope strands under their soft hands.

As the evening progressed, Captain Sergey shared a few stories with our small table, stories we imagine he always shared with his guests. The greatest hits included stories that celebrated both the dangerous adventures and heart-stopping beauty he experienced sailing the Strait of Malacca. More than his stories, Tunikov entertained us in an unexpected way. We were humbled by his leadership skills and the confidence that was palpable in the energy around him.

Seeing the way he led his crew had left us in awe; we knew that we were in the presence of a true leader who faced adversity with the confidence of someone who was highly emotionally regulated, highly capable, and highly amused by adversity.

As if reading our minds, Captain Sergey punctuated one of his stories with these words we'll never forget, "Sailing these waters requires not just skill, but also the ability to inspire confidence in your crew. You must be prepared for anything, whether it's the beauty of the sea or the threat of pirates. Leadership is about being steady and calm, no matter what challenges you face."

"Captain Sergey," I (Lori) piped up after a whistle-whetting swig of my Sling— perhaps addressing the captain was a little intimidating to me. "At what point did you stop fearing the waters, the winds, and the pirates?"

Without skipping a beat, almost as if on queue, the Captain replied, "Confidence is built through preparation and perseverance. Face your fears head-on, and you'll emerge stronger."

Today, when faced with the responsibility to act as a leader to others, we sometimes tap into the memories of this trip as we engage in incantations and somatic visualization. We inhale the heady bouquets from the Victorian Botanic Gardens in Singapore or the subtle, musty scent of old wood and salt, caked on every inch of the deck and railings of the Star Clipper from years of adventures throughout the world. And of course, in our mind's eye, we are encouraged by Captain Sergey as we visualize the Best Day Ever ahead of us as he shouts confidently, "All sails up!"

Great leaders come in all walks of life, but they all share similar traits. One thing they have in common is confidence in what they're doing.

CONFIDENCE IS A MUSCLE (YOU MUST EXERCISE)

Confidence is the secret ingredient to the cocktail of creating your Best Day Every Day life. Like Captain Sergey, when you're confident, you are more likely to take risks, try new things, and reap the rewards of your endeavors. Confidence isn't factory-installed in most people, especially not in women. In fact, some neuroscientists and psychologists even link confidence to a specific gene.

One of the notable genes associated with self-esteem is the oxytocin receptor gene (OXTR). Oxytocin is often referred to as the "cuddle hormone." It plays a crucial role in social bonding, trust, and emotional regulation. The receptor gene for oxytocin (OXTR) influences how individuals respond to oxytocin.

The Serotonin Transporter Gene (5-HTTLPR) is involved in the reuptake of serotonin, a neurotransmitter that affects mood and social behavior. Variations in this gene, particularly the length of the allele (short vs. long), have been associated with susceptibility to anxiety and depression, which can adversely affect confidence levels. People with the long allele variant tend to have higher levels of serotonin reuptake, which is associated with better mood regulation and potentially higher confidence.

Dopamine is another neurotransmitter involved in reward and pleasure systems in the brain. Dopamine Receptor Genes (DRD4 and DRD2) have been studied for their effects on novelty-seeking and extraversion. These traits can influence confidence, as more extraverted individuals and novelty-seeking may display higher levels of confidence.

The development of self-confidence, a complex interplay between nature and nurture, is often attributed to more superficial things, such as, in some studies, a man's height, with taller men being generally more confident or, as studies identify, having more self-esteem.

What we know about confidence is this: it is a muscle you must exercise. As a Certified Personal Trainer, Lori knows that consistent dedication to the body makes workouts easier over time. There's no more challenging workout than the first. Her clients find that after a few months, it's harder *not* to exercise than it is to power through their day's training. This is in part the development of muscle, and partially due to the positive hormones secreted by working out. Runners call this the runner's high, and other fitness fanatics liken exercise to an addictive drug. Thankfully, it's one we all need to get hooked on.

Confidence, like exercise, is increased with practice. With clear goals in mind tethered to a strong sense of one's values, strengths, talents, and passions, it becomes easy to visualize yourself acting confidently in a situation. To help you visualize confidence, ask yourself these questions and answer them in your Training Day #4:

What are the things that you are good at?
What brings you joy and fulfillment?

Once you have identified these things, make a plan to develop them further. You may take courses, read books, or seek out mentors or role models who can help you grow and develop in these areas. Remember, what you practice in private shows up in public. In Appendix A, we have included a Confidence Reading List to help those who don't feel confident get on the path by exercising their confidence muscle through knowledge that will empower confident action.

> *"A coward dies a thousand times; a brave man dies but once."*
> *Julius Caesar*

The above statement by Julius Caesar encapsulates the idea that living in fear and avoiding challenges can lead to a constant state of anxiety and inner turmoil. Some have said that fear is "False Evidence Appearing Real," and your authors agree. How many times have you lost sleep over rent that gets handled right in the knick of time? Or the job you weren't supposed to take in the first place? Or the subpar options on a dating app, only to meet the love of your life a few months later, perhaps somebody who was in front of you the whole time.

Being confident includes aspects of a philosophy called "stoicism." Thanks to authors such as Ryan Holiday, who wrote *The Daily Stoic* in 2016, the practice and philosophies of stoicism have become commonplace in the personal development world over the past decade. The cornerstone of stoicism is rationality, control of emotions, and wisdom for the long game.

Part of mastering the long game is learning to resist the temptation to give in to worry. Worrying about the future doesn't serve you—it robs you of your power and potential in the present moment. As the saying goes, "Don't worry about tomorrow; focus on today." Just like the birds don't stress about what's coming, yet they are always provided for, you too can trust the process. Worry doesn't add value or time to your life. Instead, focus on what you can control today, take proactive steps toward your goals, and trust that things will unfold as they should. By shifting your mindset and energy to the present, you can create a future that is abundant and fulfilling.

In his *Meditations*, Marcus Aurelius, commonly thought of as the leading Stoic philosopher, says fear stems from false perceptions. In *Meditations* Book 8, Chapter 47, he writes, "If you are distressed by anything external, the pain is not due to the thing itself, but to your estimate of it; and this you have the power to revoke at any moment."

In his work *Enchiridion*, Epictetus, another Stoic philosopher, states, "Men are disturbed not by things, but by the views which they take of them," and encourages readers not to worry about things that are out of their control.

Seneca encourages proactive preparation in place of worry. When you live the Best Day Every Day life, you're preparing your heart, body, mind, and finances to withstand any storm; with preparation, just like Captain Sergey, there is no pirate of whom you need to be afraid. Three core practices of Stoicism have been introduced in this book.

1. **Mindfulness and Meditation.** As mentioned, one godfather of this philosophy, Marcus Aurelius, even has a collection of writings called "Meditations." Reflect daily on life and rewrite daily fears with the empowering lens of the teachings in Stoic philosophy or in this book to help reduce their impact.

2. **Journaling.** Instead of burying your fears, face them head-on so that you can assess them rationally and act with clarity and confidence, as Captain Sergey did.

3. **Focus on Actions.** A few times throughout this book, we'll take a dig or two at approaches that have sold a lot of books but have no practical, everyday wisdom, such as the law of attraction. In an earlier chapter, we reminded you that the law of attraction, alas, does not work without **action.** Concentration on actions within your control and letting go of concerns about outcomes beyond your influence is critical. Without worry, you are free to visualize a Best Day Every Day life.

As you've seen in the past few chapters, this book is a passport to adventure in exotic destinations, as well as lessons from the muses and guides who captured our attention and impacted us in those destinations. One of the core tenets of our Best Day Every Day life is repetition. We repeat incantations with enthusiasm. Repeat your affirmations with devotion. Repeat your meditation routine with serenity and steadfastness. So, too, will we repeat certain concepts throughout this book to show you how they impact your life in various ways. First, we focused on meditation and visualization as it relates to brain science and manifestation. Now you see the next layer of meditation and visualization—the way it impacts confidence, emotional regulation, and mood regulation.

BECOMING A LEADER

Another notable quality of the Stoics was their leadership qualities. In Robert Greene's *33 Strategies of War*, you explore the way leaders in politics and the military applied stoicism. You see how stoicism allowed them to act with wisdom, confidence, decisiveness, and ultimately, to be victorious.

Captain Sergey, Tony Robbins, and Hattie Bickmore have all inspired Lori and William's leadership over the course of over three decades, both individually and together. The Stoic avatars over time are royalty, high-ranking military, and nobility. Stoic writings emphasize that to either obtain or keep these positions, leaders must employ Stoic practices such as those described in this book.

A few lessons that have been most impactful to your authors have been:

1. **Autonomy and Initiative.** Don't wait for someone else to take the lead. A leader creates a culture, not adapts to one. Being a leader is not just about holding a position of power or authority; it's about having the courage to influence and set an example for others.

   The first person you lead is yourself.

   When you take the lead, you inspire others to follow in your footsteps and make positive changes in their own lives. For less confident individuals, your leadership will encourage them to tap into the full breadth of their own power. When you set a precedent, you inspire others to do the same.

Leadership means sitting down with your child after a school play and emphasizing the importance of the values highlighted in the script or the compassion of characters you can model.

2. **Empathy and Understanding.** Leadership happens by showing empathy and understanding—by purchasing a bag of groceries for the stranded family outside your grocery store or giving away your unneeded (but appreciated) Christmas gift cards to a friend who just tore his ACL and is missing time on the job.

3. **Ownership of ALL Results.** Leadership means taking ownership, even "extreme ownership" as Jocko Willink writes about in his book of the same title. In this book, he details the decisions of his fellow Navy Seals during some botched missions or even mortal events, highlighting the decisions of great leaders who didn't play the "blame game" or "victim," but who owned both good and bad results equally.

4. **Vision.** Captain Sergey, Hattie Bickmore, and Tony Robbins didn't magically appear victorious in the face of pirates, at the table with world leaders, or on stages in front of thousands without vision. A leader practices Training Day 2 exercises, such as visualization. Instead of waiting for checks to appear in their mailboxes, a la "The Secret," they take decisive action to materialize those visions.

5. **Collaboration.** People who lead others also understand the importance of collaboration and teamwork and can build strong relationships based on trust and mutual respect. When you take the initiative to lead and accompany risks, you earn the respect of others who see your commitment to making a difference. There's nothing more heartwarming than the story of the CEO who took a pay cut to pay his employees higher salaries, like Dan Price, who took a pay cut from $1.1 million to just $70,000 a year. Followers love a leader who has their neck out for them, and they trust a leader who has skin in the game.

Confidence is, again, the hallmark of a good leader, as we learned through Captain Sergey Turnikov. When Turnikov told us about pirates, we were surprised and even terrified. When he explained that he was prepared and confident that he could stave them off with his sailing skills and resourcefulness, we relaxed into the voyage. If he bit his lip, darted his eyes left and right, or "hemmed and hawed" about the threat, we would have asked to get off the Star Clipper at the next port.

Part Two:
STAGING HAPPINESS

Chapter Five:
A CASE FOR BEAUTY

Situated in the First Arrondissement in the heart of Paris, France, is the Hôtel Costes. Opened in 1995, the iconic hotel is famed for a stylish and sophisticated atmosphere and is frequently tagged by celebrities and other high-profile guests who visit the "City of Lights." The interior of the Hôtel Costes is opulent and eclectic, pulling from classic Parisian elegance with modern furnishings and a glamorous ambiance.

The hotel is also known for its stunning courtyard, world-class cuisine, and a chic bar that exudes an air of sophisticated mystery and electric late-night allure. It is both a hotel and a hotspot that graces the pages of fashion magazines and has become a veritable cultural landmark despite its relative youth amidst places like the Louvre and other famous sites in this central Parisian location.

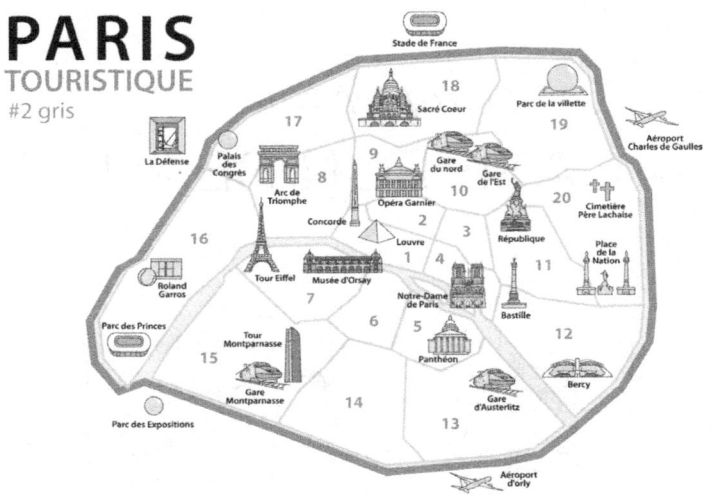

We were seated on the patio at the hotel when we encountered a woman who embodied Parisian elegance and fierceness from her head to her toes. Although in her late 70s or early 80s, she exuded an ageless charisma and even a certain sexiness that came from her vitality and vibrancy. In the years since meeting this woman, we have dubbed her the "mysterious Parisienne woman" when reflecting on her, our time at the Costes, and the impact she had on us both.

Clad entirely in black, her ensemble was a beautiful mix of textures, including silk, leather, and lace, with each piece meticulously chosen. We both, especially Lori, with expertise in fashion and design, could sense that she was a walking piece of art and sophistication. The woman's short hairstyle was chic, styled to perfection, and framed a face that teased at a life well-lived with both grace and intensity. Her commanding presence and undeniable confidence captivated men far younger than her, as evidenced by the discreet double-takes we witnessed that afternoon.

The Hôtel Costes itself is a visual marvel, a series of cozy lounges and light-flooded galleries where you can observe without being observed. The sublime-looking "5-star" fireplace casts a warm glow; its flickering flames reflect in the polished surfaces and antique mirrors. The Italian-style patio for dining is an oasis of green amidst the urban landscape. The gentle warmth of the sun, filtered through the patio's greenery, creates a comfortable and inviting atmosphere. Lush plants and elegant statues create a serene backdrop. Patrons on the terrace seemed to blend in seamlessly with the decor, each one a version of Parisian chic. For me (Lori), observing my fellow patrons and their clothes could have entertained me for endless hours.

The patio was filled with a blend of scents that tantalized our senses. The fragrance of fresh flowers from the surrounding gardens mingled with the distinctive smells of the dishes being served. From just a few feet away, the subtle hint of a classic French perfume scented with notes of jasmine and sandalwood drifted through the air, adding a layer of sophistication and mystery. The mesmerizing scene came from the mysterious Parisienne woman, who was seated next to us on the patio that day for lunch.

Her attire was a masterpiece of modern fashion with hints at a rock star's boldness and an artist's refinement. Every detail, from her statement jewelry to her perfectly-applied red lipstick, revealed a life devoted to style and substance. Her presence commanded the space, and her piercing eyes, full of wisdom as well as mischief, surveyed the scene with a knowing smile. We introduced ourselves and received a firm yet gentle handshake from the woman. Her touch conveyed a warmth that belied her fierce exterior. The variety of textures in her clothing, from the softness of her scarf to the cool metal of her jewelry, all contributed to an immediate tactile richness from the encounter.

The atmosphere at Hôtel Costes is famously underscored by a soundtrack that perfectly complements its glamorous setting. DJs, masters of their craft, spun a mix of sultry jazz, contemporary beats, and classic French chansons as we slowly sipped our first drink, wanting the meal to last for hours, if not days. The music created a relaxed and glamorous ambiance, the kind that makes every conversation feel like a clandestine affair. The gentle murmur of other patrons' conversations, the chime of toasting glasses, and the occasional burst of laughter add to the lively yet intimate atmosphere. Amidst those melodies of music and glassware was the careful cadence of the low voice from the mysterious Parisienne woman. She shared anecdotes and insights with a friend in rich tones with unforced elegance and an accent that exuded old-world refinement as well as modern flair. The cadence of her speech, punctuated by thoughtful pauses and expressive gestures, drew us into her narrative.

A waiter politely approached our table without interrupting the musings of the Parisienne woman. Without saying a word, we both looked at the woman, who took the cue and offered her advice on the menu. The three of us decided to dine together that day on the luxurious patio.

Jean-Louis Costes curates the menu at the Hôtel Costes and celebrates simple, fresh, purely delicious flavors. The Parisienne woman recommended pairing each dish with a selection from the extensive wine list, and her choices enhanced the flavors as well as the experience that afternoon. We began with impeccably prepared fresh asparagus, followed by rich, velvety, and decadent foie gras. An Asian-inspired dish called "Sua Rong Hai" followed, bursting with bold flavors and delicate textures. Next was a tender and succulent limousine-bred veal chop, which provided an epicurean delight that lingered on the palate.

The Parisienne woman savored each bite with a discerning palate; her appreciation for fine cuisine was evident in every gesture. As sumptuous as the food was, the plush velvet cushions on which we were seated were a contrast to the cool smoothness of the marble tabletops.

In our years of personal development, we've encountered people who tend to cling to either one philosophy or another about beauty. In one camp, you'll see those who are non-aesthetic. Ironically, people in this camp have a sort of pride in being unconcerned with appearance, apathy towards aesthetics, a commitment towards function or practicality rather than beauty, and a value of simplicity. Conversely, there is a movement that began in the late 19th century called the "aesthetics," which was a British intellectual and artistic movement that emphasized the importance of beauty and the arts for their own sake, with neither moral nor social purposes required. Prominent figures in the Aesthetic movement included Oscar Wilde, James Whistler, and Aubrey Beardsley. They held that not only should beauty be its own ideal, but that an art should not serve a utilitarian purpose.

Personal expression and the pursuit of beauty have been a hallmark of my (Lori's) career in fashion as well as in personal training. In politics, it's common that my (William's) colleagues could get by with a "face made for radio." This has fueled interesting discussions between us on the value and importance of aesthetics. Can somebody be beautiful in sandals and a sarong? As you'll see in this book, there is no question that some of our most influential heroes have very low aesthetic standards.

However, we want to take time in this chapter not to praise merely the beauty of the Hôtel Costes and the mysterious Parisienne woman for the sake of their beauty, but for the embodiment of art, expression, excellence, and inspiration that they inspired in us.

The mysterious Parisienne woman added layers of depth and intrigue to an already luxurious setting. Everything from her subtle but intoxicating perfume to the lace cuffs of her blouse and leather boots created a sensory experience that was powerful, vibrant, and bold. Her dedication to beauty in one of the world's most beautiful cities evoked a feeling of creation itself, as if we were witnessing the artistry behind nature's most stunning elements—animals, rivers, stars, and flowers.

THE MAGNETISM OF BEAUTY

Admit this to yourself. When someone comes to your door selling something, whether it's raffle tickets, marinara sauce, or religion, if they're dressed in an expensive suit or present themselves with beauty or professionalism, you might listen to them and probably treat them with more respect than someone who looks like a bum... unless it's a Girl Scout. Why would anybody be mean to Girl Scouts?

Whether it's a sharp suit, tall stature, or a gorgeous face, it's normal to be compelled by beauty, even magnetized by it. Taller men are promoted more than shorter men, according to statistics. Those religious zealots who come to your door know that wearing a suit instead of their favorite band t-shirt is going to make you more receptive to their message.

Humans love beauty, whether you consciously admit it or not.

Sometimes experiencing beauty doesn't need to be complicated. It can be as simple as the aesthetic joy of appreciating beauty and relishing it with present-moment awareness, which is refreshing, invigorating, and somehow makes us feel closer to the human spirit, which is beautiful.

Beautiful does not mean untouchable or "better than others."

For instance, notwithstanding her beauty, we were surprised to find that the mysterious Parisienne woman was approachable. She seemed to open up like a normal person would. As we lay in bed that night, what struck us most wasn't just how extraordinary everything had tasted, but the unexpected truth that people who seem distant are often a lot more like us than we think.

Tony Robbins, Captain Sergey, and Hattie Bickmore are larger-than-life characters with whom we experienced raw, pure, authentic, and even vulnerable interactions. The people elevated in our perceptions are generally perfectly "down to earth." But suppose these people are so down to earth. Why don't they conduct themselves like the non-aesthetics, allowing their brilliance and excellence to speak through actions rather than with the assistance of a uniform, such as Tony's booming stage voice, Hattie's perfect decorum, the mysterious Parisienne's attire, or Captain Sergey's Captain's uniform, which you'd never catch him without (we even wondered if he slept in his coat lest he be woken up in the middle of the night for an emergency and be caught without it)?

Lori is a great example of a person, like so many of our heroes in this book, who wears a uniform. Whether she's in ski clothes, workout clothes, or going to dinner, she always looks like a ten. She's put together but approachable. She's finely dressed but relatable. She's easy to open up to, but in all situations, she captivates.

Lori is magnetic. In a brown paper bag, she'd be beautiful. Still, because she has a uniform of carefully chosen attire, she also has another quality that isn't as easy to define as beauty. Whether you see us (Lori and William) at the gym, at dinner, or on the slopes, you feel, in a way, that we are trustworthy. We wake up and dress with intention, no matter where we're going. In a later chapter, we'll discuss this concept of dressing for what you want to manifest on a deeper level.

But for this chapter, we want to take a moment to celebrate the attribute of a "magnetic presence." This is a running theme among the muses and guides you'll meet in this book.

Tony Robbins, although approachable and friendly, has a magnetic presence. You find yourself listening to him intently without having to try too hard. You're not distracted by anything because of his captivating presence. Hattie Bickmore commanded a room, at once energizing those to whom she spoke while also making people feel at ease and confident in her presence. When you talk to Captain Sergey about anything from how to grind coffee to his views on political figures, you listen carefully and feel compelled to believe that he knows what he's talking about and that he's right.

The mysterious Parisienne woman was magnetic, and she may have been just as magnetic in a brown paper bag as she was in her dazzling attire. This isn't about clothes, but rather it has to do with the way one carries themself.

You'll see this in the cinema and on stage as well. We have friends who work in Hollywood, and we've learned that it isn't the best artist or actor who gets the part, but the one who can dazzle both on and off screen or both inside and outside the recording room. Listen to an audiobook read by Meryl Streep or watch the mesmerizing way John Wayne gave off his "macho man in control of all situations" vibes.

Much of this magnetic presence stems from earlier teachings about stoicism. The warrior isn't the screaming, picketing, maniacal member of the resistance, but the one carefully plodding their next move with emotional regulation and control. The one who commands attention isn't the one who spews hyperbolic or vitriolic data points to prove their argument, but the one who employs the Socratic method of asking questions and allowing the "audience" to come to their own conclusions in a safe place.

The mysterious Parisienne woman was a magnet. Men several decades younger than her turned their heads to look at her, and women leaned in as if they could capture some of her magnetism for themselves merely by standing close by.

People who are magnets aren't the loudest in the room because they're selective about where they devote their energy. They are secure and do not require outside approval. Although they may look and act like rock stars and appear to live life on their terms, they also have a charisma that draws people in. Their magnetic qualities are at once something we enjoy admiring from afar, but when interacting with them one-on-one, we feel like we've won a prize.

Another source of magnetism and beauty is vitality. One of the first descriptions in this chapter of the mysterious Parisienne woman was that she had vitality despite her age, perhaps 80 years old. Writer Andrew Solomon once said, "The opposite of depression is not happiness but vitality." This echoes Nick Seneca Jenkel's remarks about happiness being inextricably linked to the presence of a community to which one contributes. Depression might resemble a retired man or woman who wakes up, reads the paper, watches television, takes a nap, makes lunch, watches more television, microwaves dinner, watches more television, and goes to sleep in an armchair. There is literally no picture that looks more depressing than this, in your author's opinion. Not terminally ill, not burdened by financial stress, not even battling with wayward teenagers. Nothing looks more depressing than a lack of vitality. Existing solely to wake up, sleep, wake up, sleep, and repeat this cycle with no purpose or community.

When vitality is infused into any life, there isn't just more to do, but there is hope. The vital person treasures making neighbors smile as they walk past their house, treasures planning trips or activities, treasures strengthening the body in various ways, and, above all, treasures the contribution they make to a family, church, community, or hobby group. Vitality is the key to what drew eyes towards the mysterious Parisienne woman, as well as what drew people to some of the muses in this book. The vital person isn't one to be pitied but to be admired.

What if we admitted to ourselves, starting today, that being magnetic isn't merely the strength of your intelligence or the goodness of your heart but also the ability you have to magnetically draw others to you, even by valuing beauty.

PARTICIPATE IN A BIGGER GAME

A later chapter in this book is called "You Can't Manifest Your Best Life in Crocs." The title for that chapter is a bit tongue-in-cheek, but you'll understand it on a deeper level when we arrive at that portion of this book. For the time being, we want to take this moment to prime your mind and spirit for a conversation that you won't find in many other personal development or self-improvement books, and that is the concept that there is a uniform required to participate in a bigger game in life.

In all likelihood, the people you admire most participate in a bigger game. This could be somebody in the arts, sports, entertainment, or politics. These people don't live "normal" lives. They've chosen a path for their lives that would best be described as extraordinary. They decided to participate in a bigger game than "normal." This is the woman I (Lori) dreamed of becoming when I left Mansfield, and the man I (William) dreamed of becoming when I devoted myself to my studies in law.

What we learned through our early success in life, be it in Manhattan or Washington D.C., is that "extraordinary" people are more like "us" than you'd imagine. What distinguishes them is the fact that they have chosen to play a bigger game at a higher level. After reading this book, we hope that you will reject the entire notion of normal when it comes to your life.

You see, when you realize that there is no such thing as "normal," you open yourself up to new possibilities and opportunities. If a talent agent were standing in the Hôtel Costes that afternoon and met the mysterious Parisienne woman, she would be chosen for any part: rock star, model, actress, or CEO. She was anything but normal. She was extraordinary. The energy and image she exuded gave you the impression that no matter what part she played, she would win the Oscar.

Are you normal? Or extraordinary?

The prevailing narrative in society is that you can be whoever you want to be, which is true. And you are beautiful just as you are, which is also true. What is also true is that those whom we admire show up to life playing at a high level. Are you not playing at a high level today? Do you feel like you've conformed to society's low expectations for your life or success?

Then change.

The Greek philosopher Heraclitus of Ephesus said, "The only constant in life is change."

If you've read this far into our book, you have shown you're open to change. You don't believe conforming to low standards is for you. Like me (Lori), you aren't settling for the career paths laid out or the limitations an average boy from my (William's) hometown had to endure.

Change doesn't always feel good, but making small adjustments consistently makes the extraordinary your new normal. Every Training Day in this book encourages you to examine your thoughts, actions, and desires to help you break out of the patterns keeping you stuck. The heart of this book is the concept of neurogenesis: you can rewire your mind and, in turn, your life, by taking a new path, seeing things from different perspectives, immersing yourself in a new environment, and even meeting new people along the way.

It is now time for us to unveil another sneaky trick within this book. Do you know why we have carefully created twenty-one chapters and twenty-one Training Day exercises? It's been said that it takes 21 days to build or break habits. The concept originates from Dr. Maxwell Malt's observations in the 1960s. At this time, he noted that it took about 21 days for patients to adjust to changes in their physical appearance after surgery. Since then, experts have found that habits such as drinking more water or exercising regularly also fall into the "21 days to form a habit" category.

Many of our friends who don't drink discovered that after twenty-one days of eliminating alcohol—or even replacing hard liquor with wine or beer—the process became much easier. Friends who incorporate a routine of betterment through anything from reading inspiring literature to listening to educational podcasts during their commute find that after 21 days, that habit becomes second nature. It no longer becomes a challenge but an effortless part of their routine.

Twenty-one days isn't a hard-and-fast rule but a general guideline. We believe that after twenty-one Training Days in the *World of Wisdom* book and self-improvement series, you will find that introspection, visualization, and even positive habits such as meditation come more easily to you. The more you practice a new behavior, the more naturally it becomes ingrained.

Even more interestingly, the *European Journal of Social Psychology* found in 2009 that, on average, it takes about 66 days for a new behavior to become automatic, but this can range from 18 to 254 days depending on the individual and the behavior. More complex habits (such as 200 pushups per day) may take longer to take root. In addition, past traumas or psychological factors may either hinder or support your ability to form a habit that becomes ingrained or automatic.

We find that an extraordinary life has become our normal. The abnormal wonder and beauty of our lives are automatic. For that to become so, it required years of making small adjustments that led to change becoming less and less painful, and one day, our new, extraordinary lives became our baseline.

As you're reading this book today, change may feel impossible, yet that is often the sign that the time is right to make an alteration. Consider how making something different may be beneficial to you and those around you. As someone who loves their peers, family, or colleagues, does this concept inspire you to make extraordinary adjustments that lead to an extraordinary life?

Participating in a bigger game means stepping outside of your comfort zone and pursuing your passions and dreams. It means taking risks, following your heart, and making a difference in the world. It's about living a life that is fulfilling and meaningful, rather than simply going through the motions.

Choosing to participate in a bigger game also means embracing your unique talents and gifts. We all have something special to offer the world, and when we use our talents to make a difference, we feel a sense of purpose and fulfillment. The status quo is never good enough. Focus on your gifts. By playing in a bigger game, you can achieve a greater purpose and live a fully engaged life. It's not the size of the game but the impact it has on you and those around you. What does your heart desire? What does the world need? The objective is to reach the end of life deeply satisfied with how you spent your time on Earth.

What are your special talents and gifts? Everyone has things they do better than other people. Let's brainstorm what you love to do. Would your life be more fun and rewarding if you could spend more time doing the things you love? If so, why not make those activities and goals the center of your focus – "where focus goes, energy flows".

Chapter Six:
HAPPINESS IS YOUR BIRTHRIGHT

"Happiness is found in the journey, not just the destination. Embrace each moment, every sight, sound, and experience along the way, and you will discover true joy."
Satish Kapoor

"Happiness is the meaning and the purpose of life, the whole aim and end of human existence."
Aristotle

New Delhi, India, is a bustling metropolis filled with a flurry of dynamic sensory experiences. Honking vehicles and street vendors vie for the attention of passersby, who navigate their way through the chaos in cars, buses, pedicabs, and on foot. It's not unusual to hear the distant sounds of train tracks clattering as the energetic city buzzes with life.

Fragrant, freshly baked naan and street food spices blend with dust and exhaust fumes. Amidst the chaos of daily life and commuting through New Delhi, you'll be mesmerized by the deep roots of history and culture, including ancient forts and monuments, or even colonial-era buildings next to modern structures.

One afternoon in India's capital, we sought refuge from the heat and made our way to "Indian Accent," a renowned restaurant celebrated for its innovative approach to traditional cuisine. We indulged in a delightful lunch featuring dishes like the chef's signature Kashmiri Lamb, tender and fragrant with spices, alongside Dum Aloo, rich potatoes cooked in a spiced yogurt gravy. Each bite was complemented by an assortment of freshly baked naan and butter chicken, beautifully presented with a contemporary flair.

Our guides, Abercrombie & Kent, who were familiar with the logistics of traveling in India, hired a driver dedicated to safely transporting us to and from the destinations on our Indian itinerary. Our driver was Satish Kapoor, a man so unperturbed while navigating the chaotic New Delhi environment that you'd think he was out for a casual Sunday drive in the country.

Once the car escaped the sensory overload of the inner city and began to approach a rural shrine we intended to visit that day, we felt our bodies relax into the smooth leather of the car seats, embraced by the cool air conditioning. We had spent the better part of a week driving with Satish around India, traveling to sacred sites, sumptuous meals, and events with friends and colleagues who were also in the capital city.

William had imagined that on our last day together, he would ask Satish a question that had been on his mind all week. As we subconsciously sighed and the roads became more remote, William asked Kapoor, "Satish, you're a really happy guy. I mean, you're *really* content in every situation we've been in this week. What's your secret?"

Satish laughed as if he were a teacher who'd been anticipating this "ah-ha" moment from his student. He was not surprised but pleased.

"William, my happiness isn't a feeling, it's a being."

Kapoor paused to let the quip sink in. As he drove the winding streets, the car was filled with fragrant scents of marigold and jasmine garlands that

CHAPTER SIX: HAPPINESS IS YOUR BIRTHRIGHT

swayed from the rearview mirror, gifts we had given our host that morning. As if on cue, incense from a roadside shrine wafted into the vehicle. Kapoor continued, "Happiness is found in the journey, not just the destination. Embrace each moment, every sight, sound, and experience along the way, and you will discover true joy."

The vehicle hummed as we took in the wisdom, complete with the fragrance of the flowers in the car, the incense from the shrines, and the earthy scent of rain-soaked dirt across the countryside.

"Happiness is not something I'm trying to attain. My family and my appreciation for life's simple joys are all I require. I'm not looking for anything; everything I want is right here," Kapoor stated while gesturing toward the car's air-conditioned interior.

As the roads stretched out before us, winding through India's countryside, we reflected on Kapoor's wisdom: Happiness isn't a fleeting feeling, it's a state of being. His words stayed with us long after our time together, a lesson gently reinforced by every encounter, every landscape, and every sacred place we visited.

This philosophy was never more evident than in Agra, home to one of the most significant symbols of devotion and timeless beauty—the Taj Mahal. Built as an eternal monument to love, the Taj Mahal is not simply a marvel of architecture; it is a testament to the idea that what is created with deep intention and love can outlast lifetimes. The same can be said for happiness—it is not something we chase but something we cultivate, something we leave behind in the lives we touch.

Standing before the Taj Mahal at sunrise, the white marble bathed in soft golden hues, we couldn't help but think about Kapoor's words once more. The Taj wasn't built in haste or in pursuit of temporary joy. It was built with patience, care, and unwavering devotion—just like the kind of happiness that isn't dependent on external circumstances, but rather on a profound appreciation for life itself.

Much like the journey through India—its contrasts, its chaos, its serenity—happiness is not just about the peaks or perfect moments. It is about embracing the entirety of the experience. It's found not only in the grandeur of the Taj Mahal but in the simple pleasure of sharing a cup of chai with a friend, the laughter of families celebrating Diwali, or the resilience of a taxi driver navigating the labyrinth of New Delhi with an unshakable sense of contentment.

Lori and William at the Taj Mahal in Agra, India.

For us, Agra was more than just a stop on an itinerary; it was a reminder that the most extraordinary things in life—whether love, beauty, or happiness—are not instant. They are built, nurtured, and sustained. Perhaps that's the real secret to happiness: it is not found in seeking perfection but in finding the beauty that already exists.

During our travels, we learned that in India, happiness is a deeply ingrained concept, intertwined with cultural, spiritual, and social practices. It's not just about personal joy but also about collective well-being, inner peace, and fulfillment. This concept aligns with Nick Seneca Jenkel's findings that the happiest people in the world, based on a study of over 200,000 individuals in countless nations, are those who connect and contribute to others. Happiness doesn't come from money or health but from the connection one has to a community they serve.

In many cultures, happiness is often found in the warmth of family bonds, the joy of festivals, and the simple pleasures of community life. Celebrations like Diwali, Holi, and Eid bring people together, fostering a sense of belonging and shared joy. Jewish communities come together on the

Sabbath as well as during many holidays throughout the year. Christians may come together for family Sunday meals, a practice also common among Lori's Italian peers who regularly host family gatherings with several generations under one household.

Lori and William in traditional Indian attire with Tony Robbins at Platinum Partnership India 2016.

In America, these celebrations and traditions are often muted in an individualistic culture, where many people are transient, having been displaced from their communities of origin and families. This has always struck us as a depressing reality of an otherwise beautiful American life and cultural fabric: loneliness is a paramount issue associated with declining mental health in this country. Our home base is in Aspen, Colorado, where enormously high suicide rates are attributed either to the high altitude or to the isolation of "mountain people." We tend to think it's the latter, sprinkled with opioid, alcohol, and other drug abuse.

In every way, India is an anti-isolated society. Millions of people live close together in a somewhat chaotic environment. It is the birthplace of several major religions and spiritual practices, including Hinduism, Buddhism, Jainism, and Sikhism. Celebrations honoring religious practices, cultural events, and even weddings are a common occurrence throughout the year, the likes of which many of our American peers have never seen in their lives.

But the culture isn't merely concerned with a good party. Happiness for many in India is achieved through spiritual growth, meditation, and practices like yoga, which promote inner peace and harmony. Despite the complexities of life, many Indians find happiness in simple pleasures—sipping chai on a rainy day, a heartfelt conversation with a friend, or enjoying the beauty of nature.

Indian philosophy often emphasizes the importance of accepting life's ups and downs with equanimity. This resilience and adaptability contribute to a sense of enduring happiness. Because we enjoyed our time with Satish and because, in some way, he anchors us to this concept of reveling in the simple joys of life, we have stayed in contact with Satish and remain friends to this day.

Since visiting India, we have made it a part of our sacred travel routine to meditate on happiness in every location we visit. Few destinations evoke as much joy as St. Barths in the Caribbean and Lake Como in Italy. One of our dear friends, Samy Ghachem, the former General Manager of Le Sereno in St. Barths, Il Sereno on Lake Como, Italy, and now the General Manager of La Dolce Vita Orient Express, is a friend with whom we've often visited on our travels.

"Have you ever gotten used to this view?" Lori asked Samy one afternoon upon checking into Le Sereno in St. Barths. Samy stood on the balcony terrace of Le Sereno and seemed to ponder the question.

"This life and the beauty of this place are truly a gift. I cherish this view, as if it were painted just for my enjoyment! Happiness is your birthright, ready to be embraced."

Ghachem hadn't pondered the question, but the response seemed to be crafted by a philosopher or motivational speaker. It struck us as both gracious and, in a way, a bit presumptuous.

CHAPTER SIX: HAPPINESS IS YOUR BIRTHRIGHT

Did he genuinely believe the entire Caribbean Sea was painted for his enjoyment?

Did he think that luxury and beauty were inherent to our birthright?

Through time and many hours of wining and dining with Samy, we have gained insight into his philosophy on happiness and his remarkable ability to capture and replicate beauty in his life and work at the hotels. Not only does Samy believe that his birthright is an inheritance of unparalleled beauty and luxury, but he also ensures that his guests and friends understand they, too, deserve the very best.

Enjoying Samy's company one afternoon, he suggested we visit him in Lake Como and visit *Le Sereno's* sister hotel, *Il Sereno*.

That afternoon, the warm Caribbean breeze carried the scent of frangipani and sea salt as turquoise waters lapped the pristine shores. Underneath Samy's perfectly polished sandalwood brown shoes, without a single grain of sand on them, stretched a sun-kissed wooden deck pulsing with the rhythm of island life. "When will you be heading to Italy? We must plan to meet again!"

Some months later, the three friends found themselves immersed in the breathtaking beauty of Italy. The crisp Alpine air mingled with the subtle fragrance of jasmine and freshly brewed espresso as the toll of distant church bells echoed across tranquil waters. Their melody intertwined with the soft rustle of cypress trees, while the surface of Lake Como shimmered like liquid silver, reflecting the majestic mountains that stood sentinel over this Italian paradise.

PERMISSION TO BE HAPPY

The phrase 'happiness is your birthright' is often attributed to Yogi Bhajan, a spiritual leader and teacher of Kundalini Yoga. He frequently spoke about the idea that every individual has the inherent right to be happy and live a fulfilled life. Yogi Bhajan emphasized that happiness comes from within and is not something that needs to be earned, but rather something we are all entitled to by virtue of being human.

However, sometimes seeing misery around us creates a barrier between us and happiness. Although we are surrounded by beauty and every sunrise or night sky provides ample opportunities for gazing in wonder at the splendidness of our surroundings, it's common for people to feel guilty for either being happy or wanting to be happy.

We've heard variations of the following:

> *Happiness? How can you be happy when terrible things go on around the world, from wars to children being trafficked in our own country?*

> *Happy? Why don't you try being a good person? Then you'll be happy.*

> *Happiness comes from serving others. Spending time in continual self-care is selfish!*

> *The problem with this generation is entitlement! You don't deserve to be happy. You deserve to have a roof over your head. Be happy with that!*

We don't resonate with any of these messages, although we do empathize with each sentiment at face value. Happiness is not only what you deserve, but it is your duty as a "good" human. One thing reiterated time and again in science and studies of quantum mechanics is the reality of vibrational energy.

One of our favorite studies is the little-known "100th monkey" phenomenon. In this 1970s era experiment, Western scientists uncovered the presence of something now referred to as "group consciousness." We believe that this study is among many that confirm that our happiness is a duty and responsibility, as it may elevate the world around us. In fact, Dr. David Hawkins indicates that positive vibrations are so powerful that the elevated consciousness of just a handful of people can literally stop wars, as he explains in his book *Power vs. Force*. In the following chapter, you'll meet a monk, one of the muses on this journey. We can't help but thank the heavens for the men and women across the world who have devoted their lives to emitting high-vibrational energy, which we believe elevates the world as a whole.

Returning to the study of the monkeys, it remains fascinating because, to this day, there is no real scientific explanation for what was observed on the Japanese island of Kōjima. Scientists would provide sweet potatoes for the monkeys, which were a favorite treat. However, the monkeys didn't appreciate the sand that would stick to the sweet potatoes supplied to them.

One day, an 18-month-old monkey took her potato to the water to wash the sand off, a behavior that had not been observed before in the thirty years of the scientists' experiment. In time, the practice of washing potatoes with sand became common among the other monkeys on the island. Washing food soon became the new norm for monkeys all over this island. But what happened next is remarkable.

Across the ocean on another island, completely secluded from the original monkeys, the practice of washing potatoes became common among a totally separate and otherwise isolated group of monkeys. In time, the behavior was observed in five other colonies of monkeys from different islands in that area, including on the Japanese mainland. Although the concept of group consciousness is still considered esoteric, some have tried to explain the science of group consciousness by saying that, in this case, the monkeys were communicating with each other through sound waves.

In the 1970s, several books were published that included the story of the monkeys, but the phenomenon became popularized by Ken Keyes Jr.'s book *The Hundredth Monkey* in 1984. Keyes writes about the ravaging effects of nuclear war on the planet, but uses the "hundredth monkey" story as a parable to illustrate the concept of effecting positive change through vibration.

Another study that illustrates how our own positive energy may affect the world around us comes from Dr. Masaru Emoto's "Water Experiment," a classic illustration of how powerful your words are. Dr Emoto is best known for his claims that human consciousness affects the molecular structure of water. Emoto claimed that positive words, prayers, or even songs could positively affect water. Water covers 80% of our planet, and our bodies are, too, 80% water. This has led many to claim that if positive human consciousness affects the molecular structure of water, then it also affects human consciousness. Your high consciousness vibrations can positively affect the molecular structure of the bodies around you, so to speak.

Whether through Dr. David Hawkins' studies in kinesiology and consciousness, Dr. Emoto's water studies, or the group consciousness concepts from the "hundredth monkey" study, we, the authors, believe that our high consciousness and positive vibrations positively affect the world around us. Therefore, we posit that happiness isn't just your birthright but your duty.

The Christmas Wish Foundation, launched in 1984 with the support of the Rotary Club of Aspen and its inspired members, is a beautiful example of how positive intentions manifest real change. Created to uplift those in the Roaring Fork Valley facing challenges like illness, job loss, or family hardship, the foundation channels 100% of its donations directly to local families, seniors, and children—all through the efforts of dedicated volunteers.

This initiative embodies our belief that happiness and compassion are not only our birthright but our responsibility. By lifting others, we create a ripple effect that resonates throughout the community, aligning perfectly with our Best Day Every Day philosophy.

Your happiness is infectious. It elevates the consciousness around you, endears people to your cause, and makes you magnetic. Do you need more proof that happiness isn't just your birthright but your duty?

CLAIMING YOUR HAPPINESS BIRTHRIGHT

If happiness is our birthright, how do we claim it? True and lasting happiness arises when we align our actions with our deepest values, contribute to others, and consistently grow toward our full potential. Satish and Samy were aligned with their respective values, engaged with their community, and committed to daily improvement by growing, Satish in his spirituality and Samy in his profession of hospitality, where he makes it his duty to make others happy.

Across the world, therapists' offices are full of people asking the same questions: "What is the purpose of my life? Why am I here?"

Humanity has existed for a relatively short time, the mere blink of an eye in celestial terms. Our relatively small planet with its unique life-supporting characteristics is said to be 4.5 billion years old by scientists and barely 6,000 years old by many world religions. The Earth revolves around a ball of energy and light we call the sun, located in the midst of a vast galaxy we call the Milky Way, made up of billions of similar suns and solar systems. Your life, give or take, 100 years is remarkably short. And in relation to this massive solar system, how does it have any meaning? Although Earth is important to us, it's plainly insignificant in comparison to the workings of the incomprehensibly huge universe. Earth is smaller than a speck of sand in relation to the rest of the planets and celestial bodies. What's more, there are 8 billion people on this Earth who are, in so many ways, wired just like you.

This realization is not only daunting but also a revelation of how special our lives are. How do we become part of this world and existence? Why us and not someone else? Is there a purpose for our existence, or are we just the random creation of an evolving planet that started with tiny organisms that evolved over the millennia into large creatures called dinosaurs that ruled the earth for millions of years?

Contemplating the seemingly arbitrary nature of our existence and our minuscule presence in the vast universe raises that compelling question: What is the purpose of life? The quest for life's purpose has long intrigued eminent philosophers across various epochs, spanning from the ancient Greek sages to the Enlightenment thinkers. Each era has yielded profound contemplations on the essence of existence. Though no single, universally embraced answer exists, the reflections of these philosophical luminaries shed light on the many ways humanity has sought to grapple with this fundamental question.

Aristotle, one of the towering figures of ancient Greek philosophy, proposed the concept of eudaimonia as the ultimate purpose of life. Eudaimonia, often translated as "flourishing" or "well-being," is the state of living in accordance with one's true nature and fulfilling one's potential. Aristotle argued that the highest good is not merely pleasure or wealth but the realization of human virtues and the cultivation of a virtuous character. Aristotle said, "Happiness is the meaning and the purpose of life, the whole aim, and end of human existence." For him and most of his contemporaries, happiness referred not to an emotion but to the long-term pattern of action, the sum of which was one's moral character. For him, a purposeful life involves the pursuit of wisdom, courage, justice, and other virtues that contribute to the common good.

In the existentialist tradition, philosophers like Jean-Paul Sartre grappled with the inherent absurdity of existence. Sartre contended that life has no predetermined purpose, and individuals must create their own meaning through authentic choices and actions. The existentialist emphasis on personal responsibility and freedom implies that the purpose of life is subjective and self-determined. While this perspective may lead to feelings of existential angst, it also offers the potential for profound self-discovery and the creation of a meaningful narrative.

Drawing from Eastern philosophy, life's purpose is frequently articulated through the lens of spiritual enlightenment and inner balance. Within Hinduism, the notion of dharma, representing one's duty and virtuous existence, directs individuals toward a meaningful life. Likewise, Buddhism asserts that the cessation of suffering, attained through the Eightfold Path, stands as the ultimate objective. The focus on mindfulness, compassion, and detachment from worldly desires underscores a purpose centered on transcending the cycle of suffering and reaching a state of enlightenment.

Moving into the modern era, utilitarian philosophers such as Jeremy Bentham and John Stuart Mill proposed a purpose of life grounded in the pursuit of happiness and the greatest good for the greatest number. Utilitarianism suggests that ethical choices should be made to maximize overall well-being. While this perspective provides a measurable metric for evaluating the purpose of actions, it also raises questions about the potential sacrifice of individual rights and values for the greater good.

The purpose of life, as articulated by great philosophers across different cultures and epochs, reveals the richness and diversity of human thought on this profound question. Whether grounded in virtue, personal freedom, spiritual enlightenment, or the maximization of happiness, these perspectives offer valuable insights into the human experience. Ultimately, the quest for meaning is a deeply personal and subjective journey, shaped by cultural, philosophical, and individual factors. As we navigate the complexities of existence, the wisdom of great philosophers serves as a guide, prompting us to reflect on our values, choices, and the profound significance of our lives.

> *"The purpose of life is to be happy."*
> *The Dalai Lama*

Another great thinker of our time is the Dalai Lama. His Holiness is not only a revered spiritual leader but also a prominent advocate for compassion, inner peace, and the pursuit of happiness. The Dalai Lama's belief that the purpose of life is to be happy reflects the core tenets of Tibetan Buddhism and offers a profound perspective on human existence. The Dalai Lama emphasizes that true happiness is not found in the pursuit of external pleasures or material wealth but is an inner state of well-being rooted in compassion and altruism.

> *"Happiness is not something ready-made.*
> *It comes from your own actions."*
> The Dalai Lama

For the Dalai Lama, compassion is a foundational principle that underlies the pursuit of happiness. He contends that genuine happiness arises when individuals cultivate a sense of compassion not only for themselves but also for others. In his book *The Art of Happiness*, co-authored with Howard Cutler, the Dalai Lama explores the importance of compassion and its role in fostering a meaningful and joyful life. By extending empathy and kindness to others, individuals create a positive and interconnected world that contributes to their own well-being.

Another key element in the Dalai Lama's philosophy is the practice of mindfulness. Rooted in Buddhist traditions, mindfulness involves being fully present in the current moment and cultivating awareness of one's thoughts and emotions. The Dalai Lama asserts that through mindfulness, individuals can develop inner peace and a deeper understanding of themselves, leading to a more profound sense of happiness.

> *"I find hope in the darkest of days and focus on the brightest.*
> *I do not judge the universe."*
> The Dalai Lama

In a world often driven by material pursuits, the Dalai Lama advocates for a measured approach to wealth and possessions. While recognizing the importance of meeting basic needs, he warns against the excessive pursuit of material wealth as a source of happiness. Instead, he encourages individuals to find contentment in simplicity, highlighting that true happiness is not dependent on external circumstances but is an internal state of mind.

In Tibetan wisdom, it is expressed that "tragedy should be harnessed as a wellspring of strength." The Dalai Lama further emphasizes that, despite the nature of challenges and the intensity of painful experiences, the true disaster lies in the loss of hope.

The Dalai Lama's philosophy places a strong emphasis on the interconnectedness of all living beings. He contends that recognizing our shared humanity and interdependence fosters a sense of responsibility and compassion toward others. Altruism, or the selfless concern for the well-being of others, becomes a guiding principle in the pursuit of happiness. By contributing to the happiness of others, individuals enhance their own sense of purpose and fulfillment.

> *"If you think you are too small to make a difference,*
> *try sleeping with a mosquito."*
> The Dalai Lama

The Dalai Lama's belief that the purpose of life is to be happy encapsulates a profound and timeless philosophy rooted in the teachings of Tibetan Buddhism. His emphasis on compassion, mindfulness, and altruism provides a roadmap for individuals seeking a deeper and more meaningful existence. In a world marked by challenges and complexities, the Dalai Lama's teachings invite us to reconsider the sources of true happiness and the interconnected nature of human experience. By cultivating compassion, practicing mindfulness, and embracing a sense of altruism, individuals can embark on a transformative journey towards a more joyful and purposeful life, echoing the timeless wisdom of one of the world's most revered spiritual leaders. From Aristotle to the Dalai Lama, the great thinkers of human history believe the purpose of life is to be happy, and happiness is the meaning and the purpose of life, the whole aim and end of human existence.

Although we don't have the legacy of Aristotle and the Dalai Lama, it has always been our philosophy that enjoying life should be our number one goal. We share a similar outlook, a deep desire to enjoy life to the fullest. We've always made fun and joy a priority—that's the heart of this book. It's about making every day as enjoyable as it can be. It was always my (William) dream as a young boy skiing on a 300 vertical foot hill in northern Maine to live in a major ski resort one day. But, as I got older and went through college and law school, I also had the dream of having an exciting career in a major city like Washington, D.C.. After I accomplished my career ambitions, I made the decision to move to Aspen to live the life that I had dreamed about as a kid. Throughout my life, I have always sought out the most enjoyable experiences.

Lori with Samy Ghachem at Il Sereno on Lake Como, Italy

As we explored the charming town of Como and indulged in culinary delights, we marveled at the exquisite surroundings. The delicious scent of truffles filled the air, tempting our senses as we enjoyed meals at elegant restaurants. Fellow diners clinked Prosecco glasses over marble tables, seated in plush jewel-toned velvet chairs.

One evening, we found ourselves in a luxurious suite that blended modern amenities with vintage-inspired decor, creating a cocoon of elegance. Over the next several nights, enveloped in unparalleled comfort, we reflected on the words we had heard in St. Barths: "Happiness is your birthright."

As twilight fell and the first stars began to twinkle in the Italian sky, we soaked in the essence of la dolce vita. This experience was a testament to Samy's vision of hospitality, which he practiced both at *Le Sereno* in St. Barths and his sister hotel, *Il Sereno* on Lake Como. In both places, every sense was indulged, every moment savored, and happiness was not just an aspiration but a lived experience. Over countless Prosecco toasts with Samy, we uncovered keys to happiness that he carried with him to every hotel, community, and continent he visited. These lessons resonated not only in luxurious destinations like St. Barths but also in the everyday moments of our "normal" lives.

Despite my career ambitions, I (William) decided to move to Aspen to live the life that I had dreamed about as a kid. Throughout my life, I have always sought out the most enjoyable experiences.

I (Lori), hailing from Mansfield, Ohio, once dreamt of the dazzling lights of New York City and a flourishing career in fashion. Balancing my love for fitness, I carved out successful paths in both fashion and the fitness industry. The magnetic force that unites us is our shared commitment to actively pursuing and savoring life's extraordinary moments, with a shared vision of making each day the Best Day Ever.

1. Happiness is Your Job.

Along our life's journey, we've learned a few things about what brings happiness and joy into our lives. Happiness is a state of mind that most people should strive for. We all want to be happy and to lead a fulfilling life. However, happiness is not something that comes naturally to everyone, and it can be challenging to maintain a positive outlook in a world that is often full of challenges and setbacks. In this chapter, we will explore the idea that happiness is your job and discuss ways in which you can take control of your own well-being.

The idea that happiness is your job is based on the notion that happiness is something you have to work towards actively. It's not something that you can simply expect to happen on its own. Just like any other job, it requires effort and commitment to achieve. In many ways, it's even more important than any other job, as it directly impacts your overall enjoyment and quality of life.

One of the first steps towards achieving happiness is to identify what makes you happy. Everyone's definition of happiness is different, and what works for one person may not work for another. Take some time to reflect on what brings you joy and fulfillment. It could be spending time with loved ones, pursuing a passion or hobby, helping others, or simply taking some time for yourself.

Once you have identified what makes you extremely happy, you can start to make conscious choices that prioritize those things in your life. This could mean reorganizing your schedule to make time for the things that matter most, saying no to commitments that don't align with your values or interests, or changing your mindset to focus on the positive aspects of life.

Another key factor in achieving happiness is cultivating gratitude. Being grateful for what you have can help shift your focus away from negative thoughts and towards the positive aspects of life. Consider starting a gratitude journal where you write down three things you are grateful for each day. Alternatively, take a few moments each day to reflect on what you are thankful for.

Finally, it's essential to recognize that happiness is not a destination. It's an ongoing journey that requires constant effort and attention. There will be setbacks and challenges along the way, but by taking responsibility for your own peace of mind and making conscious choices to prioritize the things that bring you joy, you can create a fulfilling and meaningful life. You have the power to prioritize your own happiness today.

2. "Life Should Be a Continuous Party." - Salvador Dali

Salvador Dali, the famous Spanish surrealist artist, was known for his eccentric personality and unconventional approach to life. He was also known for his statement that "life should be a continuous party." For Dali, life was a work of art, and every moment was an opportunity to create something beautiful and meaningful. He believed life was meant to be lived to the fullest, and we should never miss an opportunity to celebrate and enjoy it. To Dali, the idea of a continuous party meant we should approach life with a sense of joy, enthusiasm, and playfulness.

Dali believed the world was full of wonders and mysteries, and it was our duty as human beings to explore them. He believed life was too short to waste on mundane activities, and we should make the most of every moment. This meant embracing the unexpected, taking risks, and constantly seeking out new experiences.

Dali was also a believer in the power of the imagination. He believed the human mind was capable of incredible things, and we should never limit ourselves or our creativity. For Dali, the continuous party was a celebration of the imagination and the endless possibilities it presented. He encouraged people to dream big, to be daring, and to take risks in pursuit of their passions.

In addition to his love of the imagination, Dali was also known for his love of pleasure. He believed life was meant to be enjoyed, and we should indulge in our senses and desires. To Dali, pleasure was an essential part of the human experience, and he saw no reason why we should deny ourselves the pleasures of life.

Of course, it's worth noting that Dali's perspective on life was not without its criticisms. Some have argued that his emphasis on pleasure and indulgence could be perceived as superficial and selfish. Others have pointed out that not everyone has the luxury of living life like a continuous party, and many people face real challenges and hardships in their lives.

However, it's also worth noting that his philosophy was not just about superficial pleasure-seeking. It was also about embracing the wonder and beauty of the world around us and approaching life with a sense of creativity and playfulness. It was about seeing the potential for joy and celebration in even the most difficult of circumstances.

While his philosophy may not be for everyone, it's a reminder that life was meant to be enjoyed and celebrated, and we should never lose our sense of wonder and curiosity about the world around us. By following his advice, we can shift our focus to the positive aspects of life, find new and exciting ways to pursue our passions, and cultivate more meaningful and stronger relationships with others. People are naturally drawn to those who radiate positive energy and joy, and by embodying these qualities, we can attract more like-minded individuals into our lives.

Engaging in activities that you enjoy can also produce positive emotions. This could be something as simple as listening to music, spending time in nature, or practicing a hobby you love. By doing things that bring you pleasure, you can elevate your mood and reduce feelings of negativity.

The grass is not greener on the other side. The grass is greener where you water it.

3. Be Boundless The Purpose of Life Is to Magnify the Human Experience

So, what can we learn from the likes of Salvador Dali? One approach is to focus on nurturing and improving your own life, rather than constantly seeking something better elsewhere. Instead of seeking external sources of happiness or success, invest time and energy in cultivating what you already have. By "watering" your own "grass," you are taking ownership of your life and actively working towards making your situation better. This could involve setting and achieving personal goals, investing in your relationships, and making positive changes to your habits and lifestyle. You have the power to create your own happiness and success. Being boundless means living without fear of failure, rejection, or criticism, and embracing the full range of possibilities and opportunities that life has to offer. It requires a willingness to step outside of your comfort zone and take risks, and a commitment to living an authentic life.

As we discussed earlier, the purpose of life is a question that has puzzled humanity for centuries. Philosophers, theologians, and scientists have all sought to answer this fundamental question, and there are many different perspectives on what the purpose of life is. One perspective that has gained popularity in recent years is that the purpose of life is to magnify the human experience.

What does it mean to magnify the human experience? At its core, this perspective suggests that the purpose of life is to make your life as rich and fulfilling as possible and to help others do the same. It is about living life to the fullest, embracing new experiences, and making a positive impact on the world around you.

To achieve this purpose, you must, as we touched on earlier, first identify what brings you joy, meaning, and fulfillment in life. For some, this may be pursuing a career that aligns with their passions and talents. For others, it may be exploring new cultures and experiences, or cultivating deep and meaningful relationships with loved ones.

To magnify the human experience, you must also strive to help others achieve this same sense of fulfillment and purpose. This can be achieved through acts of kindness, community service, and volunteering your time and resources to help those in need. Becoming an achiever of enjoyment is about cultivating a mindset of joy and fulfillment, and actively seeking out experiences that bring you happiness and contentment. It is about finding a balance between achieving your goals and pursuing the things that truly matter to you. To gain enjoyment, it is also essential to let go of perfectionism and the need for external validation. Instead, you should embrace your imperfections and focus on progress and growth, rather than perfection.

Becoming an achiever of enjoyment also requires you to cultivate a mindset of gratitude and appreciation for the good things in your life. By focusing on the positive and being grateful for what you have, you can experience greater joy and fulfillment, even in the midst of challenges and difficulties.

> *"The secret of happiness is to count your blessings*
> *while others are adding up their troubles."*
> William Penn

Don't take anything for granted in life. Everything is temporary, and the world around us can be taken away in the blink of an eye. It is a mindset to encourage you to appreciate the good things in your life and recognize their value. It is easy to become complacent and take people, experiences, and material possessions for granted. Still, by adopting a mindset of gratitude and mindfulness, you can bolster a deeper appreciation for the things you have.

One of the best ways to avoid taking things for granted is to recognize the impermanence of things. Nothing in life is permanent, and everything you have is subject to change or loss. By realizing this, you can develop a deeper appreciation for the present moment and the people and experiences in your life. Practicing mindfulness is an excellent way to cultivate gratitude and appreciation for the present moment. Mindfulness involves being fully present in the moment and focusing on the sensations and experiences around you. By practicing mindfulness and expressing gratitude regularly, you can become more aware of the good things in your life and develop a deeper appreciation for them. You can also reflect on past experiences. It can be a powerful way to avoid taking things for granted. Looking back on the difficult times in your life and recognizing how far you've come can help you appreciate the present moment. By adopting this mindset, you can appreciate and enjoy your life even more now.

Every day, we take stock of how to improve today's experience. We're always looking to upgrade and elevate our experiences—to level up. We look to do this in all aspects of our lives. We encourage you to do the same. It's not impossible to take your experiences to a higher level. Even if it's just a series of minor improvements, small improvements grow into larger improvements, and before you realize it, your life will take on a whole new level of happiness and enjoyment.

Chapter Seven:
NO REARVIEW MIRRORS

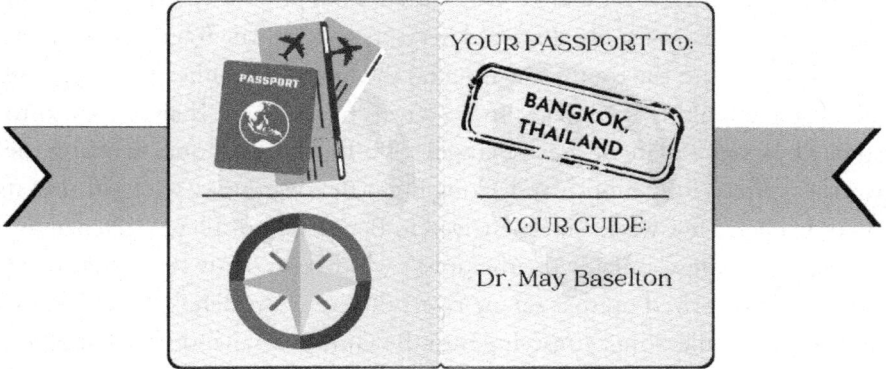

"So, what? Now it's going to end in one of those murder-suicides? Get out, Lori!"

That was the reaction from one of my "Sex and the City" girlfriends when I told her I'd just uncovered a bomb in my home—and had no idea how to defuse it.

Three years earlier, I (Lori) followed love to Colorado. Not William, but a man I thought I would build a beautiful life with. We had settled in a picture-perfect mountain community: big homes, sweeping mountain views, a golf course, and a vibrant club filled with people who hiked, skied, and played as hard as they worked. From the outside, it all looked like a dream.

But after we married, the reality behind closed doors revealed itself. I came across writings filled with despair, questioning whether life was worth living. I also learned he was on medication for struggles I hadn't known about, pieces of himself that had been carefully hidden. His behavior became unpredictable, and he often insisted on versions of events that felt untethered from reality.

Paradise had turned into a prison.

In the end, I followed my friend's advice. He left for California, and I remained in Colorado to reclaim my freedom and rediscover myself.

And thankfully, I wasn't alone.

Bangkok, Thailand

The therapist offered me herbal tea, which I happily accepted. The liquid was a soothing balm for my shattered nervous system. The fragrance of citrus fruits diffused into the room, warming up the brightly lit office in a high-rise building overlooking the Chao Phraya River in Bangkok, Thailand. Next to a tissue box was a plate of sliced mangoes. I offered myself one, savoring the sweetness after a long month and a long flight that was heavy with sadness. It had only been a few weeks since I arrived in Bangkok, but I had walked along the "River of Kings" outside the therapist's window so many times that I had the fauna memorized on that serene riverside stretch in Bangkok. The Chao Phraya is 231 miles long, emptying into the Gulf of Thailand near Bangkok.

The Chao Phraya is often called the "lifeblood" of Thailand because of its history as a key waterway for transportation, trade, and agriculture. Large cargo vessels and small passenger ferries alike traverse the waterway, and along its shores stand several cultural landmarks, including the Grand Palace, the Temple of Dawn, and many modern buildings and markets. I watched the river bustle with activity as the therapist took her seat in a chair close to me. If I had been six inches taller, our feet could have touched.

"What is happening in your life today, Lori?" The therapist opened our session with what would become her usual history-taking.

"I feel like I'm free to return to the healthy habits I enjoyed before meeting him. I'm not looking over my shoulder as much. The fear that began to dissipate on the flight here has turned from a booming headache to a minor throb in my temples."

Leaving my husband terrified me. There was the traditional "Ohio girl" in me who felt some sort of inexplicable doom at the thought of "breaking my vows, again." But there was the New York Lori who screamed, "If you don't get out of this relationship, you'll anchor yourself to a lifetime of misery—and maybe not a long lifetime. His behavior is unpredictable. You are not safe. Get. Out. Now."

As obvious as it was that I needed to protect myself by leaving a partner whose moods and behavior had become unpredictable, the process still dragged me through the predictable stages of grief. I mused upon them for a moment while Dr. May Baselton gathered her own thoughts.

How do those phases of grief go, again? Shock? Denial? Negotiation? In that order?

I experienced all the grief. And then I'd start right back at shock, again. *How did I let myself get into this situation?*

I pondered whether or not shame was part of the grieving cycle. I felt ashamed, although my intellect assured me that my husband's affliction was not my fault.

Dr. May leaned forward in her leather chair, not saying anything but staring directly into my eyes. I felt as though the therapist was transporting me into the present moment. I became aware of the soft cushions I had stuffed on my lap and behind my back—petite women rarely fit in the furniture in other people's rooms.

"Tell me about the new habits."

"I'm meditating again," I began. "And I've been celebrating what life can look like."

"What does that mean, to celebrate?" Dr. May's voice was low but soft.

"When I wake up in the morning, I take a few minutes to say affirmations aloud before I check my phone or email. When I'm working out, I listen to positive podcasts or audiobooks. When I finally do check my email, I light incense or diffuse essential oils, reminding me that whatever is in my inbox is 'out there,' but in this present moment, I am safe, secure, and serene. These habits seem to be calming my nervous system."

"Lori," said Dr. May, "habits are the invisible architecture of our lives." With that, Dr. May made a gesture out the window.

"Some of those buildings are small. Some are among the tallest in the world. A few have won awards for their design." The therapist trailed off.

"And some," she stated, "are so strong they could withstand any hurricane or tsunami. But don't worry, we don't get tsunamis here."

I smiled and may have even giggled. I appreciated the warmth from Dr. May.

"Your habits," said Dr. May, "shape your daily experiences. You have made the potential energetic assault of your email a more pleasant experience by diffusing oils or lighting incense during that practice."

I nodded.

"Our habits don't merely transform doldrums into delight, though," she continued, "They shape our relationships and our destinies, too. The key to transformation lies in recognizing these patterns and consciously replacing the destructive ones with positive actions."

As if on cue, a breeze wafted through the slightly open window, connecting me to the atmosphere and potential outside the office.

Lori enjoying the vibe in Bangkok, Thailand.

CHAPTER SEVEN: NO REARVIEW MIRRORS

Dr. May was a seasoned cognitive behavioral therapist with years of experience helping individuals navigate complex emotional terrain. She knew the disorienting pain of realizing a loved one might show traits people often link with the word "sociopath"—manipulation, lack of empathy, emotional distance. For me, it wasn't about a label; it was about facing the shock that the man I married was not the person I thought he was. She never shamed me and, periodically, she hinted at other stories she had heard as though they were analogies. I always felt like that was her way of gently saying, "Lori, you're not alone; many wonderful, bright women are misled by someone unworthy."

Of course, Dr. May didn't talk like that. She spoke with intention, clarity, and sobriety. I chose Dr. May because of her commitment to helping her clients transform negative patterns into positive actions.

Over the months that we worked together, Dr. May helped me understand that while the revelation about my now ex-husband was life-altering, it also opened a path to self-discovery and personal growth. It was the proverbial, "God closes a door but opens a window." In Dr. May's office, I discovered that by cultivating new, more positive habits, I was transitioning from jail to a glorious kingdom where I was the queen. I just had to make sure I was steadfast in leading myself. In this new world, there is no Prince Charming. I had come to accept that the only person who could save me was me. It was through the development of new habits and positive action that I not only learned how delightfully malleable my brain is, but how I could, one day, restore all I had lost and so much more.

When I left my session with Dr. May that day, I heard the words echo as I made my way back to the hotel where I was staying. "Lori, change is possible, one small habit at a time. You can eat an elephant, but you must take it in bites."

Back on my flight to Colorado, I felt invigorated to make my second start in Colorado better than the first. I was determined to stay in Aspen. To this day, I credit Dr. May's encouragement for helping to assure me that although I got off to a "rocky" start in the mountains, my dream of living in Aspen was still viable. Not only that, but this time around, it would be a greater future than any I had imagined.

HABITS FOR HAPPINESS

Who learns how to ride a bike without a few falls, a skinned knee, or even some dirt on their face?

Sometimes, sadly, relationships are like that. If you take a fall, you might even lag behind your peers. But we believe once you learn how to have a healthy, loving relationship, it's like riding a bike.

I know I'll never return to the pain of that marriage or past unhealthy relationships—I've grown beyond the patterns and choices that once led me there. I fell and got some scrapes and bruises. But I got back up, and in a later chapter, you'll learn how I called William into my life. Through healthy habits, including self-reflection and therapy to grow from my experience, I will never go back to that moment when I didn't know how to ride the proverbial relationship bicycle. Indeed, being in a healthy relationship is like riding a bike. Once you have the consciousness to be in a good one, you'll never go back to a bad one.

Funny enough, lots of things in life are like this. Healthy habits help us advance in our careers. They allow us to evolve in communication. We can become better investors. We may get better at cooking, gardening, and hobbies when we are devoted to improving ourselves. You might think adding shrimp to boiled pasta makes you fancy when you're in college, but as an adult, you may find yourself creating entire five-course meals at dinner parties with instruments and flavors that were more sophisticated than you could have fathomed back then. It is through good habits that we evolve, and habits are the cornerstone of our Best Day Every Day lives. *Your habits create the building that becomes your life - brick by brick.* The building will be either tall or short, sturdy or vulnerable, well-designed or an eyesore. You *will* create something of your life. Whether good or bad, your habits determine that outcome. Sometimes the lines are unclear. You might overdo a good habit, and then it becomes negative. For instance, working out is a healthy habit that can become an obsession or lead to injury. Beauty may involve healthy habits, but it can also lead to self-centeredness or excessive (and expensive) indulgence.

My forgiving, accepting, kind nature may have compelled me to overlook a red flag or two in that marriage, so my therapist helped me recognize patterns that would allow me to create stronger, healthier boundaries.

Today, we have made it a "habit" to design each day of our lives with a touch of something special. In time, we adopted the mantra "that was the best day ever! How can we do it again?" These little celebrations at the end of the day became our guiding principle. We committed to making each day, tomorrow, and the next the absolute best.

Our planning revolved around this motto. When organizing nights out, we asked ourselves, "How do we transform this into the best evening ever?"

Even trips to a restaurant are carefully orchestrated: "What's the best table or the prime spot at the bar? What are the must-try items on the menu?"

Even our evenings at home were a part of this mindset. We meticulously planned delightful dinners, collaborated in the kitchen, enjoyed a favorite cocktail, uncorked a cherished bottle of wine, and set a romantic ambiance with candles and soothing music. More often than not, we'll close the day with the sentiment that it was yet another Best Day Ever.

What started as a conscious effort became a habit subconsciously. Best Day Every Day was once a landmark occasion. Now it's a daily experience. We don't try to make each day the best; instead, everything we do—automatically, from the time we wake up until the time we go to bed—supports that day being the best. This is possible because of the habits you're reading about in this very book and the guides who have imparted their wisdom along the way.

DO NOT BE A WORRIER. BE A WARRIOR!

"Life happens for you, not to you."
Tony Robbins

The human mind finds a way to suffer, but the spirit knows the truth—your essence is not one of a worrier, but a warrior. You alone decide whether or not a moment has beauty. When you live in a beautiful state, you are living in your essence. Our firm conviction is that all human beings are optimists in their spirits; in their truest essences.

In a previous chapter, you met Satish Kapoor—a man whose job would spike anyone's cortisol levels. He navigates heavy traffic, races to get passengers to precise destinations on time, and likely encounters his share of less-than-polite riders. And he does all of this from behind the wheel, constantly alert in a city where a single wrong move could lead to disaster—an everyday reality in the fast-paced chaos of a typical Indian metropolis.

In our hours of conversations with Satish over the years, we admire him most for his ability to find the silver lining in the dark clouds.

Being an optimist doesn't mean you're in cognitive dissonance, unable to accept the data or reality that's directly in front of your face. Instead, you push away the negative thoughts to focus on the positive ones. You don't control circumstances, but you are in control of your response. The optimist also tends to understand that adverse events can do the following wonderful things:

1. They can help you grow.
2. They can be the proverbial "closed door" that opens a window to something greater.
3. They test our emotional regulation.
4. They help us exemplify equanimity to children or loved ones.
5. They allow us to turn lemons into lemonade.

Tony Robbins likes to say, "Life happens for you, not to you". There is light at the end of the tunnel. And every cloud truly has a silver lining. You get what you look for; so pay attention to what you are not looking for, and let that in.

Make something grueling your gift, and allow obstacles to become blessings in disguise. If you don't encounter obstacles in your life, you might be living a life sheltered from risk. That might be a life that's devoid of purpose and meaning. It might be a life that lacks relationships. Pursuing your passion and being in a relationship with somebody means you're taking risks. Therefore, if you don't have obstacles in your life, we would go as far as to say that you had better start praying for some.

A BEAUTIFUL STATE OF MIND

Humans live in two states of mind, much like the popular image of two people on a train. One person is facing a rock wall that is dark and foreboding. He thinks the world is dark and gloomy. The other passenger, seated just a few feet away, stares out at a beautiful, sunny valley. He thinks the world looks beautiful.

The passengers are seated in the same place, but they're facing different directions.

Humans have two states of mind, as illustrated in this analogy: the beautiful state or the suffering state. Living in a beautiful state means living in a state of joy, gratitude, and abundance. It means focusing on the positive aspects of life and finding great happiness in the present moment. When you live in a beautiful state, you become a magnet for positive experiences, and you attract people and opportunities that are in alignment with your highest good.

Those who live in a beautiful state are aligned with their heart's desires and passions, and they face the "sunny side" of life, which means they also attract people and experiences in that beautiful place. We'll repeat this important mantra: where your focus goes, your energy flows.

Those who live in a suffering state needn't be described; we know what it's like to play victim or see the person who seems to have pain and misery in their lives constantly. In many situations, these poor souls actually invite that misery into their lives with a suffering state of mind.

One of the surest ways to live in a suffering state of mind is to be trapped in negative emotions. Usually, that doesn't come from present moment circumstances, but past stories. Your head replays negative thoughts all day, such as "you always mess up your relationships," or "you'll always be overweight," or "nobody wants to hang out with you."

Replaying those negative thoughts in your head is a surefire way for them to manifest in your life. You attract negative things by focusing your thoughts on the negative rather than the positive. The soundtrack in your head materializes into real-world events.

Your brain has something that is referred to as the Reticular Activating System (RAS). The RAS is a network of neurons in the brainstem that plays a crucial role in filtering information. It helps you focus by tuning out irrelevant stimuli and highlighting things that align with your thoughts and beliefs. For example, if you frequently think about success or a particular goal, your RAS may make you more aware of opportunities that help manifest those thoughts into reality. It's less about literal "manifestation" and more about heightened awareness leading to action.

The brain is amazing at connecting the dots for us when we focus in the right places. Hence, where your focus goes, your energy flows. But due to the RAS, where your focus goes, the prosperity, love, and abundance in your life increase.

NO REARVIEW MIRRORS

In this book, I (Lori) have chosen to share the story of my divorce, which included experiences that felt emotionally abusive at times...but it's not a song I sing every day. It is because of my commitment to using my life (and even some bad choices) as a teaching tool for others that I bring that story into this book. Without the relationship, there would be no Dr. May. Without Dr. May, there would not have been the deep understanding of how to rise above circumstances through healthy habits. In short, I don't live life looking in the rearview mirror.

The past is your future if you live there in your mind. If you replay adverse circumstances, you live there indefinitely.

But here's something you may not know about your brain: you're in control of it. Your mind is, in fact, much less powerful than your heart. In fact, according to the HeartMath Institute,[2] the heart's electromagnetic field is about 60 times greater in amplitude than the brain's, and about 5,000 times stronger than the brain's magnetic field.

Although the brain is always in survival mode, you needn't surrender to its messages. Rewire your mind's messages by focusing on the beauty and opportunity around you. In time, your brain will understand that you can survive in this state of beauty, gratitude, and plasticity or evolution.

---

2   www.heartmath.org

Part Three:

MICRO PURPOSE

Chapter Eight:
CULTIVATING YOUR COMMUNITY

YOUR PASSPORT TO: Bolgheri, Italy, Mykonos, Greece & Varanasi, India

YOUR GUIDES: Massimo Piccin, "Stefan," "La La La" & Sister Maria DiBenedetto

A soft breeze moves through the courtyard, carrying with it the sounds of rustling leaves in the vineyard and echoes of barks and chirps from nature. We are seated at a communal table at the Sapaio Winery, where winemaker Massimo Piccin regularly brings visitors together to enjoy his forward-thinking, modern vineyard nestled in an environment where Italians have more than 4,000 years of winemaking experience.

The rhythmic ring of celebration during a communal toast is accompanied by laughter and lively conversation. The harmonious notes of a local folk band playing traditional Tuscan music provide a joyful backdrop to the gathering.

The Bolgheri wine region, nestled in Maremma along the Tuscan coast in the Livorno province, is a relative newcomer to Italy's rich viticultural landscape. Its story began in 1944 when aristocrat Mario Incisa della

Rocchetta planted the first Cabernet vineyard in Castiglioncello di Bolgheri, according to the Bolgheri DOC Consorzio.

Nestled at the foothills of the majestic Apennine Mountain range and bordered by the shimmering Tyrrhenian Sea, the Bolgheri region is a picturesque slice of Tuscany that captivates the senses. This enchanting landscape is characterized by rolling hills adorned with lush vineyards and sprawling olive groves, creating a patchwork of vivid greens and dusty browns that stretches as far as the eye can see. The gentle slopes cradle some of Italy's finest wineries, where Sangiovese and Bordeaux varietals thrive in the sun-drenched climate.

As you wander through this idyllic countryside, you'll be greeted by the intoxicating scent of ripe grapes mingling with the fragrance of Mediterranean herbs. The golden rays of the sun illuminate the historic cypress trees that line the winding roads, adding to the region's timeless charm. With its blend of natural beauty and rich agricultural heritage, Bolgheri offers an extraordinary backdrop for indulging in the pleasures of wine and cuisine, making it a truly remarkable destination for travelers seeking both adventure and serenity.

Massimo Piccin, the innovative and passionate founder of Sapaio Winery, is a key figure in the Bolgheri wine-making community. He represents the new wave of winemakers who balance respect for traditional practices with an avant-garde approach to viticulture.

What struck us the most was not the entrepreneurial side of Massimo, but his heart. Massimo believes that a strong community is essential for the continued success and evolution of Bolgheri's wine-making legacy.

We spent the week enjoying Sapaio's varietals, our senses magnified by notes of ripe blackberries, dark cherries, and plums mingling with subtle hints of spice, tobacco, and earth. The late harvest wines bore notes of dried apricots and honey that would stick to the palate long after each sip of the smooth, velvety, well-aged red.

In the warm Mediterranean sun, while admiring the elegant Sapaio emblem on a bottle in front of him, William looked up from his plate of freshly baked breads and cheeses from a local farmhouse. He asked Massimo, "I've tasted a lot of wine in my day, good ones and some bad. But there's a vitality in your wines as well as at your vineyard that I can't place my finger on. What's your special secret? How have you created wines that are so special they stand out on the palate so much?"

Lori and William with friend and winemaker, Massimo Piccin at Sapaio Winery in Bolgheri, Italy.

"It's the community here. In Bolgheri, the past and future of winemaking converge. Here at Sapaio, we honor this place and its traditions while innovating with new techniques and ideas. Our community thrives because we work together, share our passion, and strive for excellence in everything we do."

"Imagine that," William smiled. "The secret behind a product that brings people together in celebration is, well, people coming together!"

"One plus one equals eleven," says Massimo wisely. "I could never do this alone. It wouldn't be much fun, anyway."

ONE PLUS ONE EQUALS ELEVEN

Golden Hour settling over Mykonos, Greece.

Smooth, whitewashed walls contrasted with rough bougainvillea petals at the outdoor taverna. As they strolled through the streets, La La La said, "Feel these walls," running his hand along the pristine white surface.

"So smooth, yet they've stood for centuries."

"And these flowers, so delicate, yet thriving in this heat," observed Lori.

We were in Mykonos, Greece, where we enjoyed an unforgettable lunch overlooking the sea with two friends, "La La La" and Stefan, from Germany. Over the years, they had spent many weeks in Mykonos, their favorite island in Europe.

Mykonos, a gem in the Cyclades Archipelago of Greece, captivates with its blend of colorful culture and sensational landscapes. The island's iconic whitewashed buildings with blue shutters create a picturesque backdrop against the azure Aegean Sea. Strolling through the charming, narrow labyrinth streets of Mykonos Town, you'll discover quaint boutiques, art galleries, and inviting cafés that beckon you to linger. The sun-drenched beaches, from the bright shores of Paradise Beach to the serene sandy stretches of Agios Sostis Beach, cater to every mood, whether you're seeking a lively beach party or a tranquil escape.

*La La La, William, Lori and Stefan
making memories in Mykonos, Greece.*

As dusk fell, the island transformed from the peaceful, perfume-scented flow to a nighttime bustle with music pulsing from beach clubs and bars. Mykonos is not just a destination; it's a celebration of life, beauty, and the irresistible allure of the Mediterranean.

La La La and Stefan were thrilled to share their favorite details from the town they both loved with us. As they strolled, they noted the briny scent of the Aegean Sea mingled with the smell of grilling souvlaki from nearby tavernas. We caught the subtle perfume of wild herbs carried on the warm island breezes as Stefan pointed out local flora.

"Ah, breathe in deeply," La La La advised, closing his eyes. "This is the smell of Greece – sea, herbs, and grilled meat."

We inhaled deeply and both grinned. William said, "It's intoxicating. I think I'm falling in love with Mykonos all over again."

Lori and William allowed their hosts to order the meal that afternoon. The salty tang of freshly grilled octopus paired with the crisp, refreshing flavor of Assyrtiko wine delighted the group.

"Mmm, this octopus is delicious," stated William.

Stefan, William & Lori

Stefan nods enthusiastically. "Ja, it's so fresh! But save room for the baklava – it's to die for."

His German-accented English mixed with the melodic Greek conversations around the table, where they could hear waves lapping rhythmically against the shore. Seagulls occasionally cried overhead, and if you listened carefully above the chatter, you could even hear the tinkling of goat bells from the hills.

"Listen," Stefan whispered, "Can you hear the goat bells?"

"It's like music from the hills," Lori said.

"You have now experienced the smells, tastes, and sounds of Greece. But do you know what makes Greece the most beautiful country in the world?" asked La La La.

"The Sea?" Lori guessed.

"Ancient history, mythology, and monasteries?" guessed William.

"These are all beautiful things," starts La La La. "But what makes this the most beautiful country in the world is right here at this table."

Lori glanced down at her sticky, sweet baklava quizzically, and William inhaled his Ouzo, smiling wryly. "You tell me, La La La."

"It's the people," La La La responded. "The community. The love people share around a table. The care your chef put into your dishes is truly commendable. The sweat of the farmers and the drink makers. Ten thousand people were involved in bringing this food to our table, and their care is with us in every bite we take."

With that, Stefan raised his glass. "Yamas!" he offered a toast.

BE OF SERVICE TO OTHERS

"I never thought I'd be so excited to visit a place where people have seen and experienced so much pain," pointed out Lori as we traveled to Varanasi, India, at Mother Teresa's Home, a shelter for the homeless, helpless, and sick.

As we departed our vehicle, we noted that the air in front of the Home was as rich with incense and spices as the rest of the town. The pungent aroma of the Ganges River nearby mingled with the fragrant smell of fresh flowers used in daily prayers as we entered the lobby of the Home. We were struck by the distinctive, slightly pungent odor of the medicinal herbs used in the shelter's care practices. A comforting smell of home-cooked meals wafted through the corridors, bringing a sense of warmth and community.

Lori and William visit Mother Teresa's Home in Varanasi, India.

"Welcome, Lori and William! We are so grateful to have you here, and our prayer is that as you assist our staff this week, you will leave just as blessed as the residents here at Mother Teresa's Home."

Taken aback at the notion that they would receive blessing in their quest to bless others, William stated, "We're here to serve."

"Of course you are!" stated Sister Maria Di Benedetto. "That's where the greatest blessings lie, in helping others. There is no satisfaction like service. I know you will be immensely happy this week."

As they followed Sister Di Benedetto through the corridor, I (Lori) whispered to William, "I was ready to roll up my sleeves, get dirty, and be a bit miserable for the sake of the greater good, weren't you?"

"Same," replied William. "But I like her perspective much better."

"Same!" whispered Lori happily. "Her heart is infectious; I already caught the love bug!"

Over the course of the following week, Sister Maria's heart continued to bless us. We enjoyed warm, simple meals with the residents and volunteers at Mother Teresa's Home. For every five-star meal we'd enjoyed in our lives thus far, the simple cooked rice, lentils, and soft chapatis ranked just as highly at the Home.

Throughout the shelter tour, we heard the laughter of children playing, the clatter of cooking pots, and the rhythmic chanting of prayers. Outside, rickshaws honked, street vendors called in potential customers, and occasionally, we heard temple bells ringing.

Over the course of that week, Sister Maria's gentle touch contrasted with the rough, calloused hands of the people they helped. One day, as William offered a sweet cup of chai tea spiced with cardamom and ginger to a resident, she embraced him, which, while disarming, gave him a sense of being valuable to this sick patient's journey. He stole a glance at Sister Maria, bent over a resident with her coarse, pressed uniform over the smooth stone floors of the Home.

As if on cue, Sister Maria glanced back at William, a knowing smile on her face.

"I get it," William said in a whisper. "We're residents too. It's not us ministering to the sick. It's also the sick who are ministering to us."

Sister Maria Di Benedetto, originally from Rome, found her calling in Varanasi, India, working at Mother Teresa's Home, a beacon of light for the community. Welcoming volunteers from all walks of life, Sister Maria's work emphasizes the importance of cultivating a compassionate and supportive community, showing that through acts of service, we can create profound and lasting connections.

THE GIFT OF COMMUNITY

As we've emphasized before in this book, there is no measurable meaning to life without service to others. Periodically, we meet people, especially having lived in D.C., Aspen, and New York City, whose sense of value comes from spending long hours on the computer or building a business in isolation. Those are the people we worry about the most.

The essence of the Best Day Every Day philosophy is community, which is why we aren't merely providing an instruction manual from our own experiences or success, but more than thirty guides who have held our hands to inspire our lives. We would be incapable of creating the Best Day Every Day lifestyle were it not for the love and care of our communities in the United States and in many countries and continents abroad. The positive impact of their lives has rippled into our lives, and we are writing this book so that their wisdom will ripple into yours, too.

> *"We make a living by what we get,*
> *but we make a life by what we give."*
> *Winston Churchill*

There are few things more satisfying than helping others. The good news is it doesn't take mantras, meditation, or even money to make an impact through kindness, a charitable donation of time, or the simple act of listening to somebody who needs a safe place to share.

The "suspended coffee" or "caffè sospeso" tradition is one of our favorites. Naples is known for its solidarity, especially during challenging economic times. In this Italian city, the tradition of paying for two coffees but receiving only one, leaving the second as a gift for a stranger too poor to pay, was born. Pay It Forward Day is a worldwide celebration of kindness that takes place every year on April 28th, inspired by the Napolitan tradition.

Dr. David R. Hawkins believed that negative energy could affect a small percentage of people. Still, he wrote an entire book on the theory that high consciousness could exponentially affect more people. In his books, especially *Power vs. Force*, Hawkins posited that different emotional states can be ranked on a "Map of Consciousness" with a scale of 1 to 1,000, with Shame being the lowest and higher states including love, peace, and joy. The highest state? Enlightenment, vibrating at a level of 700 to 1,000.

What is the highest vibrational phrase ever calibrated by Hawkins? *"There is no cause of anything."* This represents an individual perceiving reality as an interconnected whole, transcending the concepts of cause and effect.

One of Dr. Hawkins' key ideas is that individuals vibrating at higher levels of consciousness (such as love, peace, or enlightenment) can counterbalance the negative energy of a larger number of individuals vibrating at lower levels. For example:

> *He suggested that **one person** vibrating at the level of **500** (Love) could counterbalance **750,000** people below the level of 200 (which he considered the threshold for positive consciousness).*

> *Similarly, someone vibrating at **600** (Peace) could counterbalance **10 million** people below 200, and someone at **700** (Enlightenment) could affect **70 million**.*

Buying a coffee for somebody can undoubtedly have a "butterfly effect," but a lot more goes into positive vibration than throwing money at issues or needs. High-vibrational consciousness requires a heart aligned with the ideals of love, peace, and joy. Do you ever see a politician making grandiose promises and you think, "There's no way that guy believes what he's saying."

Sure enough, when push comes to shove, many of these politicians forget the principles they so passionately campaigned on. We recognize the authenticity in the energy fields of others. The truest way to affect the world positively is to be authentically aligned in the spirit of giving, supporting, and spreading kindness to others.

We often remind ourselves of the phrase, "The secret to living is giving." Financial wealth alone doesn't guarantee happiness. While we've met many successful and joyful individuals who generously give back to their communities, we've also observed that some people—regardless of their financial situation—can struggle with fulfillment. Particularly in places like Aspen, Colorado, where the pressures of high society can sometimes weigh heavily, we've noticed that happiness isn't always tied to material success.

In some cases, families that have enjoyed wealth for generations face unique challenges. Without a sense of purpose or something to strive for, it's easy to feel unmotivated or disconnected from life's deeper meaning. The constant pursuit of perfection or superficial improvements can leave one feeling empty when there's no inner drive or passion to ignite. But through our own journey and the incredible people we've met along the way, we've learned that true fulfillment often comes from a sense of mission—serving others and being part of something larger than ourselves. With that, happiness becomes not just a possibility but a way of life.

Generosity is a quality that is highly valued in many cultures and societies around the world. It is the willingness to give to others, without expecting anything in return. Many people believe that generosity is important not only for the benefit of those who receive but also for the benefit of the giver, as Sister Mary suggested in the Mother Teresa Home.

As members of the Rotary Club of Aspen, we embrace the theme "Service Above Self," a concept at the heart of Rotary International, a global service organization with over 1.2 million members across more than 200 countries. It represents a commitment to putting the needs of others before your own and striving to make a positive impact on the world. We've both been actively involved in the Rotary Club of Aspen for several years. Not only do we enjoy the camaraderie with fellow members, but we also enjoy the opportunity to be involved in well-organized international service projects that send members to third-world countries to build water projects, support reading and education projects, and help to eliminate diseases such as polio and malaria. Through these experiences, you realize how much positive impact we can have with a small amount of money and a well-organized effort.

The idea of Service Above Self is grounded in the belief that we all have a responsibility to give back to our communities and the world at large. It is about using our talents, skills, and resources to make a difference in the lives of others and to leave the world a better place than we found it.

Service Above Self can take many forms. It might mean volunteering at a local food bank, mentoring a young person, or participating in an international service project. Whatever form it takes, the key is to approach it with a spirit of generosity and a willingness to put the needs of others first.

One of the key benefits of Service Above Self is that it helps to create a sense of connection and purpose. When you give back to your community or to the world at large, you become part of a global network of people who are working towards a common goal. This sense of connection can be incredibly powerful and can help to counteract feelings of isolation or disconnection.

Service Above Self can also help to develop important skills and qualities, such as leadership, empathy, and resilience. When you work on a service project, you are often forced to navigate challenges and overcome obstacles. This can help you to develop important skills and qualities that can be valuable in all areas of life.

Moreover, it can be incredibly rewarding. When you give back to others, you experience a sense of satisfaction and fulfillment that can't be found through material possessions or personal achievements. You feel like you are making a positive impact on the world, and this can be incredibly motivating. By putting the needs of others first, we can make a positive impact on the world and leave a lasting legacy that will inspire others to do the same.

The Rotary Four-Way Test
Of the things we think, say, or do:

1. *Is it the truth?*

2. *Is it fair to all concerned?*

3. *Will it build goodwill and better friendships?*

4. *Will it be beneficial to all concerned?*

Chapter Nine:
HEALTH IS WEALTH

"When we're healthy, our dreams seem limitless. But in poor health, our only wish is to feel well again."
Loren Lahav

Lori and William at Tony Robbins' Namale Resort in Fiji attending Life and Wealth Mastery.

"I am strong. I am vibrant. I am unstoppable." Loren Lahav's rhythmic chanting filled the seminar room as participants echoed her words in a powerful group affirmation exercise, setting the tone for the transformative journey ahead.

Loren served as the lead trainer for Tony Robbins' transformative ten-day Life and Wealth Mastery program, hosted at his impressive Namale Resort in Fiji. The five-day Life Mastery segment is designed to immerse participants in the latest breakthroughs in health, longevity, and peak fitness, providing cutting-edge strategies to revitalize the body and elevate overall well-being. Experts from around the world travel to Fiji to share their knowledge on how to stay healthy and youthful.

Nestled on the pristine coastline of Vanua Levu, the Namale Fiji Resort & Spa is a luxurious haven where lush tropical landscapes meet turquoise waters. This all-inclusive resort offered a unique blend of opulence and serenity, with lavish villas that boasted private plunge pools, sweeping ocean views, and direct access to pristine beaches. Guests could indulge in rejuvenating spa treatments infused with local ingredients, savor gourmet cuisine that showcases the flavors of Fiji, and partake in a variety of water sports, all while being enveloped in the warm hospitality that Fijians are renowned for.

The islands of Fiji are a breathtaking mix of spirited culture and striking natural beauty, comprising over 300 islands adorned with swaying palm trees and crystal-clear lagoons. Each island offers its own unique charm, from the lush, mountainous terrains of Viti Levu to the coral reefs teeming with marine life surrounding the Yasawas. The air is filled with the sound of traditional Fijian music, and the atmosphere is imbued with the spirit of "Bula!"—a warm welcome that encapsulates the islanders' hospitality. Whether you're exploring hidden waterfalls, lounging on sun-kissed beaches, or diving into the rich underwater world, Fiji promises an unforgettable escape into paradise.

CHAPTER NINE: HEALTH IS WEALTH

*Lori and William visiting a village in Fiji
with fellow Life and Wealth Mastery participants*

That morning, while Loren spoke, Eucalyptus oil diffused throughout the room, coupled with the scent of fresh organic wheatgrass from the smoothies served during that morning's break.

This wasn't just a polite weekend dedicated to her evolution through Body, Mind, and Spirit integration. We had flown all the way to Fiji for a ten-day health and fitness immersion. One of the exercises we encountered was the "Wheel of Life" well-being evaluation worksheet. As papers rustled softly, Loren reminded the audience that the purpose of this ten-day program wasn't about information, but about transformation. This training was billed as a safe space for growth and discovery where new levels of well-being and joy could be achieved.

Among the most impactful activities during this immersion was the daily time carved out for intentional meditation, coupled with wheatgrass drinks or nourishing snacks to continually help the body integrate with the soul's evolution, step by step. One such afternoon, while walking on smooth, polished stones during a mid-afternoon mindfulness exercise, invigorated by yerba mate tea that was offered as an alternative to coffee each afternoon, Lori reveled in the uniquely clean, empty space in her mind that week. Rather than overthinking the events and relationships in her life, Loren invited participants in her Health Mastery Program to be grounded in their bodies. It's a funny phenomenon how the brain resists positive change. As mentioned in earlier chapters, your brain is committed to whatever cycle has kept you alive. That's the brain's sole focus. The brain says, *"You have heartache and addictions? Well, at least you're alive - don't change a thing!"*

Loren nurtured us with the perspective that we have permission to change what doesn't serve us; to be antennas for Spirit, allowing our bodies to do more of the "thinking" and "decision making," becoming the captains of our brains. It's common to overthink and spin out when faced with stressors, but movement and life-giving, nutritious foods empower us to overwrite the programs that prohibit us from living our Best Day Every Day lives.

The training with Loren included techniques to master health, fitness, emotions, and longevity. Loren taught many of the principles from our Best Day Every Day lifestyle: creating a beautiful life requires creating automatic patterns through empowering habits. Repeating healthy habits from this book will, over time, rewire the brain. What begins as a "chore" or "checklist" eventually becomes second nature and automatic. And that is why we'll continue to remind you of that throughout the book, especially if you've encountered resistance to some of the habits we've already discussed with the previous guides and their lessons in the preceding eight chapters.

Growing up in Mansfield, Ohio, I (Lori) relished opportunities to stay active. I sensed, from an early age, that the quality of life of those who remained in continual training and movement was higher than that of those who had more sedentary lifestyles. As I grew in my understanding of the human body and how it relates to the human spirit, I became a strong advocate for fitness and health as a spiritual practice. When your body is fit and your energy moves throughout the body's energy centers, often called chakras, you also eliminate the trauma that hides your ability to seek higher states of consciousness.

A healthy body fosters life success, relationship success, clear thinking, and positive choices, enabling you to remain sober and present with those around you. Fat shaming? Of course not. But the subject of this chapter will be a call to elevate your physical wellness as a way to extend your life and improve the lives of others. Physical health and wellness are a spiritual practice.

THE SECRET NEUROSCIENCE OF HEALTHY LIVING & STRESS REDUCTION

Every day brings with it the exposure to trauma through either interpersonal relationship strife, financial stressors, or exposure to negative media, which fuels fear to sell viewers on tuning in. This wreaks havoc not only on the psyche, but on your organs. When the brain is pummeled with messages or reactions to events in the "fight or flight" mode, this stress increases cortisol levels and lowers the effectiveness of certain body functions. In some individuals, this manifests as cardiovascular problems. In others, it manifests as weight gain or addiction to substances such as marijuana or alcohol, which are in no short supply where we reside in Aspen, Colorado.

There are endless books that discuss the energy and vibration of foods and physical fitness. Still, we have often lamented that many of these books don't "hit the nerve" of what is really happening with a healthy or unhealthy lifestyle from the neuroscience perspective. That nerve is the *vagus nerve.*

Your vagus nerve is among the most important nerves in the human body. It helps regulate the parasympathetic nervous system, which controls rest, digestion, and relaxation functions. It's also the longest cranial nerve, extending from the brainstem all the way down to the abdomen, passing through the neck, chest, and a variety of internal organs. Do you ever feel a pulse like a baby kicking your stomach when you're stressed? That's the vagus nerve; you can sometimes feel it just under your ribcage, in the center of your stomach.

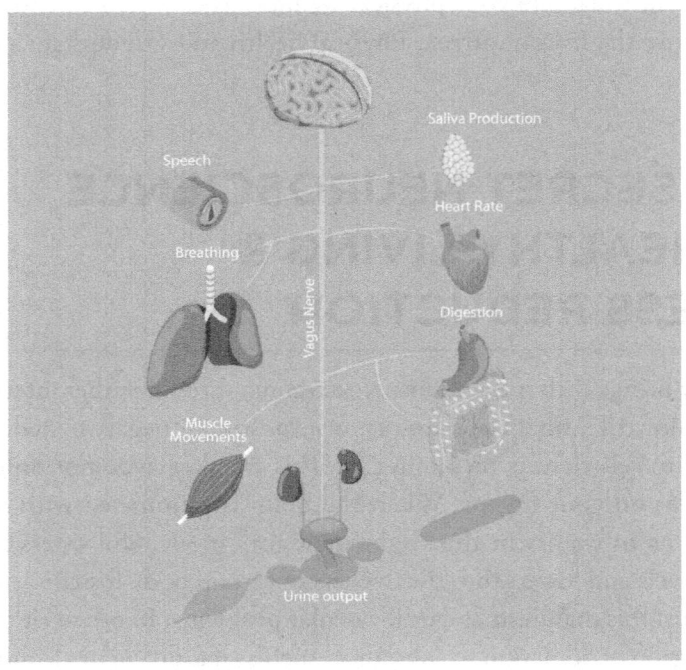

Key functions and capacities of the Vagus Nerve
Photo rights purchased at www.stock.adobe.com

The vagus nerve travels from its origination point in the medulla oblongata, part of the brainstem, down through the neck alongside the carotid artery and jugular vein. It travels down the neck alongside the carotid artery and jugular vein. It continues through the chest, innervating major organs such as the heart, lungs, and digestive tract, as shown in the image above. It helps regulate heart rate, promoting a state of calm and relaxation. This is the focus of many meditations and breathwork that is designed to help with vagal nerve stimulation. It influences your respiratory rate by helping to regulate both how frequently and how deeply you breathe.

Dr. Lauryn Lax describes the vagus nerve in her book *Total Gut Reset* as a "shoestring walkie-talkie system running from your head to the 'second brain' in your gut."

> *Your Vagus Nerve is the longest nerve in your body. It runs from the top of your brain to the top of your gut and acts like a shoestring walkie-talkie system, sending signals back and forth between these two regions—your first brain in your head and the "second brain" in your gut. Did you know that you have an entire brain inside your gut called the "enteric nervous system"? It contains 500 million neurons (brain cells) that control digestion, and 80% of all your thoughts, feelings, and emotions are directed from the gut—from cravings for chocolate or broccoli to butterflies in your stomach before public speaking or when your crush asks for your number.*[3]

This "walkie-talkie" in your body transmits information between the brain and internal organs. When you are more relaxed in the brain, your body digests better, regulates bodily functions more effectively, and finds more time to rest, digest, and heal. Stress not only hinders health but also creates an environment conducive to disease, partly because the "fight or flight" state diverts energy from the body's self-healing mechanisms.

GET "VAGAL TONED"

Fitness and health assist with the parasympathetic nervous system, a contrast to the "fight or flight" response, which comes from the sympathetic nervous system. The vagus nerve, a major component of the parasympathetic nervous system, helps you with that "rest or digest" state that reduces stress and cortisol, lowers inflammation through communication with your immune system, and supports social bonding and emotional regulation by influencing mood-related brain regions. Stronger vagus nerve function, referred to as "vagal tone," is one of the keys to true happiness, unlocking your Best Day Every Day life through optimal function both internally as well as externally in your interpersonal relationships, the subject of the previous chapter in this book.

---

[3] https://a.co/d/4WzwMi9

EXERCISING YOUR WAY TO PEACE

In the first chapter, we explored how meditation and breathing can lead to a Best Day Every Day life. In addition, cold exposure and yoga can both improve vagal tone. Additionally, cardiovascular conditioning such as walking, running, swimming, or cycling improves vagal tone. In fact, endurance exercise in particular has been shown to increase parasympathetic activity, allowing the body to switch from exertion to relaxation more easily.

In general, exercise helps your body become more resilient to stress, reducing the overall production of stress hormones such as cortisol. Deep breathing into the abdomen, called "diaphragmatic breathing," helps enhance vagal tone during and post-exercise by stimulating your vagus nerve, even when performing non-cardiovascular exercises such as weight training.

When I (Lori) realized that "health is wealth," I decided to turn my passion for fitness into a career by becoming a Certified Personal Trainer through the National Academy of Sports Medicine. I began helping clients in New York City sculpt their bodies and evolved my practice into custom-designed training programs for peak performance, injury prevention, and complete fitness. My practice is among the most successful personal training services in Aspen, Colorado, where clients are ambitious and active. Like attracts like, and I have observed that my clients share my confidence, discipline, precision, and vitality.

Sometimes the importance of health and wellness is not understood until it's too late, when the "house is on fire." We've known many friends with life-altering diagnoses who seek out holistic diets or extreme cleanses to undo decades of bad health decisions. One place many of these individuals turn is to Dr. Steven Gundry's work, notably *The Plant Paradox* or *Dr. Gundry's Diet Evolution*.

In a description for *The Plant Paradox: The Hidden Dangers in 'Healthy' Foods That Cause Disease and Weight Gain*, Gundry posits:

> Is it possible that everything you've heard about diet, weight, and nutrition is wrong? The Plant Paradox reveals the #1 danger in the American diet: a toxic protein hidden in plants called lectins. Lectins are found in hundreds of common foods, like wheat, beans, potatoes, nuts, and dairy.

Dr. Gundry's work has radically augmented our diets. We commit to avoiding high-lectin foods, substituting them for healthier plant-based options, and lectin-free recipes. Unlike many holistic health advocates, Dr. Gundry's work is praised by traditional allopathic physicians as well as alternative holistic health gurus, which is a testament to the integrity and results of his work in helping patients not only lose weight but also recover from long-standing health disorders.

> *"Happiness lies, first of all, in health."*
> *George William Curtis*

A friend of ours in Aspen recently went to Sedona, Arizona, for an intense two-day retreat where a practitioner pressed, pulled, pushed, and prodded energy release from every inch of her body over the course of eight hours on a table during these two days, which required a whole day to prepare and two days of recovery.

We asked our friend jokingly, "Why did you decide to take an entire week out of your busy schedule to have somebody basically torture you?"

The friend responded, "When I focus on healing my own body, I am in greater service to the world."

She reminded us of Steven Adler, who said, "You can have all the riches and success in the world, but if you don't have your health, you have nothing".

We both embraced health and fitness from an early age. William was an avid ski racer who leveraged vitamins and nutrition to promote better race times. In some ways, William wasn't racing merely towards a healthier life for himself, but also running away from a fear of inheriting cardiovascular disease; his father underwent a heart attack and quadruple bypass surgery at only 50 years old.

Lori found both joy and confidence in working out and high school athletics. She was inspired by women in their forties who looked fabulous, and she committed herself to achieving the same vibrancy in her forties. Now in her fifties, she is a testament to the long-term results of a life dedicated to health and wellness, receiving compliments almost daily for her fit physique and high energy.

In Fiji, during our training with Tony Robbins, we also shifted our diets and sleep patterns. This pivotal moment catalyzed a life-changing experience. Later, in June 2022, we delved into a longevity and health program by Tony Robbins that influenced his later book, *Life Force*. In Fiji, we explored Dan Buettner's research in "The Blue Zones." Drawing from this wealth of knowledge and personal experience, here are the highlights from our training.

1. EAT THE RAINBOW

Imagine a magical pill that can lower the risk of dying by up to 23 percent? In a 25-year study published by The Journal of the American Medical Association, more than 25,000 women who adhered to a Mediterranean diet lowered their risk of dying by up to 23 percent. The Mediterranean diet is common across cultures that border the Mediterranean Sea, such as in Italy, Greece, and Spain, as well as in California, Japan, and Costa Rica. At a high level, this diet includes lots of fruits and vegetables, herbs and spices, whole grains, limited meat and dairy, and avoiding processed foods or sugar.

This study is among many that support our findings that diseases can be reversed, and it's no surprise that eating the rainbow affects not only your daily energy but the health of your cells. Your cells are the building blocks of your body. They need nutrition to function optimally and fight disease. Things that can affect cells include poisons in the bloodstream, such as those found in alcohol, animal products, yeast, mold, and fungus.

Whole foods are among the most important choices you can make for your long-term health and longevity. Whole foods simply mean one-ingredient foods, such as a raw fruit or vegetable, or one prepared in a quality way, such as steamed versus fried. Whole grains, legumes, nuts, and seeds are among the whole foods you can eat to reduce the risk of chronic disease and even slow the aging process.

Exercise also improves cellular function by increasing energy and reducing oxidative stress. Lymphatic massage assists with removing waste, toxins, and excess fluids from the body and supporting the immune system.

While a plant-based diet emphasizes fiber, vitamins, minerals, and antioxidants from plants, it may include small amounts of meat, dairy, and eggs in more flexible forms. Every bite is an opportunity to nourish your cells, promote cleansing, and support detoxification.

The phrase "Eat the Rainbow" simply refers to eating a diverse range of colorful foods, each of which holds specific vitamins, minerals, antioxidants, and phytochemicals that offer unique health benefits.

Here's a breakdown of the different colors and their associated health benefits:

1. **Red**: Red fruits and vegetables, such as tomatoes, strawberries, red peppers, and beets, often contain lycopene, which may support heart health and reduce the risk of certain cancers.
2. **Orange and Yellow**: Foods like carrots, oranges, sweet potatoes, and bell peppers are rich in beta-carotene, a precursor to vitamin A, which promotes healthy vision, immune function, and skin health.
3. **Green**: Leafy greens, broccoli, kiwi, and avocados are packed with nutrients like vitamin K, folate, and chlorophyll. They support bone health, digestion, detoxification, and provide a host of other benefits.
4. **Blue and Purple**: Blueberries, purple grapes, eggplant, and purple cabbage contain anthocyanins, potent antioxidants that may have anti-inflammatory and brain-protective properties.
5. **White and Brown**: While not as colorful, white and brown foods like onions, garlic, cauliflower, mushrooms, and whole grains provide essential nutrients such as fiber, potassium, and various phytochemicals.

By incorporating a variety of colors into your meals, you ensure a broad spectrum of essential nutrients and compounds that support overall health and well-being. Aim to include a diverse range of fruits, vegetables, and plant-based foods in your diet to "eat the rainbow" and reap the benefits of a nutrient-rich, colorful plate.

Freeing yourself to live a healthier life also means overall breaking free from unhealthy habits, thought patterns, and behaviors that are holding you back from achieving optimal health and well-being. We've found that scheduling time for meditation or exercise helps us follow through, no matter what life throws at us that day. Remember: *Those who fail to plan, plan to fail. When you talk about something, it's a dream. When you schedule it, it becomes reality.*

2. YOU HAVE TO MOVE TO IMPROVE

Why is movement such a big deal? Is it all ego? I want to look sexy in a bikini (well, not William). Does a commitment to working out necessarily mean that somebody is selfish or vain? Does scheduling physical activity every day mean that you are on a path to obsession or body dysmorphia?

No, no, and no. A commitment to physical activity is a commitment to blessing the world. Your physical health keeps you alive for your family and friends. Your physical health means that your blessing to this world is extended. Your physical health improves cognitive function, regulates your vagus nerve, and ultimately makes you vibrate at a higher frequency, enhancing the lives of everybody around you.

This message is the one we've never heard other health experts tout. With her various degrees from the National Academy for Sports Medicine, Lori has read an entire library of books on nutrition and health. The good news is that you don't have to be a fitness professional like Lori to make "strides" in your physical fitness, pun intended. In fact, you don't have to have chiseled arms like Lori to make a measurable impact through physical fitness. Improving cardiovascular health, boosting one's mood, and reducing the risk of chronic diseases such as diabetes and obesity come with even just twenty minutes of moderately paced walking per day—and not up a steep mountain in Aspen, either!

On the contrary, a sedentary lifestyle is miserable. It doesn't just increase the risk of chronic diseases, but it also impacts mental health. Taking the stairs instead of the elevator, biking instead of driving, and taking periodic breaks from sitting to work at a standing desk or attending a Zoom call while engaging your legs with an exercise band literally help your circulation while improving your mood. An entire book can be written about the mood-enhancing benefits of exercise, but we've distilled the main points:

1. Release endorphins (your body's 'feel good' chemicals);
2. Boost serotonin and dopamine levels;
3. Reduce stress hormones;

4. Improve sleep;
5. Increase your sense of accomplishment;
6. Diminish negative thoughts;
7. Regulate anxiety;
8. Neurogenesis

Neurogenesis is one of the core tenets of the Best Day Every Day lifestyle. When you stimulate neurogenesis, the growth of new neurons in the brain, you improve brain function and resilience against mood disorders like depression.

Once you begin a routine that is in alignment with your current health, such as walking, biking, or swimming, make sure you gradually increase the intensity and duration of that activity. This can help reduce the risk of injury and further enhance the sense of accomplishment. Runners are great at this; they often track their mile "splits" and work to reduce the minutes (and seconds) it takes to complete a course. We have a friend who has kept splits on a stopwatch from twenty-five years ago as a reminder of his accomplishments.

3. ANTI-AGING PROMISE

What are Telomeres? Telomeres are the protective caps on the ends of your chromosomes that play a critical role in aging. Telomeres shorten with each cell division, and once they become too short, cells can no longer divide, leading to cellular aging and ultimately cell death. This process is known as cellular senescence. In short, as a person ages, their telomeres, well, *shorten.*

However, although aging is inevitable, it is possible to eliminate or reduce factors that shorten telomeres more quickly. Those factors include chronic stress, poor diet, lack of exercise, smoking, and others. Shortening telomeres can lead to premature aging and an increase in age-related diseases. In fact, one study found that individuals with shorter telomeres had a higher risk of age-related diseases such as cancer and cardiovascular disease. This suggests that telomere length may be a useful marker for predicting age-related disease risk.

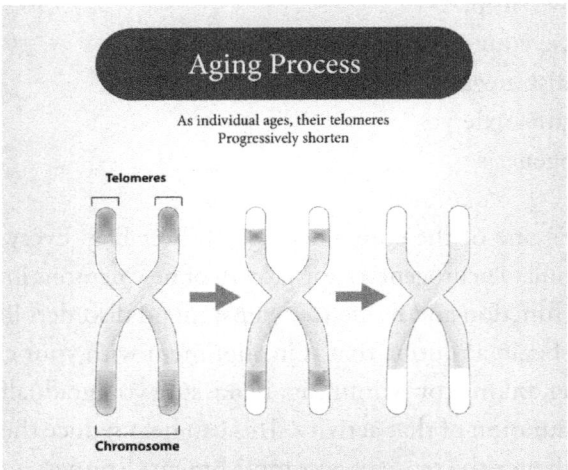

Rights for this image courtesy of Stock.Adobe.com

A sedentary life, again, wreaks havoc on your health and mental wellness, as well as telomere length. A **2008 study** found that people who engaged in regular physical activity, particularly endurance exercises, had longer telomeres than those who were sedentary. The difference in telomere length suggested that physically active individuals had cells that appeared biologically younger by as much as 10 years.

Thankfully, telomere length is not necessarily a fixed trait. Specific lifestyle changes can help to slow or even reverse telomere shortening. For example, studies have shown that regular exercise can slow telomere shortening and may even lead to telomere lengthening in some cases. There is also ongoing research into telomere lengthening therapies, including the use of telomerase, an enzyme that can lengthen telomeres. While these therapies are still in the experimental stage, they hold promise for potential future treatments for age-related diseases.

Circling back to exercise, it is believed that exercise does impact telomeres in the following ways:

1. **Reduction in Oxidative Stress**

    Oxidative stress and inflammation are key contributors to telomere shortening. Regular physical activity helps reduce oxidative damage to cells and DNA, which in turn can slow the rate of telomere shortening. Exercise also boosts the body's antioxidant defenses, which neutralize free radicals that would otherwise damage cells and contribute to telomere shortening.[4]

2. **Lower Inflammation**
   Chronic inflammation accelerates telomere shortening, and exercise is known to reduce inflammation by lowering levels of pro-inflammatory markers like C-reactive protein (CRP). By reducing systemic inflammation, exercise protects telomeres and promotes healthier cellular function.[5]

3. **Increased Activity of Telomerase**
   Telomerase is an enzyme that helps repair and extend telomeres, and regular physical activity has been associated with increased telomerase activity. Studies show that individuals who engage in moderate to vigorous exercise have higher telomerase activity, which contributes to the maintenance of telomere length and helps slow down the biological aging process.[6]

4. **Cardiovascular Health**
   Cardiovascular exercise improves heart health, enhances blood circulation, and ensures better oxygen delivery to tissues. This helps prevent cellular damage and may protect telomeres from shortening.[7]

5. **Reduced Psychological Stress**
   Chronic psychological stress is linked to shorter telomeres, as stress increases cortisol levels and oxidative damage. Exercise is a well-

---

[4] Shammas, M. A. (2011). "Telomeres, lifestyle, cancer, and aging." Current Opinion in Clinical Nutrition & Metabolic Care, 14(1), 28-34.
[5] Ludlow, A. T., et al. (2008). "Exercise telomere biology: a review." European Journal of Applied Physiology, 103, 289-296.
[6] Puterman, E., Lin, J., Blackburn, E., O'Donovan, A., Adler, N., Epel, E. (2010). "The power of exercise: Buffering the effect of chronic stress on telomere length." PLoS ONE, 5(5), e10837.
[7] Du, M., et al. (2012). "Physical activity, sedentary behavior, and leukocyte telomere length in women." American Journal of Epidemiology, 175(5), 414-422.

known stress reliever, helping to reduce cortisol levels and improve mental resilience.[8]

6. **Maintenance of a Healthy Weight**
   Obesity is associated with accelerated telomere shortening. Exercise helps manage weight by improving metabolism and reducing fat levels, which can protect telomeres from the damage associated with excess body fat and chronic inflammation.[9]

In a 2018 meta-analysis, researchers found that moderate to high levels of physical activity were associated with longer telomere length in both cross-sectional and longitudinal studies, indicating the potential for exercise to preserve telomere integrity over time. Another study of older adults found that HIIT (High-Intensity Interval Training) and resistance training had positive effects on telomere length and the body's cellular aging process.

Aerobic exercise, such as walking, jogging, or swimming, is shown to have the strongest link to longer telomeres. HITT or "High-Intensity Interval Training," strength training, and mind-body exercises such as yoga have also been linked to improvements in telomere health.

4. ACHIEVING HAPPINESS... IN YOUR SLEEP

Adequate sleep is necessary for the body to repair and regenerate. Chronic sleep deprivation has been linked to a range of health problems, including obesity, diabetes, and cardiovascular disease. Sleep allows your body and mind to recharge and recover from the activities of the day; healthcare professionals often refer to it as your body's natural "rest and digest" state, where your body does the majority of its healing, due to less energy devoted to waking functions.

---

8   Rae, D. E., et al. (2010). "Telomere length in ultra-marathon runners: implications for the role of exercise in tissue regeneration." European Journal of Applied Physiology, 109, 323-330.
9   Stamford, B. A., et al. (2015). "Telomeres and exercise: the end of the tale?" Journal of Clinical Endocrinology & Metabolism, 100(12), 4411-4414.

On the contrary, sleep deprivation has been linked to a variety of mental health issues, including depression, anxiety, and bipolar disorder. During sleep, your brain undergoes a process of consolidation, where memories and experiences from the day are processed and stored. This process is critical for your ability to learn, remember, and regulate your emotions.

In addition to its impact on mental health, sleep is also essential for your physical health. During sleep, your body repairs and regenerates tissues, releases hormones that regulate growth and appetite, and strengthens your immune system. Consistently getting enough high-quality sleep has been shown to reduce the risk of chronic conditions such as obesity, diabetes, and cardiovascular disease.

Perhaps most surprisingly, sleep has also been linked to cellular aging. Telomeres, as discussed previously, naturally shorten as you age. However, research has found that sleep duration and quality can impact the rate of telomere shortening, with sleep deprivation leading to faster telomere shortening and cellular aging.

Not all sleep is equal. Sleeping after a night of heavy drinking or drug use doesn't have the restorative effects of going to sleep while sober. What's more, it's believed that the sleep you get before midnight is more effective for healing than if you're a night owl. In fact, some professionals believe that going to sleep at the same time every night also improves the "rest and digest" magic of good sleep.

Despite its importance, many people struggle to get adequate sleep. The Centers for Disease Control and Prevention (CDC) estimates that one in three adults in the United States does not get enough sleep. While the recommended amount of sleep varies by age, most adults need at least 7-8 hours of sleep per night.

How can you get better sleep? As mentioned earlier, establishing a consistent sleep schedule is important, but so are the routines you create around that schedule. Creating a relaxing bedtime routine and creating a sleep-conducive environment (such as keeping the bedroom cool, dark, and quiet) can all improve sleep quality. Avoiding caffeine, alcohol, and electronic devices before bedtime can also help promote better sleep.

AN UNLIKELY SECRET TO ANTI-AGING

In a world of nips, tucks, surgeries, and fillers, what if anti-aging could be achieved by something as simple as buying a plane ticket? In September 2024, a study published by Edith Cowan University suggests that travel can slow down the aging process. Social interaction, mental stimulation, activity, and healthy foods all contribute to staying young, and many Western travelers enjoy these things more during travel than back at home.

Scientists found that travel "plays an important role in individual health and public health," according to principal researcher Fangli Hu to the Washington Post. When we travel, especially as Americans, we escape the onslaught of Franken-foods that are unfortunately common in our society. In fact, the EU bans over 1,570 more ingredients in cosmetics and consumer goods than the USA, where only 30 toxic ingredients are banned. Every time you smear on a potion, lotion, or pop a pill, you're likely consuming substances that can wreak havoc on your hormones and essentially do more harm than good. Likewise, every time you open a box of crackers, slurp down a fizzy drink, or eat at restaurants stateside, you are exposing yourself to an unknown quantity of mysterious chemical substances or preservatives. These toxic products are linked to the skyrocketing cancer rates in the USA, as is evidenced by the myriad of lawsuits against companies like Procter & Gamble or Johnson & Johnson.

Travel, however, kicks us out of our toxic lifestyles and into a lifestyle of holistic wellness in natural ways. We prefer walking and climbing stairs to sitting at our desks. We appreciate nature and walk barefoot on the ground, helping to recalibrate our nervous systems and electromagnetic fields. We eat foods prepared in kitchens by chefs who don't have access to the same toxic Frankenfoods that are common in the USA. Moreover, travel stimulates your mind as it requires coordination, planning, and exposure to new experiences.

Above all, travel engages your brain in neurogenesis, the process of creating new neural pathways in a new environment. Recently, a friend of ours went through a devastating breakup in Aspen. She hopped in her car for a five-day trip to the desert. At first glance, it was easy to say, "Well, Sarah, you can't run away from your problems," but we knew better. This woman was committed to rewiring the programs in her brain that said, "You are unwanted. You are unimportant. You are unloved. You are alone. You will never meet the love of your life. You are replaceable. You messed up."

Upon returning from the desert, the woman shared that her time away helped her to increase her sense of well-being, and meeting new people actually proved to her that the world is very small, and that she can "bloom" no matter where she is planted. During her travels, the woman forced herself to go on many hikes, originally dragging her broken heart behind her like an anchor. She reported that she was intoxicated with the smell of Juniper as she walked in the desert. The purchase of sandstone beneath her feet made her feel like she could run through the trails like a billy goat, and she felt more playful and silly than she had in years. The adventure of getting lost on a trail, getting lost trying to find her Airbnb, and struggling in the middle of the night to access her accommodations in a strange and foreign place helped her remember to appreciate the "little things." After a few days of mind-mushrooming about her breakup, running around the foreign desert enabled her to take a break from overanalyzing and shift her mindset to present moment awareness. This, in turn, gave her the power to enter into a time of planning for her next steps in life: the next big adventure in love and relationships.

Travel is also an appropriate time to engage in neuro-associative conditioning. If you invest time and money reaching a destination, mindfully smelling, sensing, and feeling your surroundings is a way of consecrating the experience in your mind. "Environments, stunning landscapes like forests or beaches, can help us reduce stress, boost our mental well-being, and promote physical activity. Exposure to other tourists, locals, or even animals can improve our mood and enhance cognitive function. And, travel can lead to healthy eating," reported Mr. Hu from the study.

Chapter Ten:
NEVER WORK A DAY IN YOUR LIFE

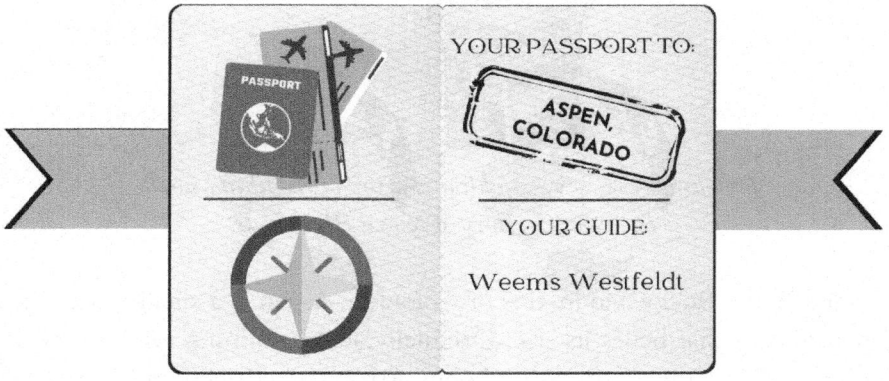

*"When you do what you love, it never feels like work.
Each day on these slopes is a new adventure,
a chance to embrace the thrill of life and find joy in every moment.
Skiing is not just a sport; it's a way of life.
It's about finding brilliance in every turn,
every breath, every moment."*
Weems Westfeldt

Lori and Weems Westfeldt at the top of Highland Bowl, the crowning glory of Aspen Highlands.

Nestled in the Rocky Mountains of Colorado, Aspen is a small town with a rich history that belies its size. Originally a silver mining town founded during the late 19th-century silver boom, Aspen transformed into one of the most iconic ski destinations in the world after World War II. Known for its breathtaking landscapes, luxury living, and rich cultural scene, Aspen attracts visitors year-round for its skiing, festivals, and natural beauty. But beyond the glamour, the town retains its charm, steeped in history and surrounded by the rugged majesty of the Rockies.

With leaves long having fallen and flowers still months away, the Aspen winter has a way of invigorating one's senses in simple ways. Crisp mountain air stabs at exposed skin, and pine needles that may be otherwise overshadowed by spring or summer scents become more pronounced, producing a slight tang in one's nose.

As Lori glided down the slopes, the crisp mountain air sharpened her senses while the powder beneath her skis felt light and forgiving. The late Weems Westfeldt, author of *Brilliant Skiing Every Day*, skied just ahead, offering precise instructions and embodying his philosophy of blending

CHAPTER TEN: NEVER WORK A DAY IN YOUR LIFE

technical skill with mindfulness. As she nailed the turn, his voice quieted, and with a glance back, he gave her a reassuring smile that said it all—Lori had mastered exactly what he asked.

The snow has a way of deadening all other noises, almost like being in a recording studio with soft, carpeted walls. In the silence of a mountain covered with a blanket of noise-canceling snow, Lori's skis carved through the silence. As she descended the slopes, she heard periodic yips and hoorahs from other skiers' laughter and the occasional call of a bird overhead. On the mountain, skiing is accompanied by little more than joyful noises.

Later on, as her face thawed out from the cold wind with a mug of hot chocolate in her hand, she chatted with Weems, whose voice was encouraging, enthusiastic, and full of wisdom as he shared stories from his rich skiing history. Inhaling cinnamon and whipped cream, fighting for space with the scent of wood smoke from the lodge fireplace, Lori felt contentment and purpose. Skiing is a hobby unlike reading or beach combing; it brings with it the opportunity to continually improve while engaging in an activity that is both adventurous and enjoyable, not to mention punctuated by some of the most beautiful landscapes in the world.

It was during this moment at the lodge that Weems explained to Lori his philosophy of never working a day in his life, even though he is arguably one of the hardest-working individuals we have met. He has dedicated himself to a craft he loves, which means that waking up early or showing up seven days a week for months on end doesn't exhaust him. His work continually regenerates more energy.

Weems Westfeldt believed that joy comes from a flow state that combines pleasure with commitment to excellence and improvement. He dedicated his life to teaching others how to find joy and excellence in skiing. His book underscores the importance of savoring every moment while committing oneself to constant improvement.

In the skiing community, Weems was known for his charismatic teaching style, his ability to connect with students on a personal level, and his unwavering passion for the mountains. At our wedding at the top of Aspen Mountain, Weems walked Lori down the aisle. He taught Lori how to dance with the mountains, and their friendship became a testament to their shared love of skiing.

WHAT IS YOUR X FACTOR?

My (William's) daughter Brigette has the ultimate competitive advantage in life. She has a powerful and unique identity. Early in her life, she was fortunate to find her passion. From the moment she could hold a crayon, she knew that she was destined to be an artist. With the support of her artist parents, she immersed herself in art programs, and now, at 23, she's carving out a thrilling career in digital art and movies. It's a lifelong passion, and she's living a life where she'll never 'work' a day.

For many of us, however, finding our passion isn't always that straightforward. Influences from parents, teachers, and friends can shape our early visions of what we should become—doctors, lawyers, accountants, you name it. It can leave us wondering if the path we're on truly aligns with our own desires.

Growing up, I (William) admired my father's friend Whit, a successful car dealer with a lifestyle that involved travel, skiing, and tennis.

In middle school, influenced by my orthodontist's charming horse ranch lifestyle, I contemplated a career in dentistry. Yet, as I progressed through college, I realized my interests were shifting. While my major was initially biology, I found myself drawn to philosophy, history, and political science. Interest tests revealed my true passions lay in business, politics, and law—not in medicine. This revelation changed everything. I shifted gears, attending law school, engaging in politics, and exploring real estate and stock investing. Today, I thrive in the political arena and real estate landscape, also investing in stocks and digital assets like Bitcoin and Ethereum.

The key takeaway?

Discovering your passion may be a journey, not a destination. It's about evolving, adapting, and aligning with your authentic self. If you're questioning your path, consider taking interest tests, exploring your curiosities, and embracing the journey of self-discovery. Your true passions could reshape your destiny, just as they did for me.

Some of our favorite professional and character tests include Enneagram, Wealth Dynamics, Meyers-Briggs, and the Kolbe A. These tests can enlighten you not only to your strengths, but also as to why specific tasks confound or frustrate you; they teach you how to avoid weaknesses so that you can focus on your strengths. This is something we refer to as focusing on your "A's," not trying to bring up your "C's."

I (Lori) dared to dream beyond the borders of a small town in Mansfield, Ohio.

Growing up, I didn't envision a grand life. I contemplated the usual paths of motherhood, teaching, or nursing. Despite being an excellent babysitter, the prospect of children, needles, and blood wasn't exactly my cup of tea. Raised in a simple family with a postman father and a secretary mother, I wasn't born into privilege. Yet, I had everything I needed—private schools, competitive sports, and a college education. However, it was my inner drive, ambition, and intelligence that set me on a unique path.

Initially enrolled in Kent State's veterinary program, my life took a turn when I discovered the "Shannon Rogers and Jerry Silverman School of Fashion Design and Merchandising" program. In an instant, I realized my talent for turning the pages of a fashion magazine surpassed all. I accelerated through my four-year program in three and a half years, setting my sights on the "Fashion Capital of the World"—New York City.

Over two decades in Manhattan, I rose through the ranks, leaving an indelible mark with fashion icons like Hugo Boss, Joseph Abboud, Donna Karan, and Tommy Hilfiger. Simultaneously, I mastered the art of physical fitness and well-being, becoming a certified personal trainer.

Today, I stand as a testament to timeless style and enduring vitality. My secret unfair advantages? A two-decade career in NYC's top fashion houses and over fifteen years as a certified personal trainer. Now, in my transformative program, *Women Over 50 Unleashed: Ageless Style & Vitality*, I share these advantages, empowering women to embrace their age with confidence, vitality, and a renewed sense of style.

DO WHAT YOU LOVE, LOVE WHAT YOU DO

The greatest gift you can give yourself is a life spent pursuing something you're genuinely passionate about. Moreover, the greatest gift you can give the world is to make your professional pursuit one that you're uniquely good at; from there, you will bless others more profoundly.

The idea of "doing what you love" may seem like a luxury or a far-fetched dream to some, but it's not. Without being melodramatic, sometimes pursuing what you love is a matter of life and death. There's nothing more soul-crushing than working in a job one hates. Few things push great minds into anesthetizing with trivial, mindless pursuits, such as binge-watching or heavy drinking, like hating their job or career. What's more, everybody knows that their lives are shorter with each passing breath. Without purpose, life doesn't seem worth living for some.

However, having a deep passion for what you do increases both happiness and success. When you do what you love, you are more likely to invest the time and effort necessary to excel in your chosen field. You become more motivated to learn, grow, and improve because you are naturally interested in what you're doing.

Moreover, when you love what you do, you're more likely to be prosperous in your work, because you're willing to go the extra mile to achieve your goals. You're also more likely to persevere through the tough times, because you're committed to something you truly care about. Of course, doing what you love doesn't mean that you won't face challenges or setbacks along the way. But the passion and love you have for your work can help you weather those storms and come out stronger on the other side.

However, it's important to note that simply doing what you love may not always be enough. You also need to learn to love what you do. This means finding joy and satisfaction in the day-to-day tasks and responsibilities that come with your work. For example, if you love writing but hate editing, you'll need to learn to love the editing process as well, because it's an essential part of the job. If you love working with people but hate paperwork, you'll need to find a way to make it more enjoyable. The key is to find ways to make your work meaningful and satisfying, even when it's not your favorite task. This may involve finding ways to challenge yourself, setting goals that align with your passions, or changing your perspective.

YOUR PROFESSIONAL X-FACTOR

The term 'X factor' generally refers to a special, often intangible quality or trait that makes someone or something stand out remarkably or exceptionally. It may refer to a person's unique talent, charisma, or personality trait. Oprah Winfrey embodies this X factor. Her authenticity, empathy, and powerful communication skills have allowed her to connect deeply with millions, making her not just influential but unforgettable. She has an innate ability to inspire and uplift, while maintaining a genuine, down-to-earth presence.

In marketing, an X factor refers to the differentiating factor that makes a product, brand, or company successful. In sports, a player is described as having an X factor when they are capable of changing the outcome of a game, performing well under pressure, or elevating their team's performance. The X factor in Brigette's art is her distinctive style, and the signature she leaves on every piece she creates makes it memorable and magnetic. In relationships, the X factor is the often indescribable quality that attracts someone to another.

You Know You Found Your X Factor When...

When you find your X factor in business, you add value beyond measure. This could be the real estate agent who consistently finds families their perfect home in record time and outperforms competing offers for their clients. This could be the financial professional who is adept at making moves for his clients at the perfect time based on markets, risk tolerance, and life events. It could be the wedding planner who consistently throws an unforgettable wedding. It could be the writer who writes one bestseller after another. This level of excellence doesn't easily come from college or by instruction; this kind of brilliance is created through the X factor of the individual performing their magical role in their perfect niche.

When you find your X factor, you will work smarter, not harder. Excelling in a career or pursuit requires effort to the point of exhaustion. It is at this point that you must realize that you haven't found your X factor or a career that nurtures your X factor. When you are working within a container that permits you to thrive in your X factor, the work becomes pleasurable; you're in a flow state, much like Lori providing personal training support or Weems while teaching skiing.

When you find your X factor, you will be more successful. When somebody has found their X factor, business becomes more prosperous. Referrals and positive client testimonials generally evidence this. You may refer to your hair stylist, accountant, yoga teacher, or surgeon as a "secret weapon" or "the best of the best." Those are individuals who have discovered and executed their X factors; they stand out above the competition, and they're rewarded with more happy clients who are willing to pay their rates with joy.

FINDING YOUR X FACTOR

You might be wondering if finding your X factor is as elusive as finding "inner peace," or "life's purpose," or even "happiness." Thankfully, finding your X factor has a clearer roadmap:

1. **Listen to your body.** Use the neuro-associative conditioning techniques from chapter three and commit to paying attention to what signals your extremities, organs, or skin provide when certain thoughts enter your brain in response to different words, images, colors, thoughts, or visualizations. These are signposts to your authentic, true desires.

2. **What gives you energy?** What is something you can do all day and never tire of it? Identify something that is the highlight of your current day, week, month, or year, and find a way to make that your full-time job.

3. **Model the right people.** Model someone who has already achieved what you desire to achieve and seek to imitate the best in the world.

Rather than trying to reinvent the wheel, piggyback on the wisdom and actions of successful entrepreneurs or men and women in industries akin to the one in which you're interested. It's been said that we are the sum of the five people around whom we spend the most time. Do you surround yourself with people who are successful, clever, and talented? Mastermind groups are a valuable resource. Friends are important, but you need a master to take you to the next professional level.

4. **Keep Notes About What Moves You.** A child may love a particular animal, bird, sport, or hobby that got "nurtured" out of him through conditioning that distracted him from his passion. To reconnect with your X factor, start by taking notice of what moves you. This could be art that catches your eye. A bird that intoxicates you with its song. Creating a perfect spreadsheet! Different people find joy and fulfillment in various ways. The busyness of families and paying bills often distracts people from immersion in the things that set their souls on fire. If you find that your life is largely uninspiring, this is where travel comes into play. Travel helps you remember the passions you understood as a child, but may have lost sight of while paying bills or keeping up with the Joneses. Events, seminars, hobbies, classes, and workshops help to remind us of what we love. Our publisher loved books, but in the hustle of paying for college, she settled for a career in finance just to work on student loan payback. She languished for years, at one point thinking she wanted to die rather than help somebody open another checking account. By attending a seminar, she was reminded of a time when she would write and journal every night or read until 3 and 4 in the morning; sometimes reading an entire book per night when she was in middle school. To honor that little girl who loved books, she then immediately applied for every position she could find in publishing and left the finance industry within just six weeks of that revelation; her inner child reminding her of her own X factor. In 2022, she wrote two Wall Street Journal bestsellers in just nine months. She finally rekindled her calling, and in her X factor, has experienced tremendous success in her field.

5. **Show Off Your Style.** To be eye-catching and unforgettable, you also need to embrace your unique personality and style. Don't be afraid to express yourself in your own way, whether it's through your fashion, your hobbies, or your personality. Be confident in who you are and let your individuality shine through.

YOUR X FACTOR ADVENTURE

One successful entrepreneur, Mike Dillard, had ten successful years in business, never grossing less than a million dollars, sometimes grossing well over $12,000,000. He was periodically working on his X factor, which was through writing stories that engaged people and sold his information courses. However, his new venture had him preoccupied with business development, vetting financial partners, and managing an increasingly large team of both employees and affiliates. Mike began to resent the business he had built around his true X factor: waking up and crafting inspiring stories that promoted products and people he believed in. He transitioned from being an untethered digital nomad to a traditional corporate CEO, facing the geographic and time limitations that come with that role. No longer could he travel or take weeks off without 100 tiny fires erupting and threatening the time he needed to recharge and do what he does best: write stories and share those stories with his online students. In time, his health began to fail. He wasn't sleeping for so many days or weeks on end that the doctors told him he was on death's door and were afraid he wouldn't make it another week with his stress load.

One day, Mike decided rather abruptly to shut down his company. He invested in hydroponic gardens, crypto, and other financial instruments, a podcast and studio, and other high-ticket items to find himself again. He took considerable risks through various holistic health practitioners, making it his job to discover what felt right for his body and spirit.

During his journey to rediscover himself, Mike invested the last of his savings, and at one point, he didn't have money to pay rent. There was less than $5,000 left to his name. At this point of rock bottom, things began to turn around for him. He found therapies that helped him regain his health and sleep better, most notably by learning how to heal from mold toxicity that was found in his home and nearly killed him.

Most excitingly, during this time, Mike not only took risks with new ventures and businesses but also interviewed one hundred of the most successful men and women on the planet to learn about their secrets to success. Mike rediscovered his passion for writing and decided to take another stab at making it his career. Today, he is living on a large ranch with millions of dollars in the bank. He has completely transformed his work from one of stress, unwanted administrative tasks, continual pressure to manage a staff and affiliates, and create content, to a life of investing his time in writing great stories. Mike has earned as much as $6,000,000 on a single email to his subscribers because his zone of genius is writing. Through writing, he promotes products and services he believes in, specifically courses that teach others how he has created wealth through crypto and the stock markets.

One thing Mike realized, as one of the greatest copywriters in the world, is that he doesn't have to fit into the corporate box. He doesn't like having employees. He doesn't enjoy networking or going to events. He is a deeply introverted person, preferring to spend six hours a day writing after a morning of trading. In the evenings, he enjoys reading and spending time with his family, including his son, his new wife, and her daughter. Mike didn't view his intense introversion as a detriment or roadblock; instead, he learned how to protect and guard his space, enabling him to thrive professionally and achieve success. His X factor is unlocked when he has ample time alone to process thoughts and write stories in his head. His X factor involves crafting copy that instills hope and promise in people. To achieve this, he must meditate on the world, current events, and the spiritual pulse of people in relation to the news and media messages they receive.

His introversion is no longer his downfall. He has found a way to make it his strength. He is contemplative, thoughtful, and empathic. Guarding his energy in silence and isolation is a superpower. The distractions of running his business in a traditional corporate way are his kryptonite.

TAKING RISKS TO DISCOVER YOUR X FACTOR

Taking risks doesn't mean you'll succeed at every adventure; it means you open yourself up to learning. One of the primary reasons we often forget the passions we had as children, which are usually signs of our deepest life's purpose and calling, is that not everybody's passion fits into traditional school curricula or their families.

Dr. Eric Anthony Johnson, CEO of AEON corporation, had a family that encouraged him to align with their culture of crime and drugs. He chose sobriety at an early age and used the game of basketball to keep himself off the streets during the 1980s crack epidemic. His family chided him, telling him he was acting "too good" for them and assuring him that he would end up on the streets or in jail like everybody else. They worked to bring him down to their level.

Eric lamented that he, his mother, and brother moved every few months, sometimes not knowing where they'd lay their heads at night when he went to school that morning. Besides basketball, Dr. Eric discovered his X factor by locking himself in school libraries where he would be safe from the crime on the streets around him. Desperate to put himself into a stable financial situation, he joined the army after high school, where he felt safer than on the streets of New Orleans. He then, although being a kid from the ghetto, applied to every internship program he could at the highest-rated schools in the world to get an education that was traditionally only afforded to middle or upper-class white kids from great schools. When he received the call that he was accepted into a White House internship program in his twenties, he was sitting on a couch in an empty apartment, wondering if he could make a single box of pizza last for a week. Eric took risks to find his X factor and excel professionally with it. Today, he has a PhD., a Harvard MBA, and two master's degrees.

Dr. Eric's X factor involves having the discipline to be a leader despite what is happening around him. He excelled as a CEO in one of the most challenging industries in the world: affordable housing and urban development. A soul passion for affordable housing drives him, and he flourishes because he learned that he is the most relentless champion of this cause he knows. Today, there is even a day named after him in New Orleans, "Eric Anthony Johnson Day."

Taking risks can be scary, but it's also one of the most rewarding things you can do in life. When you step outside of your comfort zone and try something new, you open yourself up to endless possibilities and opportunities.

Among the most soul-crushing states of being is boredom. Imagine you're watching a football game. The players are getting rained on. One team consistently knocks the opposing team to the ground in violent ways. It appears that Team A is the underdog, but they're fighting like their lives depend on it to score the winning goal.

If you're on Team A, where do you want to be? On the field. You want to be taking risks. You want to be in the game. You want a chance to contribute. If you're on the bench, you don't feel like the win is yours, even if Team A scores that final goal.

A life without risks is like being benched. You aren't in the game. You aren't on the field. You aren't learning, growing, getting bruised and beaten by life's lessons. Would you rather anesthetize with wine and Netflix every night? Or be in the game. When Lori chose to learn how to ski, to attend the ten-day workshop in Fiji with Loren Lahav, immerse herself with Geoffry Gertz in New York, or visit Dr. May Baselton in Bangkok, she got in the game. None of these experiences were spa days; they required intense physical, emotional, and psychological strength.

Chapter Eleven:
SECURING YOUR FINANCIAL FUTURE

"Having it 'all' is about creating a life of meaning and satisfaction. Money is just a tool to help you get there. It's not the destination itself."
Warren Buffet

Lori and William boarding the Glacier Express in St. Moritz, Switzerland.

Brisk Alpine air awakened our senses as we boarded the gleaming Glacier Express in St. Moritz en route to Zermatt. The Excellence Class car welcomed us with the soft scent of polished wood and leather, a prelude to the luxury that awaited us. As we settled into our panoramic window seats, the plush fabric embraced us, promising comfort for the eight-hour journey ahead.

The train glided out of the station, the gentle hum of its wheels a soothing backdrop to the breathtaking scenery unfolding before us. The crystal-clear windows offered an unobstructed view of snow-capped peaks and emerald valleys, each turn revealing a new masterpiece painted by nature.

As we approached Davos, the aroma of our first course wafted through the car—a delicate consommé infused with local herbs. The flavors danced on our tongues, a culinary representation of the Alpine landscape rushing past our window—crisp, savory, and invigorating. A sommelier presented a crisp Swiss white wine—its cool glass a welcome contrast to the warmth of the cabin.

Outside, we glimpsed the enthusiastic activity of the World Economic Forum, a curious community of the world's most powerful CEOs, journalists, and scientists who gather together for a week in discussions about how they might achieve a united one-world order with an emphasis on collectivism and sustainability, futurism and AI, and advancements in medicine and technology. The WEF Annual Summit brings together global leaders from business, finance, and government, creating a unique environment for forging strategic partnerships, exploring collaborative ventures, and accessing exclusive investment opportunities.

As the Glacier Express paused briefly, allowing us to observe the global elite hurrying through the snow-dusted streets, we knew Ray Dalio was already inside preparing. He was not here merely to attend; he was here to analyze, synthesize, and recognize patterns where others saw only complexity. Over the next five days, we experienced a whirlwind of intellectual stimulation and high-powered networking. The Congress Centre hummed with the energy of 3,000 of the world's most influential minds. The air was thick with the scent of expensive colognes and freshly brewed Swiss coffee, underscored by the faint yet distinctive smell of fondue from nearby chalets.

Throughout the week, we packed into conference rooms where the world's brightest minds explored solutions to global issues. The soft rustle of silk ties and wool suits accompanied impassioned debates on climate change, artificial intelligence, and economic inequality. Our fingers flew across our tablets as we took notes on the cool glass, a contrast to the warmth of handshakes exchanged between sessions.

Ray Dalio stood at the center of it all, absorbing the conversations like a seasoned conductor guiding an orchestra of ideas. During an invitation-only roundtable, the conversation turned to wealth preservation in an era of economic turbulence. A hedge fund manager speculated about inflationary risks. A sovereign wealth fund director debated the future of global reserve currencies. Dalio listened, nodded, then spoke, "The greatest mistake investors make is thinking the past will repeat itself exactly. It never does. But the patterns? The patterns always return in new forms. The key is knowing what phase of the cycle we're in—and positioning accordingly."

During evening receptions, we were served exquisite canapés paired with champagne as we chatted with tech moguls, heads of state, and captains of industry and innovation. The rooms were filled with a variety of different accents and perfumes from around the world; each clinking of a glass punctuating the beginning of a potential partnership or collaboration.

Later, over a fireside dinner at one of Davos' most exclusive chalets, we sipped aged Swiss Pinot as Dalio shared his reflections on the day. "Wealth isn't just about money," he mused. "It's about knowledge. Relationships. Perspective. The most valuable currency in the world is the ability to see reality as it is—not as you wish it to be."

As twilight fell each day, we stepped out onto snow-covered streets for a final reception before falling into deep sleep; our brains throbbing with stimulation. The crisp snow crunching under our feet and the twinkling lights of Davos created a fairytale atmosphere that belied the weighty discussions of the day.

After five intense days, our minds buzzing with new ideas and connections, we returned to the Glacier Express. The familiar embrace of our Excellence Class seats welcomed us back. The panoramic windows now offered a new perspective on the passing landscape.

Dalio had already moved on to his next engagement, but his words lingered, "You came here looking for answers," he had said, "but the real value is in asking better questions. What do you want to build? What principles will guide you? And are you ready to evolve when the world demands it?"

The sommelier presented a local Pinot Noir, its complex flavors echoing the multifaceted discussions we'd just left behind. Each sip seemed to unlock new insights, blending the luxury of the Swiss Alps with the medley of global perspectives we'd gained. Following the Pinot Noir, we then enjoyed a seven-course meal with dishes all representative of Swiss innovation and tradition. As we savored a delicate chocolate dessert, its rich flavor melting on our tongues, we gazed out at the passing Alps. The majestic peaks seemed to embody both the challenges and the aspirations discussed in Davos.

The gentle rhythm of the train lulled us into contemplation. The concept of "having it all" had evolved during our journey. It was no longer just about personal luxury or success, but about balancing individual prosperity with global responsibility. We didn't agree with every person or idea at the WEF Summit. Still, we were thrilled to witness five days of influential minds coming together to solve the world's problems in the best way they know how, operating at the highest levels of consciousness they have obtained.

As the Matterhorn came into view, signaling our approach to Zermatt, we felt profoundly changed. This enormous, expansive world became small for a week; so small that it fit into a tiny town the size of Aspen. The Glacier Express journey, bookending our Davos experience, was more than a luxurious train ride. It was a passage through physical and intellectual landscapes, challenging and expanding our understanding of what it means to truly "have it all" in our interconnected world.

Stepping off the train in Zermatt, Alpine air invigorated us once more. We carried with us not just the lingering taste of the many Swiss delicacies or the memory of breathtaking vistas, but a renewed sense of purpose. The journey—both on the Glacier Express and through the forums of Davos—redefined our perspective on luxury, responsibility, and the delicate balance between enjoying the world's bounties and ensuring their preservation for future generations.

DEFINING YOUR OWN "ALL"

The pre-dawn air in Omaha was crisp and expectant as we joined the growing queue outside the CHI Health Center. The scent of freshly brewed coffee from nearby food trucks mingled with the woodsy fragrance of the Midwest, energizing the crowd of eager shareholders. Excited whispers and the rustle of financial newspapers filled the air as people from all walks of life prepared for the finance and investing world's equivalent of the Super Bowl. The shareholder meeting in Omaha has been, for decades, not just a revelation of the pulse for Berkshire Hathaway shareholders, but for the entire U.S. economy.

As the sun rose, painting the sky in hues of pink and gold, the line surged forward. The buzz of anticipation grew louder, punctuated by the beeps of scanners checking tickets. We felt the smooth paper of our shareholder passes between our fingers, our ticket to financial wisdom.

Inside, the arena buzzed with activity. The sound of thousands of footsteps echoed over the polished concrete floors as attendees found their seats. The air was electric with anticipation as freshly printed annual reports were handed out.

As Warren Buffett and Charlie Munger took the stage, a reverent hush fell over the crowd. Buffett's warm, grandfatherly voice fills the arena, "The key to having it all is understanding what 'all' means to you." Beside him, Munger nodded sagely, his decades-long presence a testament to the power of partnership and shared wisdom. The finance world has often referred to them as a stock trading Waldorf and Statler, only a bit less grumpy.

Buffett continued, his eyes twinkling.

"You see, 'all' isn't just about accumulating wealth. For some, it might mean financial security to provide for their family. For others, it could be the freedom to pursue their passions without monetary constraints. And for others, it might be the ability to make a positive impact on their community or the world at large."

He paused, letting his words sink in.

"The trick is to define your own 'all.' Is it time with loved ones? Is it the pursuit of knowledge? Is it leaving a lasting legacy? Once you know what truly matters to you, you can align your financial decisions with those goals."

Munger chimed in, his voice gruff but wise, "And remember, the best investment you can make is in yourself. Your skills, your knowledge, your health - these are assets that no market crash can take away."

Buffett nodded in agreement.

"Exactly, Charlie. Having it 'all' is about creating a life of meaning and satisfaction. Money is just a tool to help you get there. It's not the destination itself."

The audience hung on every word, pens scribbling furiously as they absorbed this perspective on wealth and fulfillment. In this moment, 'having it all' transformed from a vague, materialistic concept into a profoundly personal and achievable goal, unique to each individual in the room.

Throughout the day, our senses were bombarded with everything from the taste of See's Candies on our tongues to the feel of our pens scratching against paper as we furiously took notes while studying complex financial concepts simplified on giant screens. Munger's dry wit punctuated Buffett's homespun wisdom, their back-and-forth a masterclass in financial insight.

During the Q&A, we watched as someone from the crowd asked Warren Buffett a question. The microphone passed hands, and Buffett, with his signature warmth, responded thoughtfully. Then came Charlie Munger's dry, classic humor, "I have nothing to add," which sparked knowing chuckles from the audience. The brief exchange captured their dynamic perfectly—a moment of wit and wisdom.

As the Shareholder Meeting wrapped up, the energy shifted. The scene moved to the annual Shareholders Picnic—an open-air gathering where shareholders enjoyed food, music, and relaxed camaraderie under the Nebraska sun. The air was filled with the smell of sizzling burgers from Dairy Queen and the sweet scent of Coca-Cola, both Berkshire Hathaway companies. Live music pulsed through the space, the rhythm seeming to match the beating of our hearts, still racing from the day's insights. We felt the cold condensation of a root beer float and an ice-cold beer against our palms as we navigated through the crowd, exchanging ideas with fellow shareholders from around the globe.

The taste of a warm, gooey chocolate chip cookie from Mrs. Fields (another Berkshire company) melted on our tongues as we watched Buffett challenge a shareholder to a game of table tennis, his competitive spirit as evident here as it is in the boardroom.

As the evening wound down, we embraced the cool Omaha night. The city skyline twinkled before us, each light a beacon of possibility. The day's lessons resonated in our minds, blending with the lingering notes of music and the taste of success on our lips.

In our pockets, our notebooks felt heavy with the day's insights. We inhaled deeply, breathing in the clean Midwestern air and the intoxicating scent of potential. With the wisdom of Buffett and Munger echoing in our minds, and the camaraderie of fellow shareholders warming our hearts, the path to "having it all" felt not just possible but within reach. This annual pilgrimage to Omaha once again transformed abstract financial concepts into a tangible, sensory experience of wealth, wisdom, and community.

FINANCIAL HEALTH IS NOT ABOUT BEING RICH

Being financially healthy means living the life you want, free from the stress and uncertainty of financial insecurity. As we've gone through life, we've learned valuable lessons about financial health. We've had times when we've accumulated more wealth than we've felt we could ever use. We've also had times where we've lost wealth due to bad decisions and questionable investments. There are very few of us who haven't experienced this kind of financial roller coaster and near-death financial experiences. But each financial event along our path has taught us a valuable lesson about maintaining financial health and how important that is to our ability to enjoy life. These are some of those lessons we've learned and would like to pass along about making sound financial and investment decisions.

Financial health is often misunderstood to mean being rich or having a high income. Financial health is much more than just having a lot of money in the bank. At its core, financial health is about being able to manage your finances in a way that allows you to live within your means. It is about being able to handle unexpected expenses and emergencies without falling into debt or financial hardship. When you've accomplished this, you can live a more stress-free life and focus on pursuing your passions.

Financial health is about having a long-term perspective. This means planning for your future, whether that means saving for retirement, paying off a mortgage, or saving for your children's education. It also means being prepared for unexpected events, such as job loss, illness, or other emergencies. There are five keys to financial health. They are budgeting, managing debt, saving, investing, and contributing.

CRAFTING FINANCIAL HARMONY

In the exhilarating journey of life, managing your finances is akin to navigating a complex labyrinth filled with fear, as we age, of an evil monster who can bankrupt us, steal our peace of mind, leave us stranded when in need of a personal emergency fund, or, scariest of all, leave us destitute in retirement.

As we strive to achieve financial freedom and create a future of abundance, the art and science of personal finance budgeting become our guiding stars. Welcome to the realm where strategy meets emotion, and financial success becomes not just a possibility but a certainty. In navigating this labyrinth, the key to casting out fear is self-love, self-reliance, and faith in your ability to create a life free of financial worries.

CHAPTER ELEVEN: SECURING YOUR FINANCIAL FUTURE

One of the key components of financial health is budgeting. This means creating a plan for your income and expenses and sticking to it as much as possible. A budget helps you prioritize your spending, so you can save for the things that are most important to you, while also covering your essential expenses. A budget is a financial blueprint of your life and how you want to spend it.

The art of personal finance begins with a canvas—a blank sheet on which you sketch the aspirations and dreams that will shape your financial future. It's not merely about numbers; it's about aligning your money with your values and creating a roadmap that resonates with your life's purpose. As we often say, "The only limit to your impact is your imagination and commitment."

Imagine your budget as a strategic blueprint, a detailed plan that channels the flow of your income towards your desired destinations. It's not about restricting yourself but rather about consciously directing your resources toward what truly matters. Just as an artist selects colors to evoke emotions in a painting, you allocate your funds to create a vivid picture of your financial success.

Yet, the canvas alone is not enough. Enter the science of personal finance—the meticulous calculations and data-driven decisions that transform dreams into reality. Numbers don't lie, and they provide the objective foundation upon which your financial masterpiece is built. This is where tracking expenses, setting savings goals, and understanding investment principles become the essential building blocks.

Consider your budget as the laboratory where financial experiments unfold. Experimentation is fundamental to the scientific process, and your financial journey is no exception. Test different saving and investment strategies, observe the results, and adapt your approach accordingly. In the laboratory of personal finance, failure is not a setback but a valuable lesson, propelling you toward greater financial wisdom.

THE EIGHTH WONDER OF THE WORLD

In this laboratory, the concept of compounding takes center stage. Albert Einstein once referred to compound interest as the eighth wonder of the world, and rightfully so. The art of compounding is the science of exponential growth—an ally that can work tirelessly in your favor when given time. Much like a seasoned alchemist turning base metals into gold, you can transform modest savings into a treasure trove through disciplined, long-term investing.

What is compounding interest? An example of compounding interest is when interest is calculated on both the initial principal and the accumulated interest from previous periods. Here's a basic example:

Example:

Suppose you invest $1,000 in a savings account with an annual interest rate of 5%, compounded annually, for 3 years.

Year 1:
- Principal: $1,000
- Interest: $1,000 × 5% = $50
- Total at the end of Year 1: $1,000 + $50 = $1,050

Year 2:
- New Principal: $1,050
- Interest: $1,050 × 5% = $52.50
- Total at the end of Year 2: $1,050 + $52.50 = $1,102.50

Year 3:
- New Principal: $1,102.50
- Interest: $1,102.50 × 5% = $55.13
- Total at the end of Year 3: $1,102.50 + $55.13 = $1,157.63

At the end of 3 years, your initial $1,000 investment has grown to $1,157.63, with interest building on the original amount and on previously earned interest (the "compounding" effect).

In the pursuit of financial mastery, emotions often play a pivotal role. The ebb and flow of market sentiments, coupled with personal financial challenges, can stir powerful emotions. Here, the art and science of personal finance converge. The artist within you must recognize and manage these emotions, while the scientist grounds decisions in rationality.

Picture a scenario where the stock market experiences a downturn. The artist acknowledges the fear and uncertainty but understands the importance of staying true to the long-term vision. Meanwhile, the scientist analyzes historical market trends, assesses risk, and recalibrates the investment strategy accordingly. It's the delicate dance between emotion and logic, where both partners must perform in harmony. The strategy of "buying low" and "selling high" is important to remember. Many times, investors become excited about stocks when they are at their peak, which often results in that investor "buying high." When the market is high, you hold. When the market is low, you buy. When the market tanks, fear often leads investors to sell shares before they come back, which results in a loss.

THE CANI CONCEPT

One of our mentors and muses, Tony Robbins, has a concept of "CANI" (Constant and Never-ending Improvement), which is one of his guiding principles. Apply this philosophy to your financial journey. Regularly revisit and refine your budget, seeking opportunities for improvement and optimization. Continuous improvement ensures that your financial strategies evolve with changing circumstances, keeping you resilient in the face of economic fluctuations.

Financial freedom isn't about the money you start with or even about the money you make, but how you keep and deploy what you have. Knowledge is more important than capital; any small amount of capital can be deployed wisely to beget gains. As dull as it sounds, rather than time markets, some of our most successful friends simply budget $100-$200 monthly into a stock or cryptocurrency they believe in. This is called "Dollar Cost Averaging." Friends who have invested just $100 monthly in Bitcoin over the past five years now have enough money for a new car, and they barely noticed the monthly allocation.

As you sculpt your financial future, envision your budget as a masterpiece in the making—a testament to your aspirations, discipline, and unwavering commitment to financial success. Remember, the true artistry lies not just in creating the budget but in living it, as each intentional choice propels you closer to the life of abundance you deserve.

BUDGETING TOOLS YOU CAN USE TODAY

Here's a list of 20 free budgeting tools available online that can help with managing personal finances:

1. **Mint**
   This is a popular tool for tracking expenses, setting budgets, and monitoring your credit score.
   https://www.mint.com
2. **Personal Capital**
   Offers budgeting, investment tracking, and retirement planning tools.
   https://www.personalcapital.com

3. **YNAB (You Need A Budget)**
   Known for proactive budgeting strategies, YNAB offers a 34-day free trial.
   https://www.youneedabudget.com
4. **EveryDollar**
   Developed by Dave Ramsey's team, it focuses on zero-based budgeting.
   https://www.everydollar.com
5. **Google Sheets Budget Templates**
   Customizable spreadsheet templates for budgeting and expense tracking.
6. **Microsoft Excel Budget Templates**
   Free templates to create a budget, track expenses, and manage personal finances.

7. **Goodbudget**
   Envelope budgeting app that helps allocate money for different spending categories.
   https://www.goodbudget.com
8. **PocketGuard**
   Automatically tracks spending, bills, and your disposable income.
   https://www.pocketguard.com
9. **Trim**
   A financial management tool that helps negotiate bills and cancel unwanted subscriptions.
   https://www.asktrim.com
10. **Wally**
    A budgeting app that tracks income, expenses, and financial goals.
    https://wally.me
11. **Honeydue**
    A budgeting tool designed for couples to manage finances together.
    https://www.honeydue.com
12. **Albert**
    Personal finance app with free budgeting and saving features.
    https://www.albert.com
13. **Buxfer**
    Offers free budget tracking, forecasting, and expense categorization.
    https://www.buxfer.com
14. **Clarity Money**
    Helps track expenses and find ways to save, with features for canceling subscriptions.
    https://www.claritymoney.com
15. **Spendee**
    Provides budgeting tools, bill reminders, and personalized spending insights.
    https://www.spendee.com
16. **BudgetSimple**
    Focused on simple, straightforward budgeting for individuals looking to manage their expenses.
    https://www.budgetsimple.com

17. **Money Manager Ex**
    Free and open-source personal finance software for budgeting and financial tracking.
    https://www.moneymanagerex.org
18. **Fudget**
    Simplified budgeting app for tracking income and expenses without extra complexity.
    https://www.fudget.com
19. **GnuCash**
    Open-source accounting software with budgeting and financial tracking features.
    https://www.gnucash.org/
20. **Zeta**
    Budgeting app designed for couples, allowing for shared and individual tracking.
    https://www.askzeta.com

NAVIGATING DEBT AND STRATEGIES FOR FINANCIAL LIBERATION

Debt is the downfall of both the rich and the poor. From the time we are teenagers, we are tempted by debt. Each year, many bright young students are steered toward four-year colleges, even when trade schools might be a better fit—offering practical training and, in many cases, equally or even more rewarding long-term opportunities. Houses, cars, vacations, and business ventures create debt that can saddle us with nothing left over to invest. From the eighteen-year-old facing tens of thousands of dollars in college debt to every adult bombarded with ads for everything from trips to luxury items and even homes, we are in a perpetual war with a media flood of temptations to break our budgets and oversaddle ourselves with debt.

We believe in paying off your debt as quickly as possible. Many 30-year and even 40-year home loans have lower rates, but will force you to pay more in interest than your original mortgage rate! Living within your means and avoiding unnecessary expenses can be as simple as filling a cart online, but choosing to click off the page. If the product doesn't haunt you with how desperately you need it, you probably don't need it!

The principles we'll present in this chapter empower individuals to break free from the chains of financial burden because they are just as important as the other mindset skills we've learned so far. To have a life of jet-setting to personal development conferences, you might have to say "no" to other purchases. To live the life of your dreams and work a job that doesn't feel like "work," you may need to pay off debts, build an emergency fund, and take the plunge into your dream career, even if it doesn't pay well initially.

Personal finance is as important to personal development as a yoke is to an egg. Sadly, it's also one of the most neglected subjects in the world of personal development. Coaches often "assume" people will have the money to attend their conferences without making huge sacrifices in their lives or the lives of their families. Even more obtuse is the notion that if you just "believe" hard enough (such as with the law of attraction), money will magically float into your bank account. This is hogwash, and it's a way of selling magic placebo pills that don't actually improve people's lives.

No matter the current circumstances, a strategic and intentional plan can lead to liberation from the grip of debt.

We often remind ourselves that "the secret to living is giving." By freeing ourselves from financial burdens, we empower ourselves to contribute more to our own well-being and the well-being of others. A friend of ours donates to her church weekly and to the organization "Preborn" monthly. She says that when she tires of work, she puts in extra overtime hours with tremendous joy because she knows that the additional $600 or so monthly will go to good causes in her community.

On your "Financial Freedom Canvas," a holistic plan is the brush stroke guiding your masterpiece. Your budget is the palette—each color represents a strategic allocation of resources toward debt repayment. The expertise lies not just in balancing the books—it's in crafting financial choices that harmonize with your goal of a debt-free life. This is the "art" of personal finance. But what of the "science?"

Debt management requires a disciplined and systematic approach that transforms your vision into reality. Begin by conducting a thorough assessment of your current financial landscape. List all your debts, categorize them by interest rates, and understand the terms and conditions associated with each. This scientific approach lays the groundwork for a strategic debt elimination plan. Online, you can find many debt reduction worksheets, such as the one pictured below.

Debt Reduction Calculator

vertex42
https://www.vertex42.com/Calculators/debt-reduction-calculator.html © 2007-2017 Vertex42 LLC

Balance Date: 1/1/2017

Creditor Information Table

Row	Creditor	Balance	Rate	Payment	Custom
1	Card #1	4,400.00	13.00%	50.00	2
2	Auto Loan #1	3,200.00	9.81%	30.00	1
3	Auto Loan #2	5,000.00	12.00%	55.00	3
4	Card #2	9,000.00	13.50%	110.00	5
5	Student Loan #1	4,900.00	4.00%	25.00	4
6					
7					
8					
9					
10					
		26,500.00		270.00	

Monthly Payment 500.00
Initial Snowball 230.00

Strategy: Avalanche (Highest Interest First) ← Choose a strategy

Creditors in Chosen Order	Original Balance	Interest Paid	Months to Pay Off	Month Paid Off
Card #2	9,000.00	1,744.87	32	Sep-19
Card #1	4,400.00	1,798.64	44	Sep-20
Auto Loan #2	5,000.00	2,414.68	55	Aug-21
Auto Loan #1	3,200.00	1,467.30	62	Mar-22
Student Loan #1	4,900.00	1,011.94	70	Nov-22
	-	-	-	
	-	-	-	
	-	-	-	
	-	-	-	

Total Interest Paid: **8,437.43** (Lower is Better)

Debt reduction worksheet courtesy of https://www.vertex42.com/Calculators/debt-reduction-calculator.html

Prioritization is the cornerstone of effective debt management. The debt snowball method involves tackling smaller debts first. As each small debt is conquered, a sense of accomplishment and momentum builds, propelling you toward larger debt obligations. Alternatively, the debt avalanche method prioritizes debts with the highest interest rates, minimizing overall interest payments over time.

Leverage becomes a powerful tool in the science of debt management. Negotiate with creditors for lower interest rates or more favorable repayment terms. Consider balance transfers to consolidate high-interest debts onto platforms with lower rates. By strategically leveraging available resources, you maximize your impact on debt reduction.

While actively addressing existing debt, implement preventive measures simultaneously. Develop a conscious spending habit, ensuring that each financial decision aligns with your values and long-term goals. This discipline not only aids in eliminating existing debt but also fortifies against future financial pitfalls.

Consider income augmentation as another facet of the scientific approach. Explore opportunities for increasing your income, whether through career advancements, side hustles, or entrepreneurial ventures. A higher income not only expedites debt repayment but also provides a buffer against unforeseen financial challenges.

In debt management, resilience is the secret weapon. Financial journeys are seldom linear, and unexpected setbacks may test your resolve. Embrace these challenges as opportunities for growth and learning. The ability to adapt and persevere in the face of adversity is a testament to your commitment to financial freedom.

Remember, the journey to financial freedom is not a sprint but a marathon. With discipline, resilience, and a clear vision of your financial goals, you can break free from the shackles of debt and pave the way to a future of abundance.

DEBT REDUCTION TOOLS YOU CAN USE TODAY

Here's a list of 10 free debt reduction tools along with their websites. These tools can help you tackle debt and find the best strategies for paying it off faster and more efficiently:

1. **Mint**
   Tracks spending, helps create budgets, and includes features for setting up debt repayment plans.
   https://www.mint.com

2. **Undebt.it**
   A free tool to help you create debt payoff plans using methods like the debt snowball and debt avalanche.
   https://www.undebt.it

3. **Debt Payoff Planner**
   A mobile app that helps track debt and shows your progress as you work to pay it down.
   https://debtpayoffplanner.com

4. **Savvy Debt Payoff App**
   Helps automate debt payoff using the snowball or avalanche method, focusing on reducing interest payments.
   https://savvydebtpayoff.com

5. **Unbury.me**
   A simple online calculator that helps compare the debt snowball vs. avalanche repayment methods and track debt reduction.
   https://unbury.me

6. **Vertex42 Debt Reduction Calculator (featured in the image above)**
   A downloadable Excel template that helps you create a debt reduction plan and manage multiple debts.
   https://www.vertex42.com/Calculators/debt-reduction-calculator.html

7. **Zilch Works Debt Reduction Calculator**
   Free debt reduction software that helps you generate a personalized payment schedule to reduce debt faster.
   https://www.zilchworks.com

8. **Credit Karma**
   Offers free credit monitoring along with tools to help you understand and manage debt more effectively.
   https://www.creditkarma.com

9. **Tally**
   A debt management app that helps you organize and pay off credit card debt faster by consolidating payments.
   https://www.meettally.com

10. **PowerPay**
    A free tool from Utah State University Extension that helps create a customized debt reduction plan to maximize payments and minimize interest.
    https://powerpay.org

BUILDING WEALTH BRICK BY BRICK: STRATEGIES OF SAVING

In the dynamic world of personal finance, the cornerstone of financial success lies in the art and science of saving. As we frequently remind ourselves, the key to wealth is straightforward: discover how to contribute more to others than anyone else does. Strive to become more valuable. Do more, give more, be more, and serve more—and you'll create opportunities to earn more.

At the heart of financial mastery is the understanding that saving is not merely a financial habit—it is a transformative mindset. Saving is the intentional act of allocating a portion of your income to create a reservoir of wealth. It's not about deprivation—it's about empowerment. By saving consistently, you build a foundation that allows you to take control of your financial destiny.

In the Tony Robbins playbook, saving is not just about putting money aside—it's about paying yourself first. Before allocating funds to expenses or discretionary spending, prioritize saving a portion of your income. This intentional act establishes a pattern of wealth creation, ensuring that your future self is a priority in your financial decisions.

Now, let's delve into the science of personal finance and the quantitative aspects of saving. Begin by setting clear savings goals. Whether it's an emergency fund, a down payment for a home, or retirement savings, specific goals provide a roadmap for your financial journey. The science of saving involves calculating the amount needed to achieve these goals and consistently contributing toward them.

Automation is a powerful tool in the science of saving. Set up automatic transfers to your savings account, ensuring that a predetermined portion of your income is allocated before you even see it. This systematic approach transforms saving from a sporadic activity to a disciplined habit, ingrained in your financial routine.

Consider the concept of compounding—the eighth wonder of the world, according to Albert Einstein. Through compounding, your savings not only grow over time but also generate earnings on those earnings. The sooner you start saving, the more time your money has to compound, exponentially increasing the wealth you can accumulate.

Life is unpredictable, and having a financial cushion provides peace of mind and financial security. An emergency fund acts as a safety net, allowing you to navigate unexpected expenses without derailing your long-term financial goals. Sadly, the vast majority of Americans don't have enough money saved even to cover an emergency $800 expense. What if that emergency has to do with providing life-saving healthcare support to you or somebody you love? What if the emergency is related to the vehicle needed to get to your job?

The ability to save also positions you as a steward of your own financial destiny. It grants you the power to make choices that align with your values and aspirations. Whether it's pursuing further education, starting a business, or taking a once-in-a-lifetime opportunity, having savings affords you the freedom to make decisions that enhance your quality of life.

THE INVESTOR'S TOOLKIT AND MAXIMIZING OPPORTUNITIES FOR WEALTH

Investing is also a key component of financial health, as it allows you to grow your wealth over time. However, investing should always be done with caution and with a thorough understanding of the risks involved. It's essential to diversify your investments and avoid putting all your eggs in one basket.

Tony Robbins said, "The only limit to your impact is your imagination and commitment," and in the realm of investing, these words ring particularly true.

Investing is not merely a financial strategy—it is a powerful vehicle for wealth creation and financial freedom. Investing is the intentional act of putting your money to work, allowing it to grow and multiply over time. It's not about playing the stock market—it's about strategically deploying your resources to create a future of abundance. Investing is not just about chasing returns—it's about mastering the psychology of the market.

The emotional aspect of investing often plays a pivotal role in financial decisions. We emphasize the importance of understanding your own risk tolerance, managing emotions, and maintaining a long-term perspective. By mastering the psychology of investing, you gain control over your financial destiny.

Begin by setting clear investment goals. Whether it's building a retirement nest egg, funding your children's education, or achieving financial milestones, specific goals provide a roadmap for your investment journey. The science of investing involves calculating the amount needed to achieve these goals and strategically allocating your assets to maximize returns.

Diversification is a fundamental principle in the science of investing. Spread your investments across different asset classes to mitigate risk. Diversification ensures that the performance of one investment does not disproportionately impact your overall portfolio. Through compounding, your investment gains earn returns, and those returns, in turn, generate more returns. The earlier you start investing, the more time your money has to compound, amplifying the growth of your wealth over time.

In the Best Day Every Day methodology, the importance of education cannot be overstated. Equip yourself with the knowledge and understanding of investment principles. Whether it's understanding different asset classes, grasping market trends, or staying informed about economic indicators, education empowers you to make informed and strategic investment decisions.

Consider the concept of leverage in the science of investing. Leverage involves using borrowed capital to amplify the potential returns of an investment. While leverage can magnify gains, it also increases risk. Understanding the judicious use of leverage can be a powerful tool in the hands of a knowledgeable investor.

CONTRIBUTE BEYOND YOURSELF TO FIND HAPPINESS

In the vast landscape of personal finance, where wealth creation and financial mastery take center stage, the significance of charitable giving emerges as a transformative force that we fervently advocate. We often emphasize that the essence of life is found in generosity, and in the realm of personal finance, this philosophy transcends mere financial transactions. Let's embark on a journey that unveils the profound importance of charitable giving in personal finance, guided by principles that have empowered individuals to not only accumulate wealth but also contribute meaningfully to the world.

At the core of the Best Day Every Day philosophy is the understanding that personal finance is not just about amassing wealth for personal gain; it is a vehicle for creating positive change in the world. Charitable giving is the intentional act of sharing one's resources with others, whether through financial contributions, time, or expertise. It's not about depletion; it's about enrichment—enriching the lives of others and, in turn, enriching one's own life with purpose and fulfillment.

The artistic element in charitable giving lies in the creation of a vision—a vision of a world transformed by generosity and compassion. Imagine your financial resources as instruments of positive change, capable of uplifting communities, supporting causes close to your heart, and leaving a lasting legacy. This vision becomes the driving force, motivating you to make conscious choices that extend beyond personal wealth accumulation.

Creating a holistic charitable giving plan helps turn your vision into reality. Each act of generosity becomes a purposeful step toward making a lasting and meaningful impact. The true skill isn't simply in writing checks—it's in crafting financial choices that reflect your deeper purpose of creating positive change.

In the Best Day Every Day playbook, charitable giving is not viewed as a one-time transaction; it's a mindset that permeates every financial decision. We emphasize the importance of integrating giving into your financial plan from the outset. By making "giving" a foundational principle, you ensure that as your wealth grows, so does your capacity to make a positive impact on the world.

Begin by setting clear giving goals. Whether it's supporting education, healthcare, environmental initiatives, or other causes, specific goals provide a roadmap for your philanthropic journey. The science of giving involves calculating the amount you can allocate to charitable causes while still meeting your other financial obligations.

Strategic giving is a crucial component of the science of charitable giving. Rather than scattering your contributions, focus on a few causes or organizations that align with your values and passions. This targeted approach allows you to make a more significant impact and establishes a deeper connection between your giving and your personal beliefs.

Equip yourself with knowledge about the organizations you support, their missions, and the impact they have on the causes they champion. Informed giving ensures that your contributions are directed toward initiatives that align with your values and maximize their positive effect.

Consider the concept of leverage in the science of charitable giving. Leverage involves utilizing your influence and networks to amplify the impact of your giving. Whether through encouraging others to join in your philanthropic efforts or leveraging your skills and expertise to support causes, the ripple effect of strategic giving extends far beyond the initial contribution.

Part Four:
MACRO PURPOSE

Chapter Twelve:
WILL IT AFFECT YOU SIX MONTHS FROM NOW?

As we arrived in Sicily, the enchanting town of Taormina welcomed us with its spectacular views and rich culture. Perched on a hillside overlooking the sparkling Mediterranean, Taormina is a blend of ancient history and modern charm. Its picturesque streets, lined with charming boutiques and crowded cafés, beckoned us to explore. The aroma of local delicacies filled the air, teasing our senses with the promise of culinary delights. The iconic Greek Theatre, a testament to the town's rich heritage, stood proudly against the backdrop of a vivid sunset, reminding us of the beauty that awaits around every corner. However, our excitement soon met an unexpected twist, one that would teach us valuable lessons in resilience and gratitude.

Lori and William at the ancient Teatro Antico di Taormina overlooking Mount Etna in Taormina, Italy.

There are few more infuriating puzzles than the bureaucratic labyrinth of lost luggage. We arrived in Sicily safely, but the joy of setting foot in one of our favorite places was diminished by our airline having lost our luggage. As we stood in the business center of the "Grand Hotel Timeo," a Belmond Hotel in Taormina, Sicily, a gentle hand suddenly placed two cups under our noses. The pungent tang of a bitter espresso wafted up, and we felt instantly grounded by the familiar scent and warmth.

A low voice stated, "I understand how unsettling this can be. I've seen many travelers go through this, and trust me, your bags will be found. Focus on what you can control. In six months, you'll look back and realize this was just a small hiccup in your journey."

"From your experience," William asked, "how many of these espresso cups are we gonna need?"

Giulio, the hotel's concierge, smiled warmly. "This might require more than one cup, but within a few hours, you will have very little reason to linger in this moment of frustration."

Just seconds later, a waitress arrived with a plate of delicate, buttery, fresh "cornetti", Italian croissants recommended by Giulio from the hotel's breakfast buffet. Lori closed her eyes as the flakes from her first bite melted on her tongue. After exhaling slowly, she looked at William and said, "He's right. This is just a hiccup. And nothing will stop us from making it our best day yet."

Fortified by Lori's optimism, William picked up the phone to make another call, leaning against the computer desk and studying his legs, preparing for what could be up to a ninety-minute hold, again.

"Let's try to find something funny about something, anything," William sighed. Humor is sometimes the best medicine as well as an excellent pastime while waiting. And waiting...

Within another two hours, we approached the cool marble counter at the concierge desk with paperwork that would help us track down our luggage, have it returned to the hotel or forwarded to our next destination, and place an approximate value on the contents stored. Giulio handed Lori an expensive pen and gently placed a reassuring hand on her arm, where the crisp, slightly snug fabric of a just-bought replacement shirt pulled tight. He told her everything would be okay.

Giulio spoke soothingly about the steps that would need to be taken to recover the lost bags. Beyond the desk was a hum of activity in the grand hotel lobby—a mix of footsteps, distant conversations, and the occasional clink of glasses. In the distance, church bells chimed from a nearby cathedral.

Lori looked at William and said, "As soon as we're done with this paperwork, would you like to walk off that espresso and check out the beautiful cathedral out there?"

Both Giulio and William smiled. With a wave of his arm in the air, sending the masculine scent of his cologne towards our noses, Guilio stated, "Now that's the spirit. Taormina is beautiful with or without clothes!"

With that, we laughed and filled out the paperwork quickly. William chimed in, "I don't know about you, but I'd like to grab one more cornetto on the way."

We eventually recovered our luggage, eight whole days later, but what we took from the experience was a lesson in surrender. No amount of planning or personal development can prevent you from encountering minor setbacks. Learning to keep your emotional body regulated while handling those situations with grace is critical to avoiding a relatively small, material setback from becoming a trauma in your psyche or your relationships with others.

Sometimes when we encounter situations that could easily make us anxious, we return to Taormina and listen to the church bells in our heads, taste the buttery croissants on our tongues, and wash it down with a few deep breaths before reacting to the situation.

RELEASE WHAT DOESN'T MATTER

Free yourself from the weight of temporary worries and focus on what truly matters in the long run.

Moving swiftly through negative experiences is key to your Best Day Every Day journey. Whether they are minor incidents like traffic annoyances or significant setbacks like business challenges, nobody is immune to what could otherwise be perceived as failure. Setbacks aren't a result of faulty thinking; they're a result of being alive. Don't over-spiritualize setbacks; nobody is immune to them.

Sometimes our initial judgment of an event as "positive" or "negative" doesn't predict its long-term outcome. Relationships can start well and end on a messy note—or begin with difficulty and later reveal themselves to be blessings in disguise. In our case, the unexpected end of past relationships ultimately led to the most positive outcome of all: meeting each other.

The Dalai Lama offers valuable advice on how to handle life's inevitable impacts. He emphasizes that life comprises experiences we must go through, and we alone decide how to interpret their effects. Whether an event is positive or negative, we control our responses. The key to living each day to the fullest is asking ourselves how an experience will affect us six months from now.

One of life's most horrific heartbreaks and traumas comes from ending a relationship. We have a friend who went through an inglorious heartache at the beginning of this summer and still struggles to even eat sometimes for days on end. She said that, thinking about how she might meet the love of her life six months from now, it's sometimes the only way she can get through a day without being paralyzed by grief over the man she loved choosing another woman.

A friend of ours recently went through a tough season that, while stressful, turned out to be unexpectedly transformative. She was hit by a car in the post office parking lot in Aspen. Then, shortly after arranging for repairs, she fell into a ditch, damaging the other side of her car. It was frustrating—two separate incidents, two insurance claims, and a long, drawn-out nine-month process. But through it all, she remained grateful. She walked away from both incidents unharmed and emerged from the experience with a deeper sense of resilience and patience.

Sometimes life hits you—literally and figuratively. But setbacks, as frustrating as they may be in the moment, can become defining moments of strength and growth. The same is true in relationships. It's always worth walking away from something that feels uncertain or forced to make space for something truly right—something aligned with who you are and what you need.

LOVE YOUR FAILURES

Love your failures, for they are the stepping stones to success. They are the lessons that shape your character and the catalysts for growth and resilience. This requires a shift in perspective from saying, "Oh no," to being curious and anticipatory for what may be. A phrase one of our friends often uses is, "Sometimes rejection is God's protection." This principle can be applied in both business and relationships.

Sometimes you aren't the innocent victim of life's circumstances, but you simply make a bad choice. Owning your decision-making power, for better or worse, helps you become more aware of your blind spots to make better decisions moving forward. The insights into our blind spots, including embracing defeat, enable growth. Moreover, making mistakes tests your resilience and perseverance. It teaches you to bounce back from setbacks, to develop a stronger mindset, and to persevere in the face of challenges. Embracing your setbacks means recognizing that they build your strength and resilience, preparing you for future endeavors and success.

Loving your failures involves redefining your perception of success. Instead of measuring success solely by the absence of disappointment, you understand that it is a journey of trial and error, growth, and progress. Failures help you refine your path and align your actions with your aspirations.

There's some ego involved, or lack thereof, as the case may be. Your ego fights to make you a victim instead of allowing you to admit your own failures. However, when you embrace your personal responsibility, free will, and the periodic mistakes you will make, you become more vulnerable and authentic.

Although we encourage you to own your failures, moderation is also key. Acknowledge that failing is a natural part of the human experience that does not define your worth or potential. You don't have to be the best. A mindset coach we know says, "Nowhere in the Bible does it state that Jesus was the best carpenter." That quip is a reminder that being *your* best doesn't mean being *the* best.

Failures push us to think outside the box, to experiment, and to embrace innovation and creativity. They force us to challenge conventional approaches and encourage us to explore new possibilities.

FAILURES FUEL COMPASSION

Recently, a friend went through a heart-wrenching ordeal with a family member's mental illness and shared her experiences on Facebook, X, and Instagram. As she diligently posted daily about her real-time experience moving through waves of grief, anger, and feelings of failure, she tied each post to a hopeful message that resonated with the message that in six months from now, she knows she'll be happy for the pain and grief she is currently wading through. From her posts, hundreds of messages poured in from others who wished they, too, could verbalize their grief. These messages also included vulnerable testimonies from people who shared that they felt alone going through their own trauma. Still, she made them feel like everything was going to be okay. Her recognition of her pain, as well as her own failures, made it OK for other people to share theirs.

Experiencing missteps in life can cultivate empathy and compassion for others who face similar challenges. It allows you to relate to their struggles, offer support, and share your own journey through pain. Embracing your mistakes fosters a sense of connection and understanding with others on their own paths to growth and success. Above all, it's a mindset shift that empowers you to view failures as opportunities rather than setbacks. It enables you to learn from them, grow stronger, and navigate the journey of life with a greater sense of resilience, authenticity, and compassion.

EMBRACING THE PAST

Dwelling on why a mistake happened is toxic. Questions like 'Why didn't he love me?' or 'Why did I choose that business partner?' or 'Why didn't I time that investment better?' usually distract from the lessons and opportunities that mistakes can offer. Dwelling on past mistakes doesn't help you grow—focusing on preventative measures for the future through personal development does. The Best Day Every Day manual serves as a blueprint for making wise decisions, helping you prevent future mistakes by elevating your consciousness beyond the level at which you made those mistakes.

Accepting that the past cannot be changed is an act of surrender. Letting go of negative emotions, attachments, and grudges associated with past experiences frees you to focus on the expansion that is your birthright. The past cannot be changed; what's done is done. No amount of dwelling or regret will alter the events that have already occurred. You have permission to be free from negative emotions such as anger, resentment, or sorrow that may be tied to past experiences.

Not getting hung up on former times involves cultivating mindfulness and being fully present in the current moment. Engage in meaningful experiences and create a future that aligns with your aspirations. Shift your focus from past mistakes to what you have to be grateful for currently. Being in a state of gratitude literally makes it *impossible* for your brain to be in a state of stress, so be sure to flood your system with appreciation when you are going through tough times.

Mindfulness, the practice of being fully present and non-judgmental, can help you see things as they truly are. When you observe your thoughts and emotions without attaching judgment or interpretation, you create space for clarity and objectivity. Mindfulness allows you to observe reality with greater awareness, free from the distortions of negative biases or judgments.

To avoid seeing things worse than they are, seek different perspectives and gather diverse opinions. Engage in open and honest conversations with others who offer alternative viewpoints or insights. By considering different angles, you broaden your understanding of a situation and prevent narrow-mindedness. When faced with challenges, it is easy to get caught up in the problem itself, amplifying its negative impact. Instead, shift your focus toward solutions and possibilities. By directing your energy and attention to finding creative and practical solutions, you can transform the way you perceive a situation. Seeing it as an opportunity for growth and problem-solving rather than a hopeless predicament can lead to a more constructive mindset.

YOU ARE ONLY AS GOOD AS THOSE YOU SURROUND YOURSELF WITH

It's been said that you are the sum of the five people you surround yourself with most. Do the friends or company you keep challenge you to become the best version of yourself? The qualities, values, and behaviors of the people you choose to spend time with can shape your own character, attitudes, and level of success. If you surround yourself with motivated, ambitious, and positive-minded people, their drive and enthusiasm can inspire you to aim higher, pursue your goals, and maintain a positive mindset. Their success and accomplishments can serve as a source of inspiration and motivation for your own personal growth.

The people you surround yourself with can also hold you accountable for your actions and choices. When you associate with individuals who demonstrate integrity, responsibility, and high standards, it encourages you to align your behaviors and decisions with those same values. Their presence acts as a reminder to uphold your commitments, act ethically, and strive for personal excellence.

THE HUMAN MIND FINDS A WAY TO SUFFER, BUT THE SPIRIT KNOWS THE TRUTH

The human mind is eerily adept at creating suffering with its complex web of thoughts, emotions, and perceptions. It grasps onto negative thoughts, dwells on past regrets, and worries about an uncertain future. It can become entangled in patterns of self-doubt, fear, and negativity, leading to a distorted perception of reality.

Suffering often stems from the mind's attachment to desires, expectations, and external circumstances. It convinces you that your happiness and well-being are dependent on specific outcomes or possessions. However, the truth lies in recognizing that suffering is a product of your thoughts and interpretations rather than the reality of your world, and especially that of your future possibilities.

Beyond the mind's incessant chatter lies the spirit—the eternal essence connected to the deeper truths of existence. The spirit embodies qualities such as resilience, inner peace, and a profound sense of interconnectedness. It holds the wisdom that transcends suffering, reminding you of your inherent worth, inner strength, and capacity for joy. Through the practice of mindfulness and self-reflection, you can cultivate awareness of the mind's tendencies and detach yourself from its suffering. By observing your thoughts, emotions, and reactions with non-judgmental awareness, you create space for the spirit's wisdom to emerge. This awareness allows you to navigate challenges with greater clarity and compassion.

The spirit within us knows the truth—that suffering is transient, and your true essence is untouched by it. By aligning yourself with this truth, you can free yourself from the grips of the mind's suffering. It requires recognizing that your worth and fulfillment come from within, rather than external circumstances.

Recognizing the interconnectedness of all beings, you can support one another in your journey towards liberation from suffering. By fostering connections built on empathy, compassion, and understanding, you create a space for collective healing and growth. Together, we can uplift and inspire each other to tap into the truth of our spirits.

USE YOUR MIND, DON'T LET YOUR MIND USE YOU

Harness the power of your own mind without allowing it to overpower or control you. Your mind is an incredible tool, capable of creativity, analysis, and problem-solving. However, if left unchecked, it can also become a source of anxiety, self-doubt, and negative thought patterns. Take charge of your mind and use it as an instrument of empowerment rather than being consumed by its influence.

To use your mind effectively, you must first develop the practice of observing your thoughts and emotions without judgment or attachment. By cultivating mindfulness and self-awareness, you gain insight into the patterns and tendencies of your brain. This awareness allows you to distinguish between helpful and harmful thought patterns, enabling you to choose your mental state consciously.

Your mind can sometimes become trapped in limiting beliefs and self-imposed barriers. However, by recognizing and challenging these beliefs, you can open yourself up to new possibilities. Through introspection and reframing, you can shift your perspective, transcend self-imposed limitations, and embrace a mindset of growth and abundance.

By recognizing the power of your mind and consciously harnessing its potential, you can become an active participant in your own life. You can choose to direct your thoughts, beliefs, and actions towards growth, positivity, and self-empowerment. Through self-awareness, cognitive transformation, and intentional mindset cultivation, you unlock the immense capacity of your intelligence and create a path towards personal fulfillment and success.

Chapter Thirteen:
YOUR TRUE LOVE IS OUT THERE SOMEWHERE

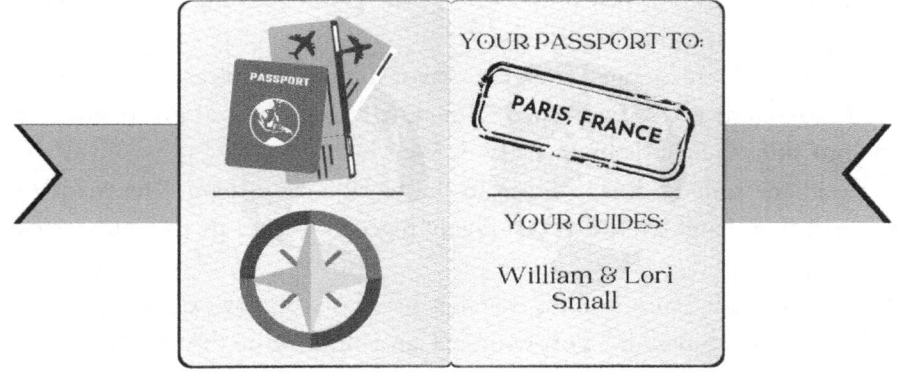

"Love finds you when you least expect it. Keep your heart open, and the right person will come along."

A nostalgic carousel at Le Jardin des Tuileries in Paris, France.

Lori and William, now inseparable, found joy in sharing their philosophy of living their Best Day Life through a book they were co-authoring. They often worked on their manuscript at a quiet corner table in the Jardin des Tuileries in Paris, located between the Louvre Museum and the Place de la Concorde, where the fresh scent of chestnut trees mixed with the sweetness of blooming roses.

As they wrote, their passion was evident in their focused expressions and the excited energy between them. Passersby could see the genuine happiness radiating from the couple's relaxed postures and occasional shared smiles. The soft scratching of pen on paper and the gentle tapping of laptop keys punctuated their quiet discussions.

Their book encouraged readers to savor life's simple pleasures.

"Close your eyes," Lori typed, "Imagine feeling the warmth of the sun on your skin, the gentle breeze ruffling your hair."

William added a line, "Listen to the world around you. The rustle of leaves, distant laughter, the soft cooing of pigeons—these are the soundtrack of life."

They included mindfulness exercises based on sensory experiences:

"Take a deep breath," Lori wrote, "Can you imagine the scent of fresh-baked baguettes from a nearby boulangerie? Or perfume floating out of a chic boutique?"

William contributed, "When you bite into a ripe strawberry, really taste it. Notice the burst of sweetness, the slight tartness, the juicy texture. This is living in the moment."

Their words flowed onto the page, distilling their philosophy into chapters that they hoped would inspire readers to find joy in everyday moments.

As the sun began to set, casting a golden glow over the garden, William suggested they continue their work at their favorite café on Rue Cler. Little did Lori know, he had a special question in mind for her that evening…

It was a balmy evening. The tinkling of glasses and the soft murmur of conversation created a cozy atmosphere. They sat at a small wrought-iron table, its cool surface a contrast to the warm evening air. As they sipped their wine—a crisp Chablis with tastes of green apple and citrus—William reached across the table. His fingers, slightly calloused from his guitar playing, gently intertwined with Lori's soft ones.

CHAPTER THIRTEEN: YOUR TRUE LOVE IS OUT THERE SOMEWHERE

"Lori," he said, his voice low and tender, audible only to her above the café's ambient noise, "these past months have been the best of my life. Every day with you feels like our Best Day Ever."

Lori's heart quickened, her cheeks flushing warmly as she met William's gaze. His eyes, reflecting the soft glow of the café's fairy lights, held a mixture of love and nervous anticipation.

"I was wondering," he continued, his thumb tracing small circles on her hand, "if you'd like to make every day our Best Day Ever... together. Will you move in with me?"

The scent of her Vetiver perfume mingled with William's Tuscan Leather cologne as Lori leaned in, her eyes glistening with joyful tears. The taste of wine still lingering on her lips, she whispered her answer, sealing this perfect moment in the heart of Paris.

Love at first sight — the night Lori and William first met at Jimmy's in Aspen with friends Geoff and Bernard.

HOW IT STARTED...

Who doesn't want a great love story? Life is made fuller by relationships. They give us the most meaning and purpose, above any other pursuit.

It was a serendipitous Friday evening, May 3, 2013, at the iconic Jimmy's in Aspen during the off-season. Lori, not planning to go out, found herself there, rocking a casual tank top, jeans, and a cashmere sweater draped over her shoulders. Meanwhile, William was at the bar, enjoying a light dinner and reconnecting with friends after several months.

As fate would have it, Lori walked in, accompanied by one of her best friends, Geoff. They were destined to cross paths with the same group with whom William was chatting. Friends for a while, they started conversing. Yet, there was a spark of intrigue mixed with a dash of dissatisfaction in Lori's eyes. So, she turned to William and popped the question, "So, what's your story?" Intrigued, William responded, "Just having dinner at the bar."

And there unfolded a spontaneous, engaging conversation, the start of a beautiful love story. After mingling with friends at Jimmy's, they ventured to Eric's Bar, another local hotspot, where a competitive game of pool sealed the deal for that night.

What transpired left both of them feeling a connection that took them by surprise. Their eagerness to meet again materialized just a couple of nights later. Bonding for various reasons, they soon found themselves missing each other when apart. This yearning intensified over the weeks, leading to a profound realization – they had found their soulmate.

HOW DO YOU FIND YOUR SOULMATE?

What does it truly mean to find your soul mate? Every relationship expert delves into it, and it's the aspiration we all share when seeking a life companion. A rare gem not easily found.

You see, both Lori and William had traversed multiple relationships before finding each other. When you meet the one you only want to be with, and every moment together is pure joy, every day becomes the best it can be.

Their journey together took a beautiful turn in the early morning light, 18 months after they first met as they departed Caneel Bay Resort, nestled on St. John within the breathtaking Virgin Islands National Park, their boat set course for Saint Thomas. The sun rose, casting golden hues across the calm waters, creating a serene and unforgettable farewell. In that tranquil moment, surrounded by the Caribbean's beauty, William asked Lori to marry him. The waves lapped gently against the boat, and their hearts soared as they embraced the promise of forever, knowing they had truly found their soulmate in each other. This unforgettable experience encapsulated the essence of their love story—a perfect blend of adventure, serenity, and profound connection, echoing the belief that true love is worth the wait.

All romantic, friendly, professional, or family relationships provide us with a sense of belonging, support, and love. They also help us to grow and develop as individuals.

Strong connections are linked to better physical and mental health, increased happiness, and greater success in life. Relationships also play a key role in our personal growth and development. They help us to learn about ourselves and others, develop empathy and understanding, and practice important social skills.

In addition, relationships give our lives purpose and meaning. When we have people to share our experiences with, we feel more fulfilled and connected to the world around us. We have a sense of purpose and belonging that enriches our lives and gives us a reason to keep striving towards our goals. Relationships are the ultimate spiritual path. The purpose of a relationship is to magnify the human experience.

Romantic relationships provide you with a deep sense of connection and intimacy that is essential to your emotional well-being. You may not find it in other areas of your life. Being in a loving relationship can help you to feel supported, understood, and validated.

RELATIONSHIPS AS A CATALYST FOR SELF-GROWTH

When you are in a relationship, you are often challenged to confront your own flaws and to work towards becoming a better version of yourself. Relationships can serve as mirrors that reflect back to you your own strengths and weaknesses. They require you to confront your own limitations, biases, and emotional wounds. This process of self-improvement can be incredibly rewarding, and it can help you to develop a greater sense of purpose and meaning in your life.

Work On Yourself First

Your relationship with yourself may be the most important relationship of all. Before you can build a truly healthy relationship, you have to first work on yourself.

Things often happen when you're not focused on finding a mate, but on the journey of self-improvement. In fact, one of the best ways to get both your head and heart in order and ready to meet your partner is through personal development, such as your journey in this book.

If you're waiting for someone else to give you the life that you want and deserve, take a look in the mirror.

Making the Right Selection

Can you imagine loving and living with someone who is your best friend and your number one fan? Not all relationships are created equal. When it comes to romantic relationships, 95% of success is based on making the right selection. This means that choosing the right partner is key to building a successful and fulfilling relationship. It is important to be intentional about the qualities you look for in a partner and to avoid settling for someone who is not a good fit.

When you have a profound connection with someone, play full out. It is important to remember that relationships require effort and investment. Relationships are not always easy, and they require time, energy, and emotional commitment to be successful. It is important to prioritize your relationships and to make time for the people who are important to you.

Whatever You Fail to Appreciate, You Will Lose

If you continue to act the way you did at the beginning of the relationship throughout the partnership, the relationship will never end. There's a popular saying that goes, "You don't know what you got til it's gone." This phrase is often used to describe the feeling of regret that comes when you fail to appreciate something until it's too late. It's a reminder that you should never take anything for granted, especially the people in your life.

In relationships, this sentiment holds even more true. When you're first getting to know someone, everything is new and exciting. You're eager to learn about their interests, their dreams, and their quirks. You go out of your way to make them feel special, to show them how much you care. You put in effort and attention, and in return, you feel valued and appreciated.

But as time goes on, the novelty wears off. You settle into routines and become comfortable with each other. You may start to take your partner for granted, assuming that they'll always be there. If you stop making as much of an effort, your partner may begin to feel neglected or unimportant.

This is where the danger lies. When you fail to appreciate your partner, you risk losing them. You risk losing the connection and the love that you've built. You risk losing the trust and the intimacy that you've worked so hard to cultivate.

You need to actively work to maintain and strengthen your bond with your partner. One way to do this is to remember what you did in the beginning of the relationship. Can you recall the things that you did to make your partner feel special? Are you continuing to do those things? You can surprise them with small gestures of love and appreciation, like leaving a note or bringing them their favorite snack. You can make time for them, even when you're busy, and you can show them that they're a priority in your life.

When you appreciate your partner, you not only strengthen your bond with them, but you also enrich your own life. You feel happier, more fulfilled, and more connected. You create a positive cycle of love and gratitude that sustains your relationship over time.

Romantic couples progress through stages of growth. But there are also phases of deterioration. Ties with one another do not end for lack of love, but for lack of intimacy. When intimacy decreases, dissatisfaction increases. The most violent act in a relationship is to take love away.

Get Out of Your Own Way

Many of us tend to let our fears, doubts, and insecurities hold us back from reaching our full potential. We seek affirmation and praise from others, hoping that they will validate our worth and our accomplishments. But the truth is, we don't need external validation to feel good about ourselves. We can learn to get out of our own way and honor others, even when it's hard.

One of the biggest obstacles to getting out of your own way is your ego. You want to feel important and valued, so you seek affirmation and praise from others. You may become defensive or competitive when you feel threatened or overlooked. You may even sabotage your own success, fearing that you won't live up to your own expectations.

To overcome this tendency, you need to learn to honor others. This means putting aside your own ego and recognizing the value and worth of those around you. You can learn to celebrate the accomplishments of others without feeling threatened or jealous. You can acknowledge the strengths and talents of those you work with or interact with, without feeling inferior or inadequate.

When you honor others, you create a positive and supportive environment that benefits everyone. You build stronger relationships and foster a sense of community. You become more open to learning from others and collaborating with them. You become humbler and more gracious, and you inspire others to do the same.

Enjoying Sex: The Ultimate Pleasure in Life

Intimacy goes beyond the physical realm and encompasses a profound understanding, vulnerability, and closeness shared between two individuals. It is about being truly seen, heard, and accepted for who you are, allowing yourself to be vulnerable and creating a safe space for your partner to do the same. Intimacy requires open and honest communication, trust, and the willingness to invest time and effort into nurturing the connection.

Physical intimacy, including sexual intimacy, serves as a means of expressing love, desire, and passion. However, it should be understood that each individual's needs and preferences regarding physical intimacy may vary. It is crucial for partners to communicate openly about their desires, boundaries, and expectations, and to approach physical intimacy with respect, consent, and mutual enjoyment.

Enjoying sex is the ultimate pleasure in life. Here are seven ways regular sex can enhance intimacy in your relationship:

1. **Emotional Bond:** Physical intimacy, including sexual intimacy, allows for a deep sense of closeness, vulnerability, and trust, fostering a stronger emotional connection.
2. **Expression of Love and Desire:** Physical intimacy provides a way to express love, desire, and attraction for one another. It allows partners to show affection, passion, and admiration, deepening their emotional connection.
3. **Stress Relief and Connection:** Engaging in physical intimacy releases endorphins and promotes relaxation, helping to reduce stress and increase feelings of well-being.
4. **Relationship Satisfaction:** A satisfying physical relationship can significantly contribute to overall relationship satisfaction. When partners feel desired, wanted, and fulfilled in the physical aspect of their relationship, it can enhance their overall happiness and contentment together.
5. **Health Benefits:** Engaging in regular physical intimacy has been associated with various health benefits, including improved cardiovascular health, stress reduction, a boosted immune system, and increased overall well-being.
6. **Communication and Intimacy:** Physical intimacy requires communication and understanding between partners. It encourages open dialogue about desires, boundaries, and preferences, promoting healthy communication and fostering intimacy in other areas of the relationship as well.
7. **Bonding and Connection:** Physical intimacy provides a unique opportunity for couples to connect on a deep, sensual level. It can

create shared experiences, increase feelings of togetherness, and strengthen the sense of partnership and unity.

While physical intimacy is an important aspect of many relationships, it is just one piece of the puzzle. Emotional connection, trust, communication, and shared values also play vital roles in maintaining a strong and fulfilling partnership. Striking a balance between all these elements is key to building a healthy and satisfying relationship.

For some couples, incorporating sex toys or erotic novels into their intimate relationship can enhance arousal, provide new ideas, and stimulate sexual exploration. It can serve as a source of inspiration and contribute to a sense of novelty and excitement. Sharing such materials can also foster open communication and lead to a deeper understanding of each other's desires and fantasies. In the early days of our relationship, physical intimacy came naturally. One night, we playfully picked up an erotic novel at a bookstore and decided to read it together. What started as a joke became something unexpected—it sparked conversations about desires we hadn't expressed before, revealing new depths in our emotional connection. By exploring our fantasies and opening up about what we truly wanted, we discovered that genuine intimacy is a powerful blend of both emotional and physical connection.

However, it is essential to approach the consumption of erotic content with caution and respect for the boundaries and values of both partners. It is crucial to have open and honest conversations about preferences, consent, and any potential concerns or insecurities that may arise. Building trust and maintaining clear communication is key to ensuring that both partners feel comfortable and respected in their exploration.

When you've discovered your soulmate and committed to nurturing your relationship as if it's the cornerstone of your existence, you unlock the power to relish the Best Day, every single day.

Chapter Fourteen:
NOBODY MANIFESTS THEIR BEST LIFE IN CROCS

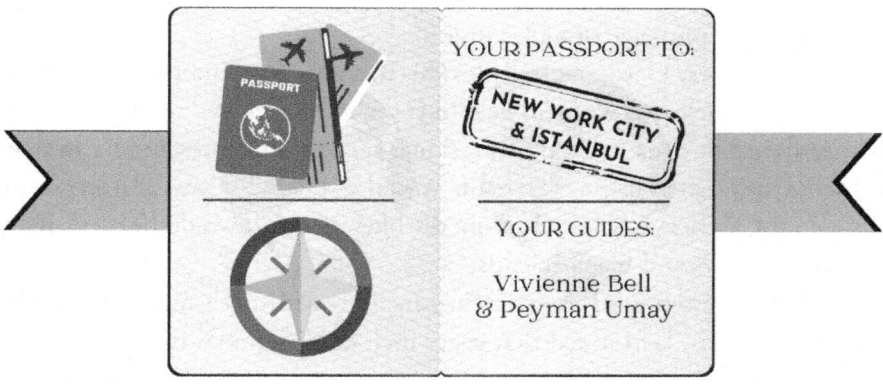

YOUR PASSPORT TO:

NEW YORK CITY & ISTANBUL

YOUR GUIDES:

Vivienne Bell
& Peyman Umay

*"Your appearance reflects your inner self.
Dress for the life you want to live."
- Vivenne Bell*

As she entered the chic offices at Saks Fifth Avenue in New York City, Lori was enveloped in a warm scent of Vivienne Bell's signature perfume, a blend of jasmine and vanilla that lingered in the air, adding a touch of mystery and allure to the ambiance. As Lori walked toward Vivienne's desk, she breathed in the rich scent of luxurious fabrics, warm cedar, and the unmistakable aroma of high-end leather from designer handbags and shoes displayed nearby. Lori sat herself across from Vivienne's desk and straightened her skirt, feeling suddenly like her own attire was too humble for the surroundings. She self-consciously adjusted her sleeves and shirt collar, wondering if she ought to wear her jacket or remove it to reveal a slender shirt cut and a fashionable leather belt she'd chosen for the day. Before she could decide, Vivienne entered the office.

She gracefully sauntered towards the desk and sat herself across from Lori in a leather chair that looked masculine, but embraced her slender frame like a gentle hug. Vivienne Bell exuded an effortless elegance and unforgettable presence with her long, dark hair cascading in waves over her shoulders. Her style was polished and sophisticated. That day, she donned an impeccably tailored designer red dress that accentuated her fit, athletic figure, maintained by her rigorous morning gym sessions. Her perfectly applied makeup highlighted her sharp features. Her piercing eyes reflected her confidence and determination. Vivienne's presence commanded attention, embodying the pinnacle of high fashion.

When Geoffry Gertz tragically lost his business, Lori interned at Patricia Clyne, where she met a womenswear buyer who emphasized the importance of appearance in personal and professional success. Lori presented a swatch of fabrics and materials that Vivienne would evaluate for next season's hero pieces in the Patricia Clyne collection; the likes of which would be on display in shop windows and magazine ads.

As Vivienne retrieved the swatch from Lori with her smooth, perfectly manicured hands, Lori noted that every inch of Vivienne was flawless.

"What do you feel drawn to among these materials?" asked Vivienne.

Not having anticipated a pop quiz that morning, Lori fished through the swatches and chose a piece of leather in a deep ruby color.

"This one seems to fit with the winter season, holiday colors, and could invite buyers to invest in the piece for holiday gatherings. It's also…"

Lori stammered, "Commanding."

"Commanding," Vivienne smirked. "That's what women really want. They don't just want to look commanding, they want to feel it."

Vivienne's voice was lively and confident as she moved through the swatches, giving her opinions on each material, generously providing Lori with style tips, and encouraging her to see the materials beyond a "low-hanging fruit" holiday theme.

"You see," she said authoritatively, "your appearance reflects your inner self. Dress for the life you want to live."

Vivienne's philosophy of using clothes as a way to command authority in her world impressed Lori. But what stuck with her even more was that she used her style as a way to create a visual representation of the trajectory she expected for her life. Her success in womenswear came not only from her impeccable taste but also from her ability to create styles that captured a woman's desire to express her feminine essence and exude confidence. Vivienne taught Lori that your wardrobe isn't merely a vehicle to survive your day, but an opportunity to manifest your best life.

WILLIAM'S STYLE MENTOR

The golden light of Istanbul's sunset glinted off the Bosphorus, casting a warm glow on Peyman as he strolled along the waterfront. The air was thick with the scent of roasting chestnuts and the briny tang of the sea. In the distance, the haunting call to prayer echoed from the minarets of the Blue Mosque, its melody intertwining with the gentle lapping of waves against the shore.

Peyman's bespoke linen suit, the color of sun-bleached sand, whispered against his skin with each step. The fabric, light and breathable, moved with him like a second skin, a stark contrast to the heavy, plastic embrace of the dreaded Crocs he'd seen tourists wearing earlier. He suppressed a shudder at the memory.

As he passed a street vendor, the spicy blend of cumin, paprika, and garlic from sizzling kebabs made his mouth water. The spices danced on the warm breeze, mingling with the sweet scent of apple tea wafting from a nearby café.

His fingers trailed along the rough stone of an ancient wall, its cool surface a testament to centuries of history. In the fading light, the city seemed to pulse with an energy all its own—a dynamic fusion of old and new, East and West, tradition and innovation.

Peyman paused, taking in the scene before him. The skyline was a mosaic of domes and skyscrapers, silhouetted against the fiery sky. As twilight descended, the city began to sparkle, thousands of lights coming to life like stars falling to earth.

In this moment, surrounded by the beauty and energy of Istanbul, Peyman felt the thrill of possibility. This was a place where dreams took flight and where style was an art form.

Peyman's influence extended far beyond the confines of his atelier, touching lives with the transformative power of impeccable style. For us, he wasn't just a designer—he was a curator of confidence, a maestro of self-expression.

William's first fitting with Peyman was nothing short of revelatory. As Peyman's expert hands took measurements, his eyes gleaming with creative vision, I watched William's posture change. With each carefully chosen fabric, each discussion of cut and style, William seemed to grow taller, even more assured than before.

Peyman's charm was effortless, his knowledge of style encyclopedic. He spoke of colors that would complement William's complexion, of cuts that would accentuate his best features. It wasn't just about clothes—it was about bringing out the best version of William.

The first time William stepped out in a Peyman Umay suit, the transformation was palpable. The perfectly tailored jacket hugged his shoulders just so, the trousers breaking precisely at the shoe. He carried himself with a newfound spring in his step, a twinkle in his eye that spoke of a man who knew he looked good.

Peyman's influence seeped into our lives beyond the wardrobe. His sophisticated approach to life—the appreciation for fine craftsmanship, the attention to detail, the understanding that true style is an extension of oneself—became a source of inspiration. Dinner conversations were peppered with discussions of texture and pattern, of the interplay between tradition and modernity that Peyman so deftly navigated in his designs.

With each new outfit, each perfectly chosen accessory, Peyman didn't just dress William—he unveiled layers of personality. He taught us both the language of style and how to speak volumes without saying a word through the cut of a jacket or the knot of a tie.

The glamor Peyman brought into our lives wasn't just about looking good for others—it was about feeling good in your own skin. It was about the confidence that comes from knowing you're presenting your best self to the world. William walked taller, smiled more readily, tackled challenges with renewed vigor—all because Peyman had shown him how to armor himself in style and self-assurance.

In Peyman, we found not just a designer, but a friend and a guide to a more refined, more confident way of moving through the world. He didn't just make William look like a million bucks—he made him feel it, from the inside out. And in doing so, he added a new dimension of sophistication and joy to our lives, a daily reminder that true style isn't about the clothes themselves, but about the power they have to reflect who we are and who we dare to become.

LEAVE AN INDELIBLE MARK ON EVERYONE YOU ENCOUNTER

"Smiling is a universal language of kindness."
William Arthur Ward

In our journey together, we've discovered that the way we carry ourselves as a couple, including our choice of attire, makes us a magnet for attention. In our presence, we strive to remind people they are loved. Our attire makes us more approachable and allows people to feel safe in our presence. Our wardrobe commands the right attention; we present as put-together, professional, and trustworthy. When attention is given to our clothes, the subconscious assumption people make is that we are responsible and caring. It illustrates our attention to detail and our commitment to taking the events, outings, excursions, and people we meet more seriously.

What you wear is a reflection of your energy. We desire to inspire others, and how we present ourselves helps us to do that. Among the many things we inspire in others is the strength of our partnership and marriage. People often remark on our attractiveness, the evident love between us, and the desire to emulate our connection as they age. Compliments such as 'You always look so beautiful and sexy,' 'Undoubtedly the best-dressed couple in town,' or 'I aspire to have a relationship like yours someday' are always appreciated. Although we don't actively seek attention, the attention we command draws others towards excellence, not slacking off and "skidding by" with less than their best. We encourage others to be extraordinary because our benchmark for every detail of our lives is extraordinary. Whether we're hitting the slopes, exploring nature, or having a night on the town, we consciously dress for the occasion.

Lori and William in Capri, Italy at sunset.

Although the Best Day Every Day mindset shines through in our interactions with others, we haven't always had such a positive outlook. But by adopting this mindset, life has transformed into a more enjoyable and fulfilling journey.

CHAPTER FOURTEEN: NOBODY MANIFESTS THEIR BEST LIFE IN CROCS

THE CASE FOR BODY LANGUAGE

Nonverbal cues, such as facial expressions, body language, tone of voice, and even your clothing, can communicate just as much, if not more, than the words you use. Speaking without saying a word can convey a range of emotions, intentions, and attitudes, often in ways that are more powerful and effective than spoken language. For example, a smile can communicate warmth and friendliness, while a frown can indicate displeasure or disapproval. Similarly, a firm handshake can convey confidence and assertiveness, while a weak or limp handshake can suggest insecurity or lack of conviction. Lori discovered the significance of a firm handshake in the fast-paced business world of New York City, and decades later, her grip is recognized as confident, commanding respect, and making her someone to be reckoned with.

Body language is another important aspect of speaking without saying a word. Your posture, gestures, and movements can convey a range of emotions, such as confidence, nervousness, or boredom. For example, standing tall and maintaining eye contact can communicate confidence and assertiveness, while fidgeting or looking away can suggest discomfort or lack of interest.

Tone of voice is also a key factor in nonverbal communication. The way you say something can convey a range of emotions and intentions, such as sarcasm, enthusiasm, or frustration. Even the volume and speed of your speech can communicate important messages, such as urgency or emphasis.

Finally, your clothing and appearance can also communicate a lot about you, without saying a word. The way you dress can convey your personality, social status, and cultural identity, and can also influence how others perceive you. Thanks to Peyman Umay, William has become an expert in the art of dressing.

Good Posture

Carrying oneself with confidence and grace involves several factors, including good posture, positive body language, and self-awareness. Good posture involves standing tall with your shoulders back and head held high. Lori developed a comprehensive program titled "Posture Please," aimed at educating participants on the significance of good posture in everyday life. This engaging class combines practical exercises, expert insights, and interactive demonstrations to help individuals improve their posture and overall body alignment. Good posture has been known to have a positive impact on a person's physical and mental health. Not only does it promote physical health by reducing the strain on muscles and joints, but it also has a significant effect on a person's mental well-being, particularly on their confidence. When you maintain good posture, you exude confidence and self-assurance, which can have a positive impact on how others perceive you. Good posture also helps you feel more in control of your body, enhancing your self-esteem and making you feel more powerful.

The Language of Connection

Positive body language involves smiling, making eye contact, and using open gestures. Body language is a powerful tool that can significantly influence how others perceive you and how you feel about yourself. When you exude confidence through your body language, you are more likely to be seen as capable and trustworthy, which can help you in both personal and professional situations. Positive body language also signals to others that you are engaged and interested in the conversation, which can help you build stronger relationships and establish a more positive reputation. By using positive body language, you can project a confident and approachable image, which can lead to greater success in both your personal and professional life.

Eye Contact

When you make eye contact with someone, you establish a direct and intimate connection and convey a range of emotions and intentions that words alone cannot express.

It has been said that "eyes are the windows to the soul."

Eye contact shows you are engaged. When you make eye contact with someone, you demonstrate your interest and engagement in the conversation. Eye contact signals to a speaker that you're paying attention to what they are saying. This can help to establish a sense of mutual understanding and respect, and can create a stronger sense of connection between two people.

Eye contact can also help to convey your emotions and intentions more effectively. When you look someone in the eye, you add layers to your communication. You express feelings and attitudes more clearly. Confidence, enthusiasm, and sincerity all increase when you're focused on somebody's eyes. On the contrary, shifty eyes imply that somebody is nervous, lying, deceiving, or otherwise up to no good. Eye contact helps you connect with others on a deeper level. What's more, making eye contact with others shows respect.

If you want to command more authority in your world, look somebody in the eyes. As mentioned, it conveys confidence. What's more, it helps establish a sense of authority. In job interviews or negotiations, eye contact establishes your credibility and influence.

Since this is a book of not just American but global wisdom, it's important to note that eye contact is not always appropriate in every situation. In some cultures, prolonged eye contact may be seen as disrespectful or aggressive, and in some contexts, such as intimate conversations or moments of grief, direct eye contact may be uncomfortable or inappropriate.

Active Listening

Active listening involves not just hearing the words that someone is saying, but also actively engaging with them, such as by asking questions. Active listening may include demonstrations of empathy and understanding, such as a hand on somebody's hand when appropriate or a gentle "I see" or "I understand," encouraging your speaker to continue without interrupting them. These can help build stronger relationships with others because you demonstrate that you're interested and engaged in a conversation, and that you value the thoughts and feelings of others.

Ask clarifying questions. By actively engaging with the other person and asking clarifying questions, you can ensure you fully understand their perspective and the meaning behind their words. This illustrates your willingness to put aside your own biases and perspectives to understand others fully.

The Handshake

As we mentioned, your handshake can say a lot about you. It's often your first interaction and impression on somebody else. Here are some things to keep in mind when it comes to what your handshake says about you:

Strength and Confidence:
A firm handshake can communicate strength, confidence, and assertiveness. It shows that you are confident in yourself and your abilities, and that you are ready to take on whatever challenges come your way.

Trustworthiness and Respect:
A good handshake can also communicate trustworthiness and respect. A handshake that is too limp or weak can convey a lack of confidence or even insincerity, while a handshake that is too forceful can come across as aggressive or even threatening. A firm, yet respectful handshake can convey a sense of trust and respect, and can help to establish a positive and productive relationship with the other person.

Attention to Detail:
The way you shake someone's hand can also convey your attention to detail. A sloppy or rushed handshake can convey a lack of attention or respect, while a well-executed handshake can demonstrate your commitment to excellence and attention to detail.

Cultural Considerations:
It's also important to keep in mind that different cultures may have different expectations when it comes to handshakes. For example, in some cultures, a firm handshake is seen as a sign of respect, while in others, a softer, more gentle handshake may be more appropriate. It's important to be aware of these cultural nuances and adjust your handshake accordingly.

Negative Body Language

Body language can be a powerful tool in attracting *or* repelling others. Gestures, postures, facial expressions, and other nonverbal cues convey messages and emotions. In fact, research has shown that body language can account for up to 70% of all communication between people.

Positive body language can make you appear more approachable and attractive to others. For example, standing up straight, making eye contact,

CHAPTER FOURTEEN: NOBODY MANIFESTS THEIR BEST LIFE IN CROCS

and smiling can signal confidence and openness. Similarly, leaning in towards someone, nodding your head, and using appropriate hand gestures can convey interest and engagement.

On the other hand, negative body language can push people away and create barriers to communication. Examples of negative body language include crossing your arms, avoiding eye contact, and fidgeting. These behaviors can signal defensiveness, discomfort, and disinterest, making it difficult for others to connect with you.

A clenched jaw and tight fists can signal anger or frustration, while a relaxed posture and open palms can convey calmness and receptiveness. Similarly, a furrowed brow and crossed arms can signal skepticism or disagreement, while a nodding head and open body language can indicate agreement and receptivity.

Lori and William at the iconic Hôtel de Paris Monte-Carlo.

> *"Sex appeal is fifty percent what you've got*
> *and fifty percent what people think you've got."*
> Sophia Loren

SEXY VS. SENSIBLE

Being Sexy

The definition of "sexy" can vary depending on cultural and individual perspectives, but in general, it is used to describe someone or something that is sexually appealing or attractive. It can refer to physical features or traits, such as a person's body shape, facial features, or voice, as well as behavior or clothing choices that are suggestive or alluring. However, it is important to note that "sexy" is a subjective term, and what one person finds attractive may not be the same for another.

A woman who is perceived as sexy is usually defined by a combination of her confidence and her looks. Vivienne Bell mastered both the energetic sexiness of her capable and commanding presence and physical sexiness by wearing makeup that accentuated her features, form-fitting clothing that celebrated her impressive fitness level, and slightly revealing clothing. She was not only comfortable in her own skin, but her radiating energy drew others towards her. Being sexy doesn't mean conforming to conventional beauty standards. There are "sexy" women with long hair or short, those like the "Mysterious Parisienne Woman" in their seventies and eighties, as well as Loren Lahav, in her fifties. Both of these guides from our book exuded a sexiness; they were both conscious of their fitness and health, but equally mindful of presenting themselves in a put-together and alluring way. There are celebrities like Kim Kardashian or Kate Winslet who have been called "overweight," but are among the most revered icons of sexiness in the world. Then some women are more waif-like, such as Nicole Kidman, who, even in her sixties, is dually an icon of sexiness. The confidence each of these five women exudes makes them magnetic, and their attention to flattering clothes puts them over the top.

Being Sensible

A woman who is seen as sensible is often characterized by her practicality, intelligence, and level-headedness. She may prioritize comfort and functionality over fashion. She may not be particularly concerned with her physical appearance or sexiness. A woman characterized as sensible may also be known for her ability to make rational decisions and think critically in high-pressure situations. Being sensible means taking responsibility for your actions, being reliable and trustworthy, and using your intelligence and reasoning to navigate life's challenges and complexities.

It is important to note that "sexiness" and "sensibility" are not mutually exclusive. Women can be both sexy and sensible depending on the situation and their individual personalities. Additionally, it is important to recognize that everyone has their own unique qualities and traits that make them attractive, and these don't always have to be related to being "sexy." Finding your style is like finding your X factor; it's different for each unique woman. A woman in our town always wears decorative hats, and we know one woman who refuses to wear black, opting instead for pink, which she associates with being happier and calmer.

Intelligence, kindness, and many other non-physical attributes are just as attractive, if not more, than physical appearance. However, combining sensibility with sexiness exponentially increases a powerful and compelling presence. Radiating healthy energy and physical fitness illustrates that you have discipline and care for yourself.

MATCHING AND MIRRORING MAGIC

Matching and mirroring is a technique used in communication to build rapport and create a sense of connection with others. The concept of matching and mirroring, often associated with neuro-linguistic programming (NLP), was popularized by Richard Bandler and John Grinder in the 1970s. They identified these techniques as effective tools for building rapport and enhancing communication by subtly mimicking another person's body language, speech patterns, or behaviors. This approach aims to create a sense of connection and understanding in interpersonal interactions. Creating rapport is 55% body language, 38% tone of voice, 7% actual words.

When you match and mirror another person's body language, you are sending a signal that you are similar to them and understand them. This helps to establish a sense of trust and comfort, making it easier to build rapport and connect with them on a deeper level. Imitate what someone else is doing, and you'll start to feel the way they feel. In addition, they will feel you, as well.

Matching and mirroring can be done in a variety of ways, such as matching the speed and tone of someone's speech, mirroring their posture and movements, and even matching the words they use. For example, if someone uses a particular phrase repeatedly, you can use that phrase too, as long as it is natural and not forced.

However, it's important to note that matching and mirroring should be done subtly and naturally, so as not to come across as insincere or manipulative. If done correctly, it can create a positive and comfortable atmosphere, allowing for more effective communication and a stronger sense of connection.

THE FIFTY FOOT RULE

What is the fifty-foot rule? The fifty-foot rule is a concept that encourages us to care about those in our proximity and to be more mindful and attentive to our surroundings. The idea behind this rule is to pay attention to the people and things within a fifty-foot radius and take action if you notice something that requires your attention or assistance. It also suggests that people should be friendly and engaging within a fifty-foot radius. The rule emphasizes the importance of making connections and creating a positive atmosphere in social settings.

Developing a fifty-foot rule can create a sense of community and connection, as well as improve your overall well-being and quality of life. When you are mindful of the people and things around you, you are more likely to notice opportunities for connection and support, as well as potential dangers or risks.

Caring about those in your proximity can also help to promote kindness and compassion. By taking action to help others and improve your community, you are not only helping those around you but also contributing to a greater sense of purpose and meaning in your own life.

SMILING

Making someone smile is a simple yet powerful act that can have a significant impact on both the person receiving the smile and the person giving it. It is a gesture of kindness and warmth that can brighten someone's day, boost their mood, and create a positive ripple effect that spreads to others. Every year on the first Friday of October, World Smile Day celebrates the simple yet powerful impact of a smile. Founded by Harvey Ball, the creator of the iconic smiley face, this day encourages spreading kindness, positivity, and joy through small but meaningful gestures. After all, a smile is contagious, and the world can always use more of them.

There are many ways to make someone smile, and it doesn't have to be a grand or elaborate gesture. It can be something as simple as a genuine compliment, a kind word, or a small act of kindness. The key is to be sincere and thoughtful in your actions, and to take the time to connect with the person you are trying to make smile.

Some ways to make someone smile include offering a sincere compliment, sending a message or letter, random acts of kindness or politeness, or sharing a laugh.

Smiling is a powerful tool for enhancing well-being. It can lower heart rate and blood pressure, effectively reducing stress. When you smile, your brain releases endorphins, the body's natural feel-good chemicals, which improve mood and create a sense of happiness. Additionally, smiling boosts your immune system by increasing white blood cell production, helping to fend off illnesses. It can also alleviate pain by triggering the release of natural painkillers, reducing both pain and inflammation. Overall, a simple smile offers a multitude of health benefits. Finally, smiling can help to enhance social interactions by making you more approachable and likable. It can also create a positive and welcoming atmosphere, which promotes social bonding and connection.

DON'T BE LATE

In life, time is one of our most precious resources; it is non-renewable. Nevertheless, many people struggle with punctuality and time management. Being late can have negative consequences in both personal and professional situations, potentially damaging relationships and reputations.

Showing up on time is more than simply being present. It demonstrates respect for others, conveys that you value their time, and affirms your reliability and trustworthiness. When you commit to a meeting, appointment, or event, you are making a promise to the other person that you will be there, ready and prepared.

Committing to being on time requires time management and, therefore, preparation. Valuable opportunities can be lost when you do not plan for contingencies. Inefficiency can create chaos. Part of being on time involves planning ahead and being accountable for potential roadblocks. If you're a parent, that means ensuring your child has their lunch or school bag prepared the night before. If you're heading to a meeting, it means preparing notes ahead of time. We have a friend who is a guest on many radio shows. She often spends up to three hours preparing a simple thirty-minute segment for radio. She ensures that her information is up-to-date, that she has tested her microphone and sound equipment, and that she is in a location that has a strong internet or cell phone signal for call-in versus screen-sharing shows, even if that involves pulling over on the side of the road while traveling.

On the other hand, when you are consistently late or fail to show up, you send a message that you do not value the other person's time or effort, and that you are not dependable. This can damage relationships and make it difficult for others to trust you or take you seriously. Moreover, assuming that others have more time to spare than you is inconsiderate. In reality, we all have a finite amount of time on this earth, and arriving late can deprive someone else of their valuable moments. It's essential to respect everyone's time as we navigate our busy lives.

Ultimately, embracing punctuality is a powerful way to enrich your life and the lives of those around you. By valuing time, you not only foster trust and respect but also create space for new opportunities and meaningful connections. Each moment is a chance to make a positive impact, and by being present, you open the door to richer experiences and relationships. Embrace each moment by seizing every opportunity to connect and share joy as you work towards creating your Best Day, every single day.

Part Five:

CELEBRATING YOUR NEW LIFE

Chapter Fifteen:
BECOME A MAGNET FOR ABUNDANCE

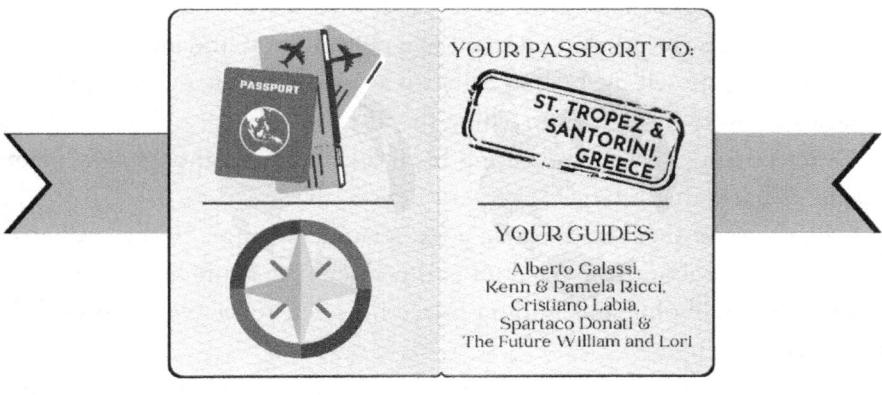

YOUR PASSPORT TO: ST. TROPEZ & SANTORINI, GREECE

YOUR GUIDES:
Alberto Galassi,
Kenn & Pamela Ricci,
Cristiano Labia,
Spartaco Donati &
The Future William and Lori

Lori and William enjoying the Saint Tropez spirit at Le Club 55.

As the sun danced upon the pristine blue waters off the coast of Saint-Tropez, we found ourselves comfortably settled on the deck of a brand-new Riva 130 Belissima, a stunning nautical creation by the Ferretti Group. The scene was straight out of a dream—a harmonious blend of Mediterranean charm and serene luxury that perfectly captured the philosophy of our friend Alberto Galassi, CEO of the Ferretti Group.

Under Alberto's leadership, the Ferretti Group has united seven premier shipyards across Italy, creating an efficient industrial operation paired with the finest in Italian artistry. Alberto's approach exemplifies the power of vision and a relentless commitment to excellence. On this day, from the sun-kissed terrace of his magnificent yacht, he revealed what it truly means to "have it all" and how we can develop our own magnetism for abundance.

"We are not selling boats," Alberto explained. His conviction was apparent in every word. "We're selling the lifestyle."

After pursing his lips and tilting his head slightly in thought, William asked, "What is that lifestyle… to your buyers, that is?"

"I've learned that this lifestyle goes beyond owning a yacht," Alberto responded. "It's about true freedom and privacy. The allure lies in escaping the hustle of daily life and finding solace in quiet, reflective moments on open waters."

Alberto paused, tilting his own chin confidently upwards towards the sun, as if he were inhaling the sea air for the first time that morning. He exhaled slowly and deeply, as if to slow time down in that moment to illustrate his next point.

"At its core, owning a Ferretti yacht is a commitment by our clients to making the experiences that allow us to unplug, breathe deeply, and savor the beauty around us a priority. Were they to always be frantic, no amount of money could compensate for the trauma that would be inflicted upon their families, their bodies, and their own very psyches," he stated with conviction.

"When you put it that way, I suppose it's our duty to invest in a yacht, like our lives depend on it!" Lori suggested cheerfully. William smirked at his wife's cleverness.

"We don't just sell a story, we have the product to back it up," continued Alberto.

"If you stop investing in product development, you become old very quickly," he emphasized. His passion for innovation was palpable.

Thanks to diligent research, development, and a willingness to embrace change, the Ferretti Group placed itself at the forefront of the yacht industry. We felt a kinship with the Ferretti commitment to refine their niche and continually expand their horizons.

Alberto often compared managing a brand to raising a gifted child: both require focused attention, discipline, and care. "It takes hard work to protect a brand," he said many times. During these philosophical musings, he'd draw parallels to a Formula One driver or a promising young athlete as examples.

Alberto didn't just pontificate on the concept of famous brands or influencers; he knew them personally. Over the years, Alberto has crossed paths with an astonishing array of individuals, including global icons, reclusive innovators, and just about everyone in between.

"In this business, I've met people you wouldn't believe exist," he says with a grin. "But you also work hard to gain their respect."

"The brand is a duty, a discipline," he observed. "Enjoying life's luxuries is a privilege, but it also demands diligence."

He went on to explain how Ferretti serves as mindful stewards of their yachts, their clients, and the environment, with equal consideration to preserving heritage or ensuring sustainable practices as to revenue-generation.

Onboard the Riva 130 Belissima, exquisite detail abounds. Alberto runs his hand along a mahogany railing. "The lifestyle we provide extends beyond luxury—it includes events, relationships, and a sense of belonging," he explained.

"In the same vein, we shape the world around us both for ourselves as well as for those around us to create memories that last a lifetime," quipped Lori.

"Exactly," Alberto said affirmingly. "By immersing ourselves in each experience and engaging every sense, we discover the joyful essence of truly living."

"No rearview mirrors," he continued, "the past literally doesn't exist." Alberto mused about the importance of being anchored to the present moment while keeping an eye on the future.

"I see," offered William. "The past can offer lessons, but it should never constrain our potential."

"Cento per cento," Alberto exclaimed. "Exactly."

"Embracing a forward-looking mindset encourages us to remain open to new possibilities, ever ready to seize life's next adventure," Lori said while staring across the waters as if visualizing her own future with William, and the adventures to come.

As the yacht's sleek lines cut through the gentle waves, we basked in the realization that we weren't just standing on a masterpiece—we were sailing on one.

"The fingerprint of Italian craftsmanship is unmistakable," William said.

"We have that special Italian touch," Alberto smiled. "Design, elegance, and attention to detail are modus operandi; the Ferretti nature is rooted in excellence. This spirit urges us to cultivate elegance and excellence in all we do. Seeking beauty, perfecting our craft, and honoring cultural heritage can enrich each area of our lives."

Stepping off the Riva 130 Belissima at sunset, one carries away more than memories of an extraordinary day on the water. You leave with a revitalized sense of what it means to "have it all." For Alberto Galassi, abundance surpasses mere wealth or status; it encompasses a holistic way of life—one that thrives on freedom, innovation, the bonds we form, and a heartfelt devotion to living in the brightest, boldest way possible.

Later on that evening, while returning to our hotel hand-in-hand, we were struck by the emphasis Alberto put on personal relationships throughout the day's conversations. His ability to genuinely connect with people seemed to make him a magnet for abundance.

"They say we're the sum of the five people we spend the most time with," William began. "And it's true—surrounding yourself with the wrong energy can pull you off course."

"Your tribe creates your vibe," Lori nodded. "The people around you shape your mindset, your motivation, even your sense of what's possible."

"Exactly," William continued. "When your circle supports your growth, they help you rise. But if you're surrounded by low energy or negative influences, it can hold you back in ways you don't always see right away."

"And not just professionally," Lori added. "It can affect your confidence, your decisions—your whole outlook on life."

CHAPTER FIFTEEN: BECOME A MAGNET FOR ABUNDANCE

"Becoming a magnet for abundance," William said, "isn't a solo mission. It's a team sport."

And with that, we gripped one another's hands a little tighter and walked the rest of the way towards our hotel, relishing in the warmth of our connection in the balmy French coastal air.

IT'S NOT ABOUT THE DESTINATION...

Santorini glowing in Cycladic white and blue.

This chapter is a vision board of our future five years from now. In this vision, twelve years have passed since we (Lori and William) began our journey together. Now, inspired by our dear friends Kenn and Pamela Ricci—whose visionary leadership in private aviation has redefined luxury travel—we find ourselves embracing a new chapter of life, one of imagining the next level of adventure and possibility.

As Lori settled into the supple leather seat of their friends' Gulfstream G650, she inhaled the crisp, clean scent of the cabin. Across from her, Kenn and Pamela sat comfortably, enjoying the journey as much as the destination. The gentle hum of the engines provided a soothing backdrop as the cabin attendant poured them all a glass of Billecart-Salmon Brut Rosé, the effervescent bubbles tickling their noses.

"You know," Lori mused, her voice soft against the white noise of the jet, "what really matters isn't just where you're going—it's how you get there."

Kenn smiled knowingly. "Exactly—it's about embracing every experience along the way."

William nodded, the golden sunlight streaming through the window highlighting the contentment in his eyes. "No matter how good your life may be, there is always another level. It's about allowing ourselves to dream bigger, to reach higher."

Pamela leaned in, her voice warm. "And to share that journey with those who inspire and uplift us."

Upgrading our lives isn't just about material possessions, but about expanding our horizons and experiences. And in this case, quite literally.

We first met Kenn and Pamela Ricci by chance one evening in Cartagena, Colombia, over dinner with friends. Conversation flowed effortlessly as we discovered how much we had in common. From similar backgrounds to a shared passion for adventure, we quickly realized we were kindred spirits.

Kenn, a pioneer in private aviation and the Founder and Chairman of Flexjet, has spent over four decades shaping the way people experience flight. With more than 300 aircraft in operation and a portfolio spanning fractional ownership, jet cards, and cutting-edge aerospace engineering, his vision has transformed an industry. But beyond business success, what makes Kenn and Pamela truly extraordinary is their unwavering commitment to living fully and giving generously.

Their philanthropic impact is as inspiring as their achievements. Their groundbreaking $100 million donation to the University of Notre Dame set a new benchmark for giving, ensuring future generations benefit from expanded educational opportunities. They have championed Able Flight, an organization that empowers individuals with disabilities through aviation training, proving that flight is not just a privilege but a powerful tool for transformation. Their contributions to medical research, including the Cystic Fibrosis Foundation, reflect their dedication to leaving the world better than they found it.

They embody what it means to live the Best Day Every Day lifestyle—a seamless integration of success, adventure, abundance, meaningful relationships, and purposeful generosity.

CHAPTER FIFTEEN: BECOME A MAGNET FOR ABUNDANCE

One afternoon, as we sat together reminiscing about past travels, Kenn and Pamela extended an invitation: "Why don't we take the jet and escape somewhere incredible?" It was a spur-of-the-moment idea, but those are often the best kind. Within hours, we were soaring over the Aegean, heading toward Santorini.

As we touched down in Santorini, the salty Mediterranean breeze greeted us, carrying hints of sun-warmed stone and blooming bougainvillea. Our private cliffside villa offered a panoramic view of the caldera, the deep blue of the sea meeting the crisp white of the buildings in a breathtaking vista.

That evening, as we dined on the terrace with Kenn and Pamela, the smoky char of grilled octopus and the velvety richness of fava purée came together in a perfect harmony of flavors, leaving a lasting impression with every bite. The rich, fruity notes of Assyrtiko wine complemented the meal perfectly. The sound of gentle waves splashing against the shore below provided a rhythmic accompaniment to our conversation.

"Upgrading our lives is a holistic experience. It's been about curating moments, like these," Lori explained, gesturing to the dazzling sunset before us. "About surrounding yourself with beauty, inspiration, and extraordinary people."

William added, his fingers intertwined with Lori's, "And sharing that abundance with others. It's not just about what we have, but how we use it to enrich our lives and the lives of those around us."

Kenn smiled, raising his glass. "It's about leading with passion. Aviation has always been my love, but the true joy is in creating opportunities—whether it's through flight, philanthropy, or inspiring others to reach new heights."

Pamela, ever the gracious hostess, added, "It's also about making sure that every step of the journey is filled with purpose. Whether we're supporting the next generation of aviators or giving back to causes that touch our hearts—it's about using what we've built to elevate others."

As night fell, the sky transformed into a glittering canopy of stars. The scent of night-blooming jasmine drifted through the air, its sweet fragrance a reminder of life's simple pleasures.

Upgrading our lives isn't just about seeking luxury, but about expanding our perspectives, embracing new experiences, and using resources to create meaningful moments and lasting memories. It's about dreaming big while savoring the journey. The plush sheets of a five-star hotel are a delight—but so is the thrill of stumbling upon a hidden local gem. Private travel offers unmatched ease, yet there's something gratifying about crafting the adventure yourself.

As we fell asleep that evening to the gentle lull of the Aegean Sea, we knew that the real luxury in life was the freedom to choose your path, to grow continuously, and to share your journey with those you love.

More than that, Kenn and Pamela have shown us that true success is measured not by what you achieve, but by what you give. Their legacy isn't defined by the aircraft they own, the homes they've built, or the business empire they've cultivated, but by the lives they've touched, the dreams they've inspired, and the communities they've uplifted. They exemplify the greatest luxury is a life lived with intention—a life where every experience is an opportunity to give, to grow, and to create something meaningful.

But perhaps the most inspiring lesson they've imparted is that true love is the foundation upon which everything else is built. As Kenn once said, "It has been said that love is not about finding someone to live with, but rather, finding someone you can't live without. I'm so fortunate to have found my Pam." His words, spoken with the sincerity of a man deeply devoted to his wife, resonated profoundly with us. Love, in its purest form, is not just about companionship but about an unbreakable bond that lifts and sustains.

Watching Kenn and Pamela together—partners in adventure, business, and life—reinforced in us that success and fulfillment mean little without someone special to share it with. In following their example, we realized that our own journey isn't just about experiencing the best life has to offer, but about sharing it, paying it forward, and ensuring that our success becomes a bridge for others to cross toward their own dreams.

CHAPTER FIFTEEN: BECOME A MAGNET FOR ABUNDANCE

Lori and William boarding Flexjet's Gulfstream G650.

EMBRACING LIFE'S SIMPLE PLEASURES

*"Food and wine are not just sustenance for the body;
they are a celebration of life's flavors and a feast for the soul."*
Unknown

Learning to embrace life's simple pleasures is the key to turning each day into the best it can be. Our philosophy revolves around making every day extraordinary, often by exploring the treasures right in our own backyard. Picture this: a perfect day skiing on Aspen Mountain or Aspen Highlands, crowned by a delightful picnic amidst the breathtaking mountain vistas.

A winter picnic moment at Aspen Mountain.

Our quest for the ideal picnic spot takes us to carefully chosen tables spread across Ajax and Highlands, offering world-class views. Armed with a specially designed picnic backpack featuring complete place settings for two and a wine cooler, we set the stage for a memorable experience. A tablecloth is laid, and our favorite cheeses, fresh breads, nuts, fruits, cold cuts, and wine transform an ordinary day into something extraordinary.

Salotto Nights with friends Cristiano and Spartaco.

On the subject of adding richness and enjoyment to your everyday experiences, we owe a special thanks to two friends and muses who introduced us to one of our most cherished traditions: Cristiano and Spartaco from Rome. These dear friends not only taught us about the beauty of "salotto" nights but have been a part of every gathering since, helping us turn these evenings into something extraordinary. Through their Roman roots, Cristiano and Spartaco have shared the joy of good food, fine wine, and the Italian way of bringing people together.

Our "salotto" nights, inspired by the Italian word for "living room," are intimate monthly gatherings that have become a beloved ritual over the past decade. These nights fill our home with the delicious aromas of pizza and Roman pasta dishes, prepared under their expert guidance, and accompanied by incredible Italian wines. Each salotto night is more than just a dinner party; it's a celebration of friendship, laughter, and the beauty of the moment, made richer by their presence and hospitality.

Cristiano and Spartaco have taught us that true richness is found in the warmth of shared experiences, in the sparkle of conversation, and in the simple joy of a meal enjoyed with friends. They remind us that home truly is where the heart is—and ours is filled with laughter, love, and the spirit of Italy, brought to life by friends who embody its essence.

Our travels have been deeply enriched by the connections and friendships we've made across Italy. Whether they're guiding us through a bustling Roman market or recommending friends to meet in a little-known Tuscan village, they've introduced us to some of Italy's most remarkable people. Through them, we've had the privilege of sharing stories with local artisans, dining with vineyard owners who pour their passion into every bottle, and laughing with chefs whose cooking is a true art form. Cristiano and Spartaco have introduced us to a side of Italy only a local could reveal, enriching our understanding and deepening our love for Italy's beautiful country. Their connections and generosity have guided us to hidden corners, where every experience holds layers of meaning. Through them, we've come to understand that life's beauty is found in the present—in savoring, connecting, and living by our shared motto: *Don't let it pass you by.*

As avid travelers, we find joy in savoring the local cuisine of our host countries. Before each trip, we meticulously research the best dining spots known for their unique offerings, be it in food, location, or views. From planning a leisurely lunch to a delightful dinner or aperitivo, each experience is crafted to be a special occasion. You can explore many of our favorite places, detailed on our popular website, https://bestdayeveryday.com.

In the remaining portion of this chapter, we'll share how you, too, can arrange and relish these types of enriching experiences.

1. ENJOY GREAT WINE

Wine is one of life's great pleasures—a journey of discovery where each glass tells a story of history, landscape, and cultural tradition. Whether you're savoring a bold Shiraz in Australia or a crisp Assyrtiko in Santorini, each region's wine reflects its unique heritage and environment. Visiting wineries around the globe allows you to not only sample distinct flavors but also to experience the narrative of a place through its winemaking traditions.

Enhance your life with fine wine, gourmet food, travel, and more by embracing the art of wine tasting. Educate yourself on diverse varieties, regions, and tasting techniques. Attend wine tastings, explore vineyards, and immerse yourself in the local culture by visiting small villages and renowned wineries alike. These experiences enrich your understanding of how each region's natural landscape and historical evolution have shaped the wine they produce.

Traveling broadens your perspective and creates lifelong memories. Whether you're enjoying a humble vin de table in a quaint village or exploring famed wine regions known for their storied vineyards, each encounter is a celebration of tradition and terroir. Plan trips that pique your interest—destinations where authentic culinary experiences and the art of winemaking converge to create moments of genuine connection and enjoyment.

2. ENJOY GREAT COMPANY

Entertaining is a key to cultivating high-vibrational individuals around you. Upgrade your social gatherings and create memorable experiences by incorporating fine wine, gourmet food, and a touch of elegance. Host wine and cheese tastings, themed dinner parties, or outdoor gatherings with carefully curated menus and pairings. Create an ambiance that reflects your personal style and pays attention to detail, enhancing the overall enjoyment for yourself and your guests.

The use of fresh, well-prepared ingredients enhances the taste and enjoyment of food. In addition, enjoying great food can be enhanced by sharing the experience with others. Appreciate the artistic aspect of food, including its visual presentation. Aesthetically pleasing food can add to the overall delight and elevate the dining experience. Plus, it brings about a sense of pride and accomplishment.

While the pleasures of fine wine, gourmet food, and travel are enriching, it's equally important to invest in personal development, which makes you one of the more interesting guests at any party. Seek opportunities for self-improvement, growth, and meaningful connections. Establish a *World of Wisdom* book club, with each section culminating in a party and an in-depth discussion. Engage in activities that expand your knowledge, challenge your perspectives, and contribute to your personal and professional development. Balance the indulgences with pursuits that align with your long-term goals and aspirations.

Remember that while indulging in the finer things in life can bring joy and enrichment, it's essential to maintain a holistic approach to upgrading your life. Balance your desires for luxury with personal growth, health, and meaningful experiences that contribute to your overall well-being and fulfillment.

3. ENJOY GREAT FOOD

I (Lori) remind my clients who want to look and feel their best to eat the rainbow... and more! Refer to Chapter Nine, Section One, for a detailed description of "eating the rainbow" with references to our MD health guru, Dr. Gundry.

Enjoying great food means taking pleasure and deriving satisfaction from the experience of eating. It involves fully engaging in the flavors, textures, scents, and presentation of the food, allowing yourself to indulge and appreciate the culinary delights before you.

It is best to engage in mindful eating by savoring each bite, being fully present in the moment, and paying attention to the sensory experience. In somatic workshops, participants are encouraged to drink a rich tea or cup of cacao very slowly, even sensually. It's not uncommon that women's workshops commence with mindful chocolate eating, the ultimate icebreaker for feminine energy. Refer to the beginning of Chapter Nine to see how Loren Lahav incorporated textures, flavors, and temperatures into the sensory experience of her retreat in Fiji.

The environment in which you dine is critical. Create an ambiance that complements the enjoyment of your meal. Set the table, dim the lights, play soft music, or indulge in a dining experience that captivates long after the last bite. Make sure to engage in conversations about food, recipes, and culinary experiences with others who share your passion. Sharing recommendations, tips, and stories can enhance the enjoyment of great food and create a sense of community. Lastly, don't ignore the traditions of your friends and family members. Embrace and celebrate them and their cultural practices. Open your mind, explore traditional recipes, participate in food-related festivals and events, and learn about the stories and histories behind various dishes.

Keep in mind that enjoying great food is not just about the taste but also about the entire experience surrounding it. It is about indulging in the flavors, appreciating the craftsmanship, and fostering connections through the shared enjoyment of delicious cuisine.

You can also expand your culinary horizons by exploring gourmet cuisine. Experiment with new recipes, flavors, and cooking techniques at home. Dine at fine dining restaurants or seek out local establishments known for their gourmet offerings. Consider taking cooking classes or workshops to refine your culinary skills and learn from expert chefs, especially when you are traveling abroad. Delight in the creativity and refined technique of gourmet food while indulging in exquisite flavors and presentation.

If your budget is a temporary restriction, you can purchase exotic foods or spices to cook with at home. Herbs de Provence is easy to incorporate into cooking or as a flavor enhancer when added to olive oil or butter for dipping. Rolling sushi at home is another way to turn a meal into a "salotto" night, where each family member or guest can choose their preferred ingredients for their rolls, such as vegetables, fish, or herbs. Farmers' markets offer fresh, organic produce that you can learn to use in innovative ways. For example, you can use tomato leaves in tomato sauce, achieving a taste similar to basil, or incorporate root tops into salads that are typically discarded before reaching grocery shelves. We have friends who have become avid "sprouters," adding powerfully healthy broccoli sprouts to their meals for added kick and depth to the dish.

While indulging in fine wine and gourmet food can be enjoyable, it's essential to maintain a balanced and healthy approach. Focus on quality over quantity and practice mindful eating, savoring each bite, and paying attention to your body's cues of hunger and fullness. Balance indulgences with a nutritious diet and regular exercise to support your overall well-being.

4. ENJOY INVESTMENT IN YOURSELF

When you learn a new skill or hobby and invest in yourself, you will change the world. We reflected this sentiment in Chapter Ten: *Never Work A Day in Your Life*.

Learning a new skill or hobby can help you expand your knowledge, broaden your horizons, and discover new passions and interests. Whether you want to pick up a new hobby for fun or to improve your career prospects, there are a few key steps you can take to make the learning process smoother and more enjoyable.

Firstly, it's essential to choose a skill or hobby that you are genuinely interested in. Think about the things that you enjoy doing or learning about, and consider how you can develop those interests further. Do you want to learn a new language, take up painting, write a book, or try your hand at coding? Whatever it is, make sure it's something that you feel motivated to pursue and that aligns with your goals and values.

Once you've identified your new skill or hobby, it's time to start learning. There are many ways to go about this, depending on the nature of the skill or hobby and your personal learning style. Some people prefer to take formal classes or courses, while others prefer to learn independently through books, online resources, or practice.

If you're taking formal classes or courses, make sure to research the options available to you and choose a program that fits your schedule, budget, and learning preferences. If you're learning independently, look for reputable resources and materials that can guide you through the learning process. Consider joining online forums or communities where you can connect with others who share your interests and ask for advice or feedback.

As you start learning your new skill or hobby, it's essential to set realistic goals and expectations for yourself. Don't expect to become an expert overnight, but instead focus on making steady progress and improving your skills over time. Break down the learning process into manageable steps and set small goals that you can achieve along the way. Celebrate your achievements, no matter how small they may be, and use them as motivation to keep going.

Make sure to practice regularly and consistently. Learning a new skill or hobby requires time and effort, so make sure to set aside dedicated time each day or week to work on your craft. Make it a priority in your schedule and stick to your commitments. Remember, the more you practice, the faster you'll improve.

Finally, don't be afraid to make mistakes or ask for help. Learning a new skill or hobby can be challenging, and it's normal to encounter obstacles or setbacks along the way. But by embracing these challenges as opportunities to learn and grow, you can develop resilience and a growth mindset that will serve you well in all areas of life.

5. ENJOY YOUR APPEARANCE

Dress to impress; you only have one chance to make a first impression, and it only takes one tenth of a second for somebody to make a judgment about you that can last a lifetime, according to Princeton University researchers Janine Willis and Alexander Todorov. In 2006, they released a study titled "First Impressions: Making Up Your Mind After a 100-Ms Exposure to a Face." In the study, they demonstrated that people make judgments about attractiveness, likability, trustworthiness, competence, and aggressiveness in just a tenth of a second.

The study showed that longer exposure time (up to 1 second) didn't significantly change these initial judgments. What's more, people's snap judgments remained largely consistent even when given more time to evaluate. The traits most quickly assessed were trustworthiness, which was reiterated in Chapter Fourteen: when you dress well, people feel that you are capable and trustworthy. These rapid judgments activate the amygdala, the brain's emotional center, which is why we consider the valuable habit of dressing well to be a form of mind control! That underscores the importance of first impressions and explains why a poor first impression can be so challenging to overcome, even when it's inaccurate. The saying, "dress to impress," may seem like a cliche, but there's actually some truth to it.

What's more, the way we dress can have a significant impact on how others perceive us, and even on our own confidence and self-image. Whether you're going to a job interview, a business meeting, or a social event, what you wear can make an impact on how others perceive you. A well-chosen outfit can convey professionalism, confidence, and attention to detail, while a sloppy or inappropriate outfit can give the opposite impression. We covered this in greater detail in Chapter Fourteen.

Here are some tips for dressing to impress:
1. **Dress for the occasion** - The first step to dressing to impress is to know the dress code for the occasion. Are you going to a formal event, a business meeting, or a casual gathering? Dressing appropriately for the occasion shows that you respect the event and the people you're meeting.
2. **Choose clothes that fit well.** Ill-fitting clothes can be unflattering and uncomfortable, and can even make you appear less confident. Take the time to find clothes that fit well and flatter your body shape.
3. **Pay attention to details** - Details like accessories, shoes, and grooming can make a big difference in how you're perceived. Make sure your shoes are clean and polished, your hair is neat and styled, and your accessories are appropriate for the occasion.

4. **Be yourself** - While it's important to dress appropriately for the occasion, it's also important to stay true to your personal style. Don't try to be someone you're not. Choose clothes that reflect your personality and individuality.
5. **Confidence is key** - Ultimately, the most important factor in dressing to impress is confidence. When you feel good in what you're wearing, it shows in your body language and demeanor. Choose clothes that make you feel confident and comfortable.

Naturally, clothes don't define who you are. At the end of the day, it's your actions, character, and values that truly matter. However, by taking the time to dress appropriately and confidently, you can make a positive impression and set yourself up for success.

6. ENJOY IMMERSION IN PLEASURABLE ACTIVITIES

To immerse yourself means to fully engage and involve yourself in an activity, experience, or environment. It entails giving your complete attention, focus, and energy to the present moment and allowing yourself to be fully absorbed in the experience.

When you immerse yourself, you let go of distractions and external influences that might hinder your engagement. You become deeply involved and invested in what you are doing, feeling a sense of flow and being "in the zone." Immersion often leads to heightened concentration, creativity, and a more profound connection with the subject matter or the people involved.

Immersion may involve exploring a new culture by traveling, learning a new language, or embracing local customs and traditions. It can also refer to immersing yourself in an activity or skill, such as playing a musical instrument, painting, writing, or practicing a sport, where you become fully absorbed and dedicated to improving your abilities.

7. ENJOY THE COMPOUND EFFECTS OF CONSISTENCY

The statement "consistency is power" emphasizes the impact of habits. An activity performed consistently becomes more effortless, as seen in Lori's earlier example of working out. When consistency becomes a habit, it becomes a powerful force that propels you forward and helps you overcome obstacles and setbacks.

By consistently taking action, you create momentum towards your goals. Each small step builds upon the previous one, gradually moving you closer to your desired outcome. Over time, your dedication to small steps compounds, and you'll find that moving towards your goals feels a lot less like climbing a mountain and much more like skiing down a steep slope.

When you establish yourself as somebody committed to consistency, you're perceived differently. The characteristic of consistency builds trust in the eyes of others, as well as in yourself. When you consistently deliver on your commitments, meet deadlines, and follow through on your promises, you earn a reputation for reliability and dependability.

Moreover, consistency helps you more easily overcome challenges. By constantly showing up, even when it feels difficult or uncomfortable, you develop resilience and the ability to persevere in the face of obstacles.

By consistently engaging in actions aligned with your goals, you reinforce positive behaviors and reduce the likelihood of falling back into old patterns.

It is through constant effort and habit formation that progress is made towards your life's goals.

8. ENJOY LIFE'S DANCE

Life is a dance, an ever-flowing rhythm of experiences, choices, and emotions that shape our journey. We move to different beats, transition through various steps, and adapt gracefully when the tempo changes. Embracing the fluidity of life allows you to flow with its rhythms and find harmony in the transitions.

Dance is a form of self-expression, and life provides you with a canvas to express your unique self. You have the freedom to choose your steps, create your choreography, and shape your own narrative.

Dancing requires trust in oneself and in the partnership with others. Although you must trust yourself enough to let go while dancing, you must also surrender control to your dance partner sometimes, trusting the flow and allowing for synchronization and collaboration with others.

When we dance, we feel joy. Dance is the hallmark of a proper celebration. Celebration is the act of acknowledging and rejoicing in the moments, big or small, that bring you happiness, fulfillment, and growth. It involves recognizing achievements, milestones, and personal victories, as well as appreciating the simple pleasures and blessings that enrich your life.

Embracing life as a dance means surrendering to its rhythms, finding joy in its movements, and allowing yourself to be fully present in each step. It reminds you to cherish the beauty, embrace the challenges, and celebrate the journey.

9. ENJOY BEING GLAMOROUS

Glamour, in its essence, represents an element of enchantment, allure, and elegance that adds a touch of magic to your life. While it may be seen as superficial by some, there are reasons why glamour is often cherished and valued. Glamour has the power to transport you to a world of fantasy, beauty, and inspiration.

In your everyday life filled with routine and responsibilities, glamour offers an escape—an opportunity to indulge in the extraordinary, to dream, and to imagine a life beyond the ordinary. It sparks your creativity, stirs your imagination, and infuses your reality with a sense of possibility. Glamour can be a powerful tool for self-expression and boosting self-confidence. It allows you to curate your appearance, style, and demeanor in a way that reflects your unique personality and inner desires. It empowers you to embrace your individuality, to celebrate your own beauty, and to express yourself authentically. It can be a source of confidence, enabling you to radiate a magnetic presence and embrace your own worth.

In addition, glamour invites a sense of celebration and joy into your life. It encourages you to embrace the finer things, to appreciate aesthetics, and to revel in moments of luxury and indulgence. Whether it's dressing up for a special occasion, creating an elegant ambiance, or simply pampering yourself, adopting a sophisticated style adds a touch of excitement and celebration to life's experiences, making them feel extraordinary and memorable. Having an attractive or alluring style can inspire and captivate others.

When you embody glamour, whether through your appearance, style, or demeanor, you can become a source of inspiration and admiration for those around you. Your confidence, poise, and ability to create an enchanting atmosphere can inspire others to embrace their own beauty, to pursue their passions, and to live life with a touch of charisma.

While glamour should not be the sole focus of your life or a measure of your worth, embracing it can add a layer of delight, inspiration, and confidence to your existence. It is a reminder to cultivate your own unique brand of magic, to cherish the enchanting moments, and to create a life that is as extraordinary and captivating as you desire.

In life's intricate design, each chapter unfolds with unique rhythms and melodies, inviting us to dance to the ever-changing beats. Whether savoring the richness of great wine, indulging in the pleasures of fine food, learning new skills, dressing with purpose, immersing ourselves in the beauty of the present, or embracing the enchantment of glamour, every step we take contributes to the fabric of our lives.

As we explore the nuances of life, it becomes clear that consistency is the powerful thread that weaves through each note, transforming efforts into accomplishments. The dance of life, celebrated with gratitude, appreciation, and a beautiful state of mind, resonates with the magic found in every moment.

So, let's continue this dance, cherishing the unique melodies of each chapter, finding meaning in every step, and holding onto the glamour that adds a touch of enchantment to our journey. In embracing our ageless selves, we unveil the extraordinary in the ordinary, creating a life that is not just lived but celebrated with each beat of our hearts.

Chapter Sixteen:
ENJOYING CULTURE AND GREAT WORKS OF MANKIND

Lori and William in Florence, Italy.

The warm, inviting scent of fresh espresso wafted from a nearby café as Lori licked the last bite of a smooth, velvety gelato off a paper spoon. "Do you know the only thing more delicious than pistachio and dark chocolate gelato?" she asked William.

Inhaling, William smiled and looked at his wife. "Let me guess, an espresso pairing?"

Without speaking a word, we turned forty-five degrees and made our way towards the sumptuous smells coming from a nearby café.

We stood on a tile floor in the open-air bar and sipped our espressos quickly; we were eager to meet up with Sofia Rossi, a seasoned art historian and Florentine guide.

The smell of coffee beans was soon replaced with the earthy scent of aged stone and varnish that permeates the historic Galleria dell'Accademia.

"Welcome to Florence, the cradle of the Renaissance," a voice echoed in the grand hall amidst the soft murmurs of other visitors, peppered with footsteps on the marble floors.

Turning slightly, we faced our guide for the day. "Sofia, we're so happy to meet you. How did you know it was us?"

Sofia smiled wryly. "It was a good guess. Follow me." She walked slowly, an invitation for us to follow her.

"Today, we will explore some of the most iconic masterpieces that have inspired countless generations. Our journey begins here at the magnificent Galleria dell'Accademia, home to Michelangelo's David."

When we arrived in front of "David," William found himself touching the cool, polished marble railing around the perimeter of the iconic statue. As Sofia explained the story of the statue, the artist, and the history of its commission and life over the past five hundred and twenty years, William leaned in, admiring the details.

"I've read so much about David, but seeing it in person is something else entirely."

"Indeed. Michelangelo's David is more than just a statue; it represents the pinnacle of human creativity and ambition. Michelangelo was only twenty-six years old when he started working on this masterpiece. Can you imagine? He saw a giant block of marble and envisioned this perfect form within it. It's a testament to his genius and perseverance."

"What can we learn from Michelangelo's approach?"

Sofia grinned. "That's a great question. Michelangelo believed in the concept of 'non-finito'—the idea that every block of marble has a statue within it, waiting to be revealed. This philosophy teaches us to see potential where others see obstacles. David, in particular, embodies the spirit of Florence—strength, beauty, and defiance. Let this masterpiece inspire you to pursue your own greater works, to push the boundaries of what you think is possible."

"It's incredible to think about the dedication and vision required to create something like this."

"Absolutely. And Michelangelo's work on David was just the beginning. As we walk through the Uffizi Gallery and the Palazzo Pitti, you'll see how he and his contemporaries reshaped our understanding of art, science, and the human spirit. These masterpieces remind you that your ambition can be as vast as the sky and your creativity as deep as the ocean."

> *"Culture is the widening of the mind and of the spirit."*
> *Jawaharlal Nehru*

Enjoying culture and great works of mankind combines pleasure and excitement with self-improvement by osmosis. During our formative years, neither of us truly grasped the significance of art, music, theater, and literature, despite being exposed to these elements both at school and in our homes.

William's Introduction to Culture

In my pre-teen years, my mother insisted my sister and I take piano lessons, dance instruction (including ballet and tap dance), and later, guitar lessons. Growing up in Presque Isle, a quaint town with a population of 12,000 in Northern Maine, my parents regularly took me and my sister to community concerts and local theater performances. At the time, I may not have fully appreciated the significance of these experiences. However, in hindsight, I now realize how crucial those early encounters were in shaping my understanding and appreciation of the cultural arts.

Lori's Introduction to Culture

In contrast, my upbringing revolved around sports, and I also showcased my musical talents by playing the saxophone in the school band. Hailing from Mansfield, Ohio, the highlight of the small town was the Miss Ohio pageant, a widely attended event. The impact of this spectacle was so significant on me that I decided to participate in the Miss Teen USA pageant. William likes to remind me that I *actually* came in first place—but because the runner-up had a family member on the judge's committee, I was *officially* awarded second.

For my talent performance, I sang "Over the Rainbow" from The Wizard of Oz. With the collaborative efforts of all my uncles, my stage was magnificently arranged. In Mansfield, local theater and community concerts didn't hold as much significance, although the symphony was a source of enjoyment for everyone.

Cultural Exposure 2.0

It was only when we started residing in major cities—New York for Lori and Washington, D.C., for William—that we truly immersed ourselves in the pinnacle of cultural experiences. Both New York City and Washington, D.C., boast world-class cultural institutions, including iconic venues like the Smithsonian Museums, Kennedy Center for the Performing Arts, and Ford's Theatre in Washington, D.C., as well as the Metropolitan Museum and Broadway in New York.

Initially by chance and later by choice, William spent countless weekend afternoons exploring all twenty-one Smithsonian Museums. The abundant access to cultural events in Washington, D.C., motivated him to seize every opportunity the city had to offer. Over a span of two decades living in Washington, he attended numerous performances at the Kennedy Center and Ford's Theatre. It was during this period that he developed a profound appreciation for exceptional cultural experiences.

Broadway proved to be an exhilarating and unparalleled experience for Lori, unlike anything she had encountered back home in Ohio. She immersed herself in classic Broadway shows, and each performance left a lasting impact on her. Sharing these theatrical moments became her favorite activity when friends and family visited the city.

In addition to Broadway, Lori also developed a fondness for attending live jazz performances in various jazz clubs around the city, introducing her to a new and different cultural scene.

We both left those big cities to move to Aspen, Colorado. What we find unique about Aspen is the great access to world-class culture. In Aspen, you'll find a great collection of private galleries, the "Aspen Art Museum," and art centers like "Anderson Ranch." We never go wanting for the visual arts. Aspen also has world-class ballet troupes and performing arts centers like "Theatre Aspen" and the "Wheeler Opera House."

Aspen also hosts Food and Wine Magazine's annual trade show, the "Aspen Food and Wine Classic." It is home to world-famous events such as the "Aspen Music Festival" and the Aspen Institute's "Ideas Festival." Aspen also has a great jazz show organized by "Jazz Aspen Snowmass." For a small town of 7,500 people, we have access to world-class cultural events. As part of enjoying great works of mankind, we try to take full advantage of our Aspen cultural scene.

Travel As A Means of Connecting With The World

Travel is a means of connecting with the world, gaining a deeper understanding and appreciation for the richness of human experience, and cultivating a broader perspective on life's challenges. Exploring new cultures, ideas, and topics enhances our appreciation for the complexity of the world and nurtures diverse skills and interests. Spending time in nature fosters a sense of awe and tranquility.

We've chronicled our travels over the past decade on our website: https://bestdayeveryday.com. On this platform, we strive to document our favorite destinations, cultural encounters, culinary experiences, exceptional hotels and resorts, and noteworthy events. We invite you to explore https://bestdayeveryday.com to discover the places we've been fortunate to experience. Whether you share our passion for global exploration or prefer delving into cultural opportunities closer to home, let's explore how cultural experiences can enrich our lives, making each day the best it can be.

TRAIN YOUR BRAIN WITH ARTS & CULTURE

Nourishing your mind is just as important as nourishing your body. By reading regularly, learning something new, practicing mindfulness, engaging in intellectual conversations, and taking breaks from technology, you stimulate your mind and improve your overall well-being. Incorporate these practices into your daily routine, and you'll notice a positive difference in your mental health and cognitive function.

Exposure to culture and the arts can improve cognitive function, including memory, attention, and processing speed. Studies have shown that engaging with music, visual art, and theater can improve mental performance and slow down age-related cognitive decline. In addition, studies have shown that engaging with art and music can lower cortisol levels, the hormone associated with stress, and promote feelings of calm and relaxation. Witnessing great works of mankind enhances emotional well-being. This exposure also stimulates creativity and imagination. One artist in our area regularly spends months studying other artists' innovations and techniques before he begins a new oil painting series. The cleverness of others fuels his desire to improve and elevate his own techniques, rather than getting stuck in his comfort zone. He evolves through osmosis; masterpieces from other artists inspire him to paint better.

Engaging with culture can even enhance problem-solving skills. Artistic expression can inspire new ways of thinking and encourage experimentation, which trains your brain to be more creative in all areas of life.

Above all, exposure to other cultures increases empathy and emotional intelligence by providing a glimpse into different perspectives and life experiences. By seeing the world through the eyes of others, you can develop a greater understanding of people. By experiencing the visual arts, sculpture, theatre, food, wine, architecture, music, and literature of other people, you may find that you understand places and societies that were otherwise foreign and mystical; this doesn't merely beget compassion and appreciation of others, but it makes a big world a bit smaller, and even less intimidating. In this way, immersion in other cultures fuels your confidence and courage—the world becomes more accessible.

And you'll be a much more interesting conversationalist to boot!

Chapter Seventeen:
THE JOY OF TRAVEL

Shailen with Lori and William in Monaco and Saint Tropez.

The scent of the salty sea air mingles with the fragrance of blooming jasmine and the occasional drift of cologne from passersby. We are walking with our friend Shailen, a former lawyer from London who has spent a ton of time (with both of us) in the US and the South of France, and happens to be pretty knowledgeable about Monaco. This insight stems from his years of attending the Monaco Formula 1 Grand Prix and Cannes Film Festival (where he met William), as well as his unforgettable 40th birthday celebration in Monaco — the occasion where he first met Lori, soon after she began dating William. We stop at a chic sidewalk café where Shailen waves gently towards the waiter. As he lifts his arm, we smell his own faint scent of sandalwood and citrus, a signature blend that leaves a subtle yet memorable impression.

"Your finest rosé, please," Shailen asks the waiter. When it's brought to our table, we relish the crisp, refreshing taste, which perfectly complements the warm, sun-drenched afternoon. In a moment, we are served a platter of perfect Mediterranean nibbles, including succulent olives, creamy burrata, and fresh seafood, which was caught that very morning. The vibrancy and saltiness of the fare harmonize with the wine.

Shailen looks at home in the opulence of Monaco. He turns heads with his handsome face, strong physique, and perfectly tailored white linen suit, which hints at his London roots. He looks every bit at home on the Mediterranean, with dark hair styled cleanly, catching the golden sunlight. His ever-present aviators reflect the azure skies of Monte-Carlo.

Once we've dined, we stroll down the iconic "Casino Square." The night falls, and sunlight is replaced with a glittering spectacle of luxury cars catching the last moments of the Riviera sun. Ferraris, Lambourghinis, and Bentleys line the streets; each more extravagant than the last. The grand façade of the Casino de Monte-Carlo dominates the square, its Belle Époque architecture a testament to a bygone era of elegance and excess.

As we stroll, the air is alive with sounds, such as the gentle hum of high-end engines, the clinking of champagne glasses from nearby restaurants, and the distant roll of the Mediterranean waves against the rocky shoreline. Shailen's laughter, rich and infectious, cuts through the ambient noise.

"I have the perfect spot," he states. We follow our guide, strolling into a casino, making a beeline over the smooth, cool marble of the casino steps for a cove of plush velvet seats in an exclusive club.

He shares an anecdote from his latest DJ set in Ibiza, his British accent adding a layer of sophistication to his tales. Lori sips a drink, and Shailen offers her a fine silk pocket square with a flourish, which she happily receives.

With Shailen as our guide, our time in Monaco was nothing short of extraordinary. His deep knowledge of the hottest spots and hidden gems, combined with his magnetic personality, ensured that every moment was filled with excitement and wonder.

From glamorous rooftop parties to intimate jazz clubs, Shailen knew how to curate the perfect travel experience, leaving us with memories that sparkled as brightly as the lights of Monte-Carlo at night. What we learned from him went beyond where to go or what to wear—it was about how to be. He reminded us that style isn't just appearance, and luxury isn't just access—it's presence. It's about savoring every detail, moving through life with confidence and curiosity, and making every experience feel intentionally elevated. With Shailen, we didn't just explore Monaco—we experienced the art of living well.

The city hummed with a rich medley of rhythmic guitars, while the soulful wail of trumpets drifted through the air. From nearby cafés, the mingling and chatter of locals was interrupted by the occasional clip-clop of horse-drawn carriages.

Havana's air was thick with a blend of sweet tropical flowers, the salty tang of the sea breeze, the exhaust fumes of classic American cars hailing from the 30s, 40s, and 50s, and the occasional whiff of a Cuban cigar, rich and elegant.

"Let me introduce you to the flavors of Cuba," our guide Julian Torres Rizo said while leading us into a local paladar. Julian had a fascinating background. As a young man, he had spent 10 years in New York City as part of the Cuban mission to the United Nations. Later, he served as the Cuban Ambassador to Grenada in 1983 when the United States invaded the Caribbean Island during the Reagan administration. He was an expert on Cuban history, the revolution, and the Cuban Missile Crisis. Within minutes, our table was full of Cuban flavors, including a robust, freshly brewed Cuban coffee, as well as plates of ropa vieja and yuca frita, which tantalized our taste buds with their hearty, savory goodness.

As he washed down the yuca frita with a palate-cleansing swig of strong Cuban coffee, Julian offered a story. "One of the most inspiring stories of our people is in the network of campesinos in the Sierra Maestra mountains. Although extremely poor and at risk of brutal repression, they supported Castro's rebels. They fed and sheltered revolutionaries while also serving as lookouts and messengers. All the while, they suffered under unfair land ownership systems and, to boot, they knew that if they got caught, they faced torture or death from Batista's forces. Many campesino families sent their sons and daughters to join the rebel army, and women played vital roles both as combatants and in support networks."

"I can't imagine sending my daughter to fight in any war, no matter the cause. These people are truly remarkable," stated William.

And smart, too. These rural communities developed a system of communication using everything from lanterns at night to laundry hanging patterns during the day. These warnings alerted rebels to approaching government troops. This grassroots intelligence network was so effective that Batista's forces were rarely able to ambush the rebels successfully.

"And the revolution succeeded through a true people's movement," Lori remarked.

"Yes, ordinary Cubans risked everything for the hope of a better future. Solidarity among the Cuban people taught the whole world about human resilience and collaboration."

"That merits dessert," Julian smiled. He ordered a creamy flan. It melted in our mouths, signifying a sweet conclusion to the culinary journey and the story.

Julian gestured beyond the cobblestone streets outside the café window. "The guerrilla warfare phase of the Cuban Revolution was conducted from the Sierra Maestra mountains with just eighty-two fighters who survived the Granma yacht landing in 1956. From this small group, the revolutionary forces grew to overthrow Batista's army of 37,000 troops eventually."

"Now let's go and meet some of these remarkable people," said Lori.

We began walking out of the café as Julian's voice, articulate and resonant, blended into the mix of sounds on the cobbled streets of Old Havana. As we strolled, we were captivated by the variety of colors surrounding us. Pastel-hued buildings with ornate balconies stood proudly, their colonial architecture whispering tales of bygone eras. The grand plazas were alive with activity, street performers adding splashes of movement and excitement against the backdrop of historic cathedrals and fortresses and classic American cars.

Lori and William in Havana with Ernesto, Julian Rizo, and members of the Buena Vista Social Club at Hotel Nacional de Cuba.

Julian's presence exuded a blend of diplomatic grace and deep cultural understanding, dressed in a crisp guayabera shirt that spoke of both tradition and sophistication.

With Julian Torres Rizo as our guide, our journey through Havana was profound and enriching. His ability to intertwine the city's economic, social, cultural, and political narratives ensured that every step we took was laden with meaning and insight. From the majestic edifices of Old Havana to the elegant neighborhoods of Vedado and Miramar, Julian's expertise transformed our visit into a vivid exploration of Cuba's past and present. Whether delving into the revolutionary fervor at the Museum of the Revolution or soaking in the literary legacy at Hemingway's La Vigia estate, every moment with Julian was a step deeper into the heart of Havana.

YOUR TICKET TO MINDFULNESS

When you travel, you gain the chance to see the world in a way that everyday life simply doesn't allow. Whether you're navigating the bustling streets of Tokyo or hiking along the breathtaking trails of the Cinque Terre, encountering different cultures, cuisines, and people offers a fresh perspective—a new lens through which to view the world.

When you immerse yourself in a new culture, you gain a deeper understanding of the people, customs, and traditions. You also develop a burning desire not to disturb them, but to preserve these traditions and absorb their experiences and wisdom. The future of humanity depends on preserving the diversity of the world and learning from the best wisdom of diverse cultures.

Trying new foods is more profound than satisfying hunger; it's an experience of sharing in the habits and wisdom of many generations; it's a way of literally tasting history. Trying new foods is a way of showing respect and support to the people you're visiting while celebrating their land and the regions or animals from which your food was harvested.

The people you meet while traveling are among the most interesting people you'll ever meet. Whether you're in a five-star hotel or a guesthouse, traveling surrounds you with people from different corners of the globe who are committed, like you, to exploring and experiencing new things. Surrender to the guides that appear in your life, whether it's a fellow traveler you meet on a train or a local who offers to show you around their hometown. Unlike the USA, most regions we've visited don't boast having supremely busy citizens who can't squeeze in time to floss their teeth. In fact, it would be unusual for us to wander around almost any town or city where there isn't a healthy handful of people who are willing to lend their free time to foster a relationship or even join us, the "strangers," for tea or a glass of wine. The unplanned connections we make often prove to be our most valued memories of a trip.

On the subject of busyness, we tend to fill our schedules to the brim during "normal life." We suspect that one of the reasons travel lends itself to such remarkable memories is that we hold the space to be mindful in the present moment. Watching sunrises over beautiful beaches or exploring winding streets in an ancient city does make the average calendar in American life. However, unlike your pilates class or board meeting, these moments more deeply seed themselves into our consciousness. They inspire us to appreciate the beauty of the world. Above all, they inspire us to plan more trips, slowing down to take in the world's magnificence.

The world is waiting for you to explore it and to enrich your flavor encyclopedia. We challenge you to take a leap and begin planning your next adventure right this moment. Whether it's a weekend getaway or a months-long trip, the joy of seeing the world is waiting for you, filled with sights and experiences that few others may experience.

YOUR TICKET TO ONENESS

The act of exploration triggers our brains into a fertile environment for new neural pathways. If you've ever heard somebody rave about being "transformed" after a trip, they aren't being melodramatic. When you enter a new environment with unfamiliar sights, smells, triggers, and languages, it interrupts the "tape" of what's going on in your head. If the messages and patterns going on in your head bring anxiety or sadness, travel isn't just exciting, but healing, too.

Among the most transformative parts of travel is the people around you. When you immerse yourself without interruptions from work or screens, you latch on more deeply to the world around you. You can live in an apartment for three years without counting the number of parking spaces in front of your house, but while traveling, you tend to notice and pay more attention to what's around you. In these few sentences alone, we've illustrated not only a pleasurable experience, but the activation of several cranial nerves that are often ignored in our daily routine, or, as it were, rut.

When you step out of your comfort zone, you create a fertile environment for new thought patterns. On the airplane, instead of watching a movie or playing a game on your phone, we challenge you to write a mantra or journal. Repeat your new mantra while you travel; you can consecrate new thoughts much more quickly while traveling than while in your day-to-day rhythms at home via the process of neurogenesis, mentioned earlier in this book.

Exploration while traveling (i.e., not sitting in the air-conditioned hotel room watching Netflix) also helps you experience the interconnectedness of all things. You may feel a sense of awe and wonder as you gaze up at the Aurora Borealis or stand at the foot of the Dolomite Mountains. You may feel a deep sense of peace and tranquility as you sit by the sea in Sardinia or walk through Sherwood Forest in England. These experiences can help you feel more connected and grounded when you return to your own life. They have illustrated to your brain that you are competent, courageous, and capable of overcoming challenges, alongside anchoring you to beauty beyond the four walls of your typical day.

When Lori embarked on a quest to learn about her father's life, her curiosity evolved into an obsession with Italy, the country from which her grandparents emigrated. In researching her roots and reconnecting with her Italian heritage, it became evident that she had a claim to Italian citizenship by descent (Jure Sanguinis) and a path to an Italian passport.

With the expertise of teams in Italy and the US, her Italian experience began in the small village of San Pietro Avellana, the land of tartufo, or truffles (not to be confused with the chocolate treat). This commune of approximately 600 residents today is where Lori's grandmother, Maria Raffaela D'Achille, was born in 1888. She arrived in New York in 1899 with her mother, Filomena Frazzini, and her brother, Agostino. They reunited with her father, Pasquale D'Achille, who arrived in the US five years earlier.

At 3,150 feet above sea level in the Apennine Mountains of Molise, where the rarest and most expensive kind of truffles are literally shaved onto every dish, San Pietro Avellana was Lori and William's temporary home. At the same time, they established residency, explored Lori's family tree, uncovered jaw-dropping family history, and savored memories that Lori unearthed from within her DNA. Lori never imagined that one day she would live in the same Italian village as her grandmother, walk in her footsteps, and become an Italian citizen.

One of the most magical aspects of traveling is the way it can help you connect with your loved ones. Whether you're traveling with family, friends, or a significant other, exploring new places and trying new things together can be a truly bonding experience.

Don't forget to collect memories along the way. Whether it's taking photos, keeping a travel journal, or simply reflecting on the experiences you've had, taking the time to document your vacation can help you relive the magic and beauty of your trip long after it's over. Digital frames at home are the perfect way of keeping your memories alive.

YOUR TICKET TO EXTRAORDINARY EXPERIENCES

If you want to create extraordinary outcomes in your life, you need to seek out extraordinary experiences. It's only by pushing yourself out of your comfort zone and exploring new horizons that you can develop the skills, insights, and perspectives that will enable you to achieve greatness.

Seeking out amazing adventures isn't just about achieving personal growth and development. It's also about creating outstanding outcomes in your life and in the world around you. When you challenge yourself and seek out new horizons, you inspire others to do the same. You create a ripple effect of positive change that can touch the lives of countless people and make the world a better place.

Embrace every experience as an opportunity to learn and grow. Explore new destinations, connect with diverse individuals, and welcome challenges, witnessing a transformative journey unfolding right before your eyes. The world has even more to offer than you might imagine.

Chapter Eighteen:
HOW TO LIVE IN A BEAUTIFUL STATE EVERY DAY

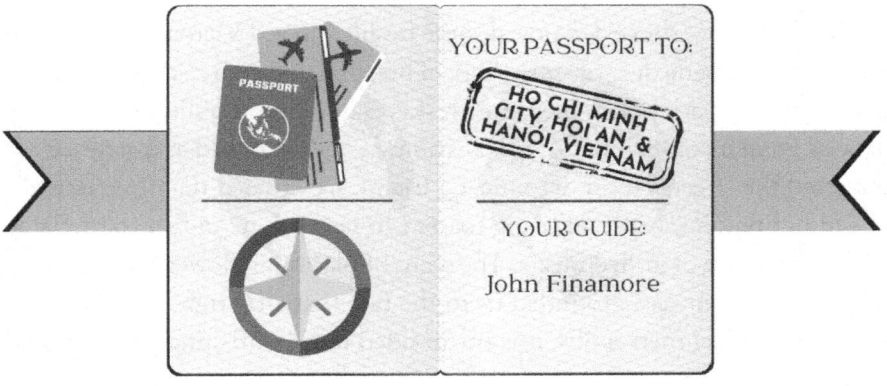

Lori and William with John Finamore exploring Vietnam.

We woke up in the economic heart of Vietnam, Ho Chi Minh City, which was formerly and famously called "Saigon." Despite the motorbikes weaving through the streets at all hours like schools of fish, with riders balancing everything from towering goods to entire families as passengers, we were cocooned in the soft embrace of "The Reverie Saigon." The haute Ho Chi Minh City hotel provided a sweet harmony to the city's skyscrapers and open-air nightclubs. Lori was wrapped in a soft, smooth silk traditional ao dai scarf. Colorful carpets, walls, hand-blown glass, and textures make walking through any room or hallway in the Reverie's decor like walking through a psychedelic forest.

"I could stay here. What about you?" asked Lori.

"I suspect this hotel is only the beginning of the intoxicating sights and colors we'll see here in Vietnam," said William.

With that, we dressed, enjoyed some freshly brewed Vietnamese coffee in the hotel, and made our way into a city of breathtaking contrast. Lotus flowers danced in city park ponds underneath sky-high modern buildings, squarely next to French colonial buildings; a striking contrast of old and new. As we traversed the streets en route to meet a friend, we inhaled the diverse smells of simmering pho, banh mi being toasted to perfection, and the tantalizing smoke fragrance of grilled meats. The scent of blooming flowers and the salty tang of the nearby sea grounded us to the fact that although Ho Chi Minh City is a bustling metropolis, it is surrounded by a flourishing, verdant, and complex landscape.

Lori stopped to mindfully inhale the delicate sliver of smoke from incense burning on an altar outside a café.

"If you think that smells good, you should get a whiff of their Pho; it's a revelation," blurted an American voice. We turned around; the voice belonged to our dear friend John Finamore, who greeted us with friendly handshakes and heartfelt hugs. "I have lots to show you today," said John.

John, who originated from Ohio but lived most of his adult life in Denver, had made it his mission over several years to explore the many parts of Vietnam and learn its unique culture.

John's eyes lit up as he pointed out the Ben Thanh Market and the historic Reunification Palace, his excitement palpable. It was common for John to stop, enthusiastically high-fiving a friend on the street and charming them with stories of his various travels or golf game with his easy Midwestern charm. After exploring the city on foot, we were famished. We stopped for "bun cha," a delightful combination of grilled pork, noodles, and fresh herbs, before returning to our hotel sanctuary to rest up for another big day.

The following morning, we left with John for the city of Hoi An. We began the trip with a visit to a local eatery John swore by for "cao lau," a dish unique to the town with its chewy noodles and savory broth. Each meal with John in Vietnam was a sensory journey, enhanced by stories of his own culinary adventures in various countries and sites around Vietnam and, of course, the friends he's made along the way.

Hoi An, with its ancient charm, offered a more tranquil visual feast than Ho Chi Minh City. Lanterns of every color imaginable lined the streets, casting a warm glow over the yellow-walled shops and riverside cafés. The Japanese Bridge, with its intricate carvings, stood as a testament to the town's varied cultural influences. John's appreciation for the town's beauty was evident as he guided us through its narrow alleys and thriving night markets. The gentle lapping of water against the riverbanks offered a melodic backdrop to the occasional notes of traditional Vietnamese music in the air.

In a few days, John led us to Hanoi, a city whose soundscape was a mix of Ho Chi Minh City and peaceful Hoi An. Returning to the nonstop rhythm of an energetic town, replete with motorbikes and street vendors, was initially overwhelming to our senses after the serenity and gentle pace of Hoi An.

We readily immersed ourselves in the intricate dance of commerce and survival beneath the looming shadows of French colonial architecture and gleaming skyscrapers in Hanoi. The hustle and bustle of the city was met with the serene sounds of nature—Hanoi is rich with lakes and public parks. We found serenity at the Jade Emperor Pagoda, where the heavy scent of incense carried our thoughts skyward as elderly devotees whispered prayers among tortoise ponds and elaborate wood carvings that seemed to hold centuries of unspoken wisdom.

John's voice, warm and engaging, tied these auditory experiences together, his laughter and stories adding depth to every moment.

In Hanoi, the serene Hoan Kiem Lake, with its "turtle tower" in the center, contrasted sharply with the animated Old Quarter, where street vendors sold everything from fresh produce to handcrafted goods. John's favorite spots included the Temple of Literature and the tranquil West Lake, where he often found peace amidst the chaos.

John Finamore reminded us that living in a beautiful state every day is a tangible reality. His joy for life, curiosity, and deep connections with people and places transformed our journey through Vietnam into a profound and uplifting experience. From the dynamic streets of Ho Chi Minh City to the serene alleys of Hoi An and the historical depths of Hanoi, John's presence ensured that each day was filled with beauty, wonder, and the heartfelt connections that make life truly extraordinary.

LIVING IN A BEAUTIFUL STATE

*"Every new day is a chance to make each moment count,
turning ordinary into extraordinary.
Embrace the opportunity to create your Best Day Ever,
one positive choice at a time."*
Lori and William Small

We've cultivated the habit of waking up each morning with the determination to turn the day into something extraordinary. Whether our schedule is packed or it's a regular day in Aspen, we actively seek opportunities to make it exceptional.

When we're jet-setting to our favorite destinations, discovering exciting activities, indulging in memorable meals, and exploring new surroundings, crafting a fabulous day feels almost effortless.

However, even during our routine days at home in Aspen, we're on the lookout for chances to infuse a touch of magic. It might mean carving a few exhilarating runs down the slopes, then lingering over lunch at a favorite

CHAPTER EIGHTEEN: HOW TO LIVE IN A BEAUTIFUL STATE EVERY DAY

mountain spot—glass of wine in hand, surrounded by a breathtaking atmosphere.

In the summer, a scenic bike ride to Pine Creek Cookhouse or a brief hike in the mountains allows us to immerse ourselves in nature for a couple of hours. In the evenings, a candlelit dinner at home paired with a splendid bottle of wine becomes a cherished ritual. We make it a point never to let a day pass without seizing an opportunity to make it truly special.

All of us encounter circumstances that challenge our inner state of being. We may find ourselves caught in the trap of expectations, constantly yearning for something different or better. However, by making a conscious choice to live in a beautiful state every day, regardless of external circumstances, you can transcend suffering and find joy, peace, and fulfillment. Among the most critical, immutable laws of living our Best Day Every Day is this: trade expectation for appreciation.

Living in a beautiful state starts with recognizing that you have the power to choose your state of mind and emotional well-being. Despite the external events and challenges you face, you can consciously decide to respond with positivity, gratitude, and appreciation. This power lies within you and can be harnessed to shape your experience of life.

Expectations can be a major source of suffering. When you constantly cling to specific outcomes or idealized versions of reality, you set yourself up for disappointment and frustration. By releasing your expectations and embracing the present moment as it is, you free yourself from the burden of attachment and open the door to a more beautiful state of being.

Trading expectation for appreciation involves shifting your focus from what you lack to what you already have. By cultivating a practice of gratitude, you train your mind to notice and appreciate the blessings, big and small, that surround you. Through this shift in perspective, you uncover the inherent beauty and abundance in your life, leading to a greater sense of fulfillment and contentment.

Living in a beautiful state requires you to immerse yourself in the present moment fully. By being fully present, you become attuned to the richness and beauty that exists in every experience. Whether it's the simple pleasures of nature, the warmth of human connection, or the joy of self-expression, you learn to savor and appreciate the beauty that unfolds before you.

Life is a constant flux of change, and clinging to fixed expectations can hinder your ability to adapt and find joy in the evolving nature of existence. By accepting and embracing impermanence, you open yourself up to the possibilities that each moment holds. You learn to let go of resistance and flow with the ever-changing rhythms of life, finding beauty and growth even in the face of uncertainty.

Choosing to live in a beautiful state requires cultivating a positive mindset. By consciously directing your thoughts towards optimism, self-compassion, and kindness, you create an internal environment that nurtures joy and well-being. Through daily affirmations, positive self-talk, and surrounding yourself with uplifting influences, you pave the way for a more beautiful life.

Chapter Nineteen:
FIND JOY IN THE JOURNEY, NOT JUST THE DESTINATION

Lori and William with Arrigo Cipriano at Harry's Bar in Venice, Italy.

The golden light of a Venetian sunset shimmered across the Grand Canal as we stepped off a sleek Riva wooden water taxi onto the worn marble steps leading to Harry's Bar. The air was thick with the briny scent of the lagoon, mingled with the subtle fragrance of centuries-old palazzos and the sweet smell of fresh pastries drifting from nearby bakeries.

As William pushed open the heavy wooden door, the sounds of the spirited city gave way to the gentle murmur of sophisticated conversation and the soft clink of crystal glasses. The warm glow of art deco lamps bathed the intimate space in a golden hue, highlighting the polished wood paneling and gleaming brass fixtures that have borne witness to decades of Venetian history.

Arrigo Cipriani, Author of *Harry's Bar - The Life and Times of the Legendary Venice Landmark*, is the embodiment of timeless elegance and quiet confidence. He greeted us with a firm handshake and a knowing smile. His presence filled the room, not with bravado, but with an air of assured competence that speaks volumes about true leadership.

"Welcome to Harry's Bar," he says, his voice a rich baritone that carries the weight of generations. "Here, we don't just serve drinks; we serve experiences, memories, and a taste of La Dolce Vita."

As he guided us to a coveted corner table, our fingers brushed against the smooth, cool surface of the white-clothed tabletop. The fabric was crisp and pristine, a testament to the unwavering attention to detail that has made Harry's Bar a legend.

The first sip of the bar's famous Bellini was a revelation—the delicate sweetness of white peach puree danced on our tongues, perfectly balanced by the crisp effervescence of Prosecco. It was a sensory embodiment of Cipriani's philosophy: simplicity elevated to an art form.

As plates of carpaccio—paper-thin slices of raw beef—arrived, the bright red provided a stark contrast against the white china. Arrigo shared tales of the bar's illustrious history. His words painted vivid pictures of Hemingway bent over his notebook, Orson Welles holding court at the bar, and countless other luminaries who graced those hallowed walls.

The rich, savory smell of risotto al nero di seppia (risotto with squid ink) drifted through the air, its inky darkness a culinary metaphor for the depths of experience that inform true leadership, like Arrigo's. As we savored each perfectly al dente grain of rice infused with the essence of the sea, Cipriani's

CHAPTER NINETEEN: FIND JOY IN THE JOURNEY, NOT JUST THE DESTINATION

wisdom flowed as smoothly as the Amarone he'd selected to accompany the meal.

"Leadership," he mused, swirling the deep red wine in his glass, "is like crafting the perfect cocktail. It requires precision, balance, and a deep understanding of your ingredients—in this case, people. But most importantly, it demands confidence—not in oneself alone, but in one's vision and in those who help bring it to life."

As the evening progressed, the sounds of Venice filtered through the open windows: the gentle lapping of water against gondolas, the distant toll of church bells, the melodious Italian conversations floating on the breeze. These sounds mingled with the stories and laughter within Harry's Bar, creating a chorus of *la bella vita*.

The cool touch of the marble bar top, the soft leather of the bar stools, and the delicate stem of our wine glasses were all sensations that reinforced the night's greater lesson: true luxury, like true leadership, lies in the details.

As the night drew to a close, we stepped out onto the Calle Vallaresso. The cobblestones beneath our feet were still warm from the day's sun. The taste of Harry's Bar lingered as we strolled through Venice—not just the flavors of exquisite food and drink, but the essence of confidence, leadership, and timeless style that Arrigo Cipriani embodied.

Venice represents a labyrinth of possibilities illuminated by the soft glow of street lamps. In this moment, infused with the wisdom and charisma of Cipriani, we felt ready to navigate our own paths with newfound confidence and grace, inspired by the living legend of Harry's Bar.

Venice, Italy, with its unique canals, historic architecture, and rich culture, offers visitors profound experiences and life lessons. Here are three key life lessons that can be learned from a visit to this iconic destination:

1. EMBRACE ADAPTABILITY AND RESILIENCE

Adaptability is essential for overcoming challenges.

Venice is a city built on water, facing constant challenges from flooding, rising sea levels, and erosion. The city's historical resilience is evident in its architectural adaptations, such as the raised foundations and innovative flood defenses like the MOSE project.

Venice teaches us that facing environmental and situational challenges with creativity and determination is vital. Just as the Venetians have adapted their city over centuries, we too can approach our personal and professional obstacles with flexibility and innovative thinking.

As you walk through Venice's alleys and observe the city's infrastructure adapting to its unique environment, you may find inspiration in adaptive features like floating barriers and elevated walkways, inspiring you to embrace change and find solutions in your own life.

2. CHERISH AND PRESERVE CULTURAL HERITAGE

Protecting cultural heritage is essential for future generations.

Venice is a UNESCO World Heritage Site, known for its striking architecture, art, and history. The city's preservation efforts are a testament to the importance of maintaining cultural heritage for future generations to appreciate and learn from.

Venice reminds us of the value of preserving our own cultural and historical legacies. This can extend to safeguarding family traditions, supporting local arts, or contributing to the conservation of historical sites.

While visiting the Doge's Palace or St. Mark's Basilica, you see how Venice preserves its rich history through art and architecture. These experiences can motivate you to support conservation efforts and appreciate the cultural heritage in your own community.

3. FIND JOY IN THE JOURNEY, NOT JUST THE DESTINATION

The journey itself can be as rewarding as the destination.

Venice's charm often lies in the leisurely exploration of its labyrinthine canals, hidden squares, and quaint shops. The city's allure comes not just from famous landmarks but from the experience of wandering through its streets and soaking in the ambiance.

Venice teaches us to savor the journey rather than just focusing on the final goals. It's a reminder to enjoy the process of reaching your objectives, cherishing the experiences along the way rather than just anticipating the end result.

While taking a gondola ride or a slow walk through the winding streets of Venice, the pleasure is in the exploration and discovery of the city's hidden gems, mirroring the idea that finding joy in the journey is essential for a fulfilling life.

Chapter Twenty:
LESSONS FROM OUR FATHERS

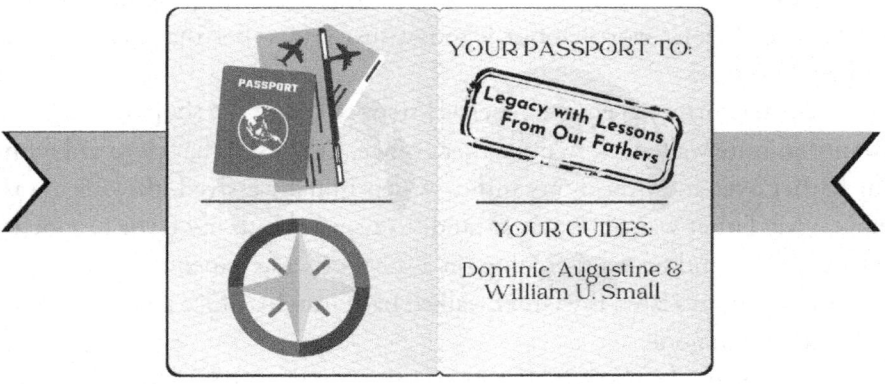

YOUR PASSPORT TO:

Legacy with Lessons From Our Fathers

YOUR GUIDES:

Dominic Augustine & William U. Small

WILLIAM U. SMALL
William's Father

I was eight years old when my father left me at the barber shop by myself to get my haircut near the end of my school year. He had finished his own cut and left to go back to the office. Now it was my turn. As I sat in the giant barber's chair, I watched the barber in the grandiose mirror. He had cut my hair for as long as I could remember with an adept flurry of his scissors and barber's shears. The barber kept the conversation going by asking me about what I was doing that summer and if I had plans to go to summer camp. I responded to his questions as best I could, occasionally daydreaming.

After half an hour, he was done. He took off the giant cap and shook my hair from it. He then gave me a dusting around my neck with a soft brush that bore an equally soft scent. I climbed down from the chair and reached into my pocket to give him the fifty cents my father had given me to pay for the cut. As he reached over to take the money, he said, "Oh, I recently raised my price to seventy-five cents." He pointed to a poster on the wall.

Not knowing what to do, I froze. Fifty cents was all my dad had given me. For a moment, I thought of all the worst scenarios that could result in my inability to pay. Was he going to hold me hostage? Would he call the police and have me arrested like on TV?

I didn't know what to do, so I started to cry. Sensing my distress, he kindly said, "Don't worry about it today, just remember that next time it will be 75 cents."

I felt an enormous sense of relief as I stepped out of the shop. During the twenty-minute walk back to my father's office, I replayed that close call with the barber over and over in my mind. When I finally arrived, the office was empty. My father was out on an errand, so I settled into my favorite spot at the extra desk and began sketching on a sheet of scrap paper.

A few minutes later, my father walked back into his office and asked how my haircut had gone.

"It was okay," I answered. Then I casually mentioned that the barber had increased prices to seventy-five cents for a haircut.

"Don't worry about it," responded my dad. He silently reached into his pocket and pulled out a quarter.

"I want you to walk back to the barbershop and give him this quarter."

"Do I really have to? He said not to worry about it. And, besides, it's a twenty-minute walk both ways."

"Yes, you're going to learn a valuable lesson today."

I reluctantly took the quarter and walked the twenty minutes back to the barbershop. When I walked in, the barber, who was working on another customer, looked at me, puzzled. I walked up to him, pulled the quarter out of my pocket, and gave it to him.

"This wasn't necessary," he said. But he thanked me, anyway.

"My father insisted," I replied.

"Your father wants you to learn a valuable lesson today," he smiled.

I left and walked the twenty minutes back to my father's office. I felt a sense of dignity. In fact, I felt even more relieved than when I'd gotten a discounted cut. My guilt was gone. I realized that even though I didn't need to do what I had just done, it really felt good. I learned that day that doing the right thing, even when it's complicated or inconvenient, is empowering. I have always remembered that day. That feeling represents a powerful lesson I learned.

DOMINIC AUGUSTINE
Lori's Father

I was nine years old, trailing behind my father as he navigated a new postal route near our home in the rolling hills of Mansfield, Ohio. It was one of the first sunny Saturdays I truly felt like myself again after a terrifying health scare. I had recently recovered from an Arbovirus infection—a mosquito-borne illness that can attack the nervous system, sometimes leading to encephalitis or meningitis. My stiff neck had sent doctors into high alert, and I was quickly incubated, isolated for weeks under the assumption I might be contagious. It was a serious ordeal, and while I fully recovered, the experience stays with me to this day.

My dad, always the noble protector, never stopped worrying about me after that. He found little ways to keep me close, like inviting me along on his mail route. It wasn't just about showing me his world—it was his way of reassuring himself that I was honestly okay.

To my father, being a mail carrier was more than delivering envelopes and packages; it was about service, reliability, and quiet pride in a job well done. As we strolled through the neighborhood together one afternoon, he explained the importance of delivering each piece of mail promptly and with care. Letters held stories—wedding invitations, college acceptance letters, paychecks, and sometimes, final goodbyes. Every delivery mattered, no matter how small.

One day, we faced an unexpected challenge: a missing mailbox.

"There's supposed to be one here," my father said, squinting at his route map, puzzled.

I watched him scratch his head, contemplating its whereabouts. Just as he was about to move on, I noticed something unusual. Eager to help, I trudged through the overgrown grass, and there it was—a small, weathered mailbox, nearly swallowed by tangled vines.

My father laughed, a mix of relief and pride. "You found it! Great job!" He showed me how to tuck the letters inside, emphasizing the importance of persistence and attention to detail.

That moment left an imprint. It wasn't just about finding a hidden mailbox—it was about problem-solving, teamwork, and the satisfaction of making someone else's life a little easier. Walking back to the truck, I felt empowered by my contribution. Even then, I understood: The smallest efforts can make the most significant difference.

My father was a man of quiet strength and an unwavering work ethic. He wore his postal uniform with pride, not because it was glamorous, but because it represented something bigger—service, community, and commitment. He often went beyond the call of duty, keeping an eye on elderly neighbors, holding packages for vacationing families, and offering a kind word to anyone having a rough day.

Years later, while immersed in the glamorous world of high fashion and earning more money than my father ever did as a mailman, I couldn't shake the feeling that something was missing. I had achieved what many would call success, yet fulfillment escaped me. My father's quiet wisdom stayed with me: "Success is about finding meaning in what you do and who you become along the way."

That realization sparked a change. It was time to shift gears and contribute to something greater. Fitness has always been a passion of mine. Ever since my days as a student-athlete, I loved the way working out made me look and feel. It gave me strength, clarity, and confidence. So, I channeled my internal drive, set new standards, and mastered the art of physical fitness and well-being, becoming a certified personal trainer at the age of forty.

But my actual "aha moment" came five years after my father's passing. He had fought cancer for 25 years—a quarter of a century defined by resilience, grit, and grace. I watched my dad transition from a strong, active man, retiring at 53, to someone gradually slowed by illness. Seeing his once-powerful stride falter lit a fire within me.

I embarked on a quest to stop poisoning my body, to invest in my health, and to become a living example of vitality. It wasn't just about personal transformation. It was about honoring my father's legacy. If he had taught me anything, it was that life's true riches lie not in what you accumulate but in how you show up—for yourself and others.

My father's journey taught me the power of resilience, the importance of purpose, and the value of human connection. He may not have worn designer clothes or closed million-dollar deals, but he lived a life of quiet significance—one mailbox, one conversation, one act of kindness at a time.

Today, I stand as a testament to enduring vitality and timeless style, fueled by the lessons my father unknowingly imparted. His legacy lives on with every client I inspire and every moment I choose health over complacency.

Being the postman's daughter taught me that true success is about delivering more than what's expected. It's about showing up, doing your best, and leaving the world a little better than you found it. And in that pursuit, you discover the richest reward of all: a life well lived.

CONCLUSION

"Our power lies in staying steady, no matter how hard the impact."
Lori & William Small

Lori Small

It was 9:00 p.m. in Denver on December 22, 2019.

We had just spent the weekend in New York with my best girlfriends, returning from a "Sex and the City" reunion. This was our thirtieth year of celebrating a "Christmas Luncheon," a tradition rooted in the glamorous fashion world where my friendships with these women were born.

This flight from JFK to Denver seemed routine enough. The flight attendant announced that we were on our final approach to Denver, and William, immersed in the last chapter of his Clive Cussler novel, only half-listened. Outside my window, the white peaks of the DIA terminal glowed against the night sky, a striking contrast to the inky darkness around us. We were ready to be home. It's always a joy to return—but especially to Aspen, with its breathtaking alpine peaks and crisp mountain air.

William mentioned being nervous about the tight connection to catch our connecting flight from Denver to Aspen. He muttered something about "comfortable shoes in case we have to run."

I didn't feel the anxiety; I was still reveling in the festivities and energy of the city we'd left behind, unaware that we were about to have the scare of our lives.

When the passengers on UAL Flight 1211, approaching Denver Airport from New York, heard from the cockpit, "Denver Approach, this is United 1211 descending to 12,000, information Charlie."

Denver Approach responded, "United 1211, turn left heading 180, maintain 7,000 until established on the localizer, cleared ILS runway 16R approach."

The captain on our flight responded, "Denver Tower, United 1211, with you on the ILS runway 16R," to which Denver Tower replied, "United 1211, Denver Tower, wind 150 at 10, runway 16R cleared to land."

Our captain responded, "Cleared to land runway 16R, United 1211."

However, when the plane approached the runway, we heard an explosive bang, followed by the deafening thud of metal meeting tarmac. Sparks flew past the windows like fireworks gone wrong, illuminating the night. The Boeing 757 lurched violently, swinging back and forth as the cabin lights flickered. The plane was skidding out of control.

We instinctively grabbed each other's hands as the chaos around us unfolded. It felt like the world had turned upside down in a matter of seconds. No turbulence, no warning, no time to prepare—just panic. The plane continued to veer, sliding across the runway at what felt like an impossible speed. Outside, sparks cascaded from the left engine as the metal screeched against the concrete, leaving an eerie trail of orange in the dark.

Amid the confusion, the older gentleman seated next to us, Gregory, remained unfazed. A retired commercial pilot with decades of experience, he sat calm and composed as if this were just another day in the skies.

"You don't always get a warning," he said, his voice steady, almost serene. "Life doesn't always give you time to brace yourself. It hits when it hits, and the trick is to find your center, no matter how hard the impact."

His words were grounding, a thread of calm running through the storm. The plane finally came to a stop, and the silence that followed was deafening. In those quiet, tense moments, Gregory's wisdom sank in. Life, much like that landing, often takes sudden, unpredictable turns. It throws sparks at you when you least expect it, but real strength is found in how you choose to respond. Resilience isn't about avoiding the rough patches; it's about how you handle them when they come.

A few moments later, the pilot came on the loudspeaker. "Ladies and Gentlemen, the landing gear on the left side of the plane collapsed as we hit the runway," he explained. "There is no fire, but we're waiting for emergency vehicles to arrive."

Through the window, we could see the flashing lights of fire trucks and ambulances racing toward us. Everyone sat in stunned silence, processing the fact that we had just crash-landed in Denver. We were shaken, but safe.

CONCLUSION

As we finally disembarked using emergency staircases, we carried Gregory's calm with us. He had given us a powerful reminder—resilience is forged in moments of chaos, not calm. When life sends sparks flying, the greatest wisdom is staying grounded, no matter how unexpected or intense the descent.

And in the end, as incredible as it seemed, we still made our connecting flight to Aspen that evening, arriving home on schedule. Because even when life veers off course, there's always a way to regain your footing—and often, still arrive precisely where you're meant to be.

The crash landing taught us a powerful lesson: resilience isn't about avoiding life's sudden, jarring moments, but about how we respond to them. Sparks will fly, chaos will erupt, and it's in those moments that we learn our true strength. Gregory, with his calm presence, reminded us that when things don't go according to plan, our power lies in staying steady, no matter how hard the impact.

Life is unpredictable, but as you train your brain and strengthen your mind with the exercises in this book, even unexpected setbacks become easier to navigate. The key is not to avoid unfavorable circumstances, but to move through them with strength and intention.

Airlines lose luggage. Storms cause delays. Jobs are lost. But when your mind is a place of peace, even life's disruptions become more than just manageable—they can become catalysts for joy and growth.

Neuroscientists agree that rewiring the brain happens through one of two experiences—one far more desirable than the other. The first is a sudden shift brought on by trauma. Needless to say, we don't recommend that path to personal growth! The second is through consistent habit formation.

Throughout this book, we've shared stories and insights from over three dozen guides across more than thirty cities, illustrating how we've spent a lifetime building habits that lead to a beautiful, fulfilling life. The best part?

The journey never truly ends. The rewards of self-improvement will continue to unfold—right up to your very last breath.

By deciding to live in a beautiful state every day and shifting your focus from expectation to appreciation, you unlock the keys to a more fulfilling and joyful existence, which we like to refer to as living the Best Day Every Day. By trading expectation for appreciation, you let go of the need for external validation and instead cultivate a deep sense of self-acceptance and inner peace. You become the author and director of your life and the architect of your own happiness.

True fulfillment lies not in the pursuit of external achievements but in your ability to cultivate a beautiful state of mind, regardless of circumstances. Each day, choose to embrace the beauty that surrounds you, to appreciate the abundance in your life, and to live in a state of gratitude and love. In doing so, you'll create a life that's not just successful, but truly worth celebrating.

We're grateful for your interest in reading our book. We hope to cross paths with you on your journey, guiding you towards making your days, weeks, months, and years the best and most enjoyable they can be.

To your Best Day Every Day,

Lori and William Small

A POEM FOR MY DAD

BY LORI SMALL

"If I Could Only"

If I could only...
Take one more walk on the beach with you,
Find one more shark's tooth in the sand with you,
Watch one more sunset on the horizon with you,
Reel in one more fish from Lake Erie with you,
Play one more hand of poker with you,
Dance one more polka at a wedding with you,
Sing one more song at church with you,
Listen to one more beat of the drums with you,
Hop from one more garage sale to another with you,
Share one more piece of banana cream pie with you,
Sunbathe just once more by the pool with you,
Husk one more ear of corn with you,
Pick one more strawberry from the fields with you,
Churn one more batch of homemade ice cream with you,
Roast one more marshmallow over the fire with you,
Play one more April Fool's joke on you,
Visit one more amusement park with you,
Go to Midnight Mass one last time with you,
Have one more Valentine's Day with you,
Blow out one more candle on my birthday with you,
Shoot one more basketball in the hoop with you,
Perform yo-yo tricks in the basement with you,

Play one more round of golf with you,
Watch one more football game with you,
Choose one more Kentucky Derby horse with you,
Build one more snowman in a blizzard with you,
Find one more mailbox and deliver the mail with you,
If I could only say, "I love you" one more time.
Still…If I could only…

"Don't cry because it's over,
smile because it happened."
- Dr. Seuss

Appendix A: RESOURCES FOR CONFIDENCE TRAINING FURTHER STUDY

"33 Strategies of War"
by Robert Green
Find on Amazon at https://amzn.to/3KSJYYJ

"Becoming Supernatural"
by Joe Dispenza
Find on Amazon at https://amzn.to/46A0NjP

"Bliss Brain"
by Dr. Dawson Church
Find on Amazon at https://amzn.to/46AvzsL

"Bowling Alone"
by Robert Putnam
Find on Amazon at https://amzn.to/4pUSxlQ

"Choose Yourself!"
by James Altucher
Find on Amazon at https://amzn.to/4gXQycD

"Enchiridion"
by Epictetus
Find on Amazon at https://amzn.to/4889tiy

"Dodging Energy Vampires: An Empath's Guide to Evading Relationships That Drain You and Restoring Your Health and Power"
by Christine Northrup
Find on Amazon at https://amzn.to/3KxCcUa

"Extreme Ownership"
by Jocko Willink
Find on Amazon at https://amzn.to/42otfCM

"Flow"
by Mihaly Csikszentmihalyi
Find on Amazon at https://amzn.to/3KzwFfM

"Getting Things Done"
by David Allen
Find on Amazon at https://amzn.to/477X0dF

"Gut Feelings: The Intelligence of the Unconscious"
by Gerd Gigerenzer
Find on Amazon at https://amzn.to/46P9UMdn

"How To Have Confidence and Power In Dealing With People"
by Leslie T. Giblin
Find on Amazon at https://amzn.to/3ITdWLK

"Leadership & Self-Deception: The Secret to Transforming Relationships and Unleashing Results"
by the Arbinger Institute
Find on Amazon at https://amzn.to/3ITdWLK

"Letters on Ethics"
by Lucilius Annaeus Seneca
Find on Amazon at
  https://amzn.to/4gTMGJD

"Lifetide: A Biology of the Unconscious"
by Lyall Watson
Find on Amazon at
  https://amzn.to/4gTMGJD

"Mating in Captivity" by Esther Perel
Find on Amazon at https://amzn.to/4o279hK

"Maybe You Should Talk To Someone: A Therapist, HER Therapist, and Our Lives Revealed"
by Lori Gottleib
Find on Amazon: https://amzn.to/3VOLpd5

"Meditations"
by Marcus Aurelius
Find on Amazon at https://amzn.to/3IU9c8z

"Mindset: The Psychology of Success" by Carol Dweck
Find on Amazon at https://amzn.to/4o2a0ak

"Power Vs. Force: The Hidden Determinants of Human Behavior"
by David Hawkins
Find on Amazon at https://amzn.to/4o2a0ak

"Rethinking Narcissism: The Secret to Recognizing and Coping with Narcissists"
by Craig Malkin
Find on Amazon at https://amzn.to/3KzBK7V

"Rhythms of Vision: The Changing Patterns of Myth and Consciousness"
by Lawrence Blair
Find on Amazon at https://amzn.to/3KzBK7V

"Should I Stay Or Should I Go? Surviving A Relationship with A Narcissist"
by Ramani Durvasula, PhD
Find on Amazon at https://amzn.to/4o7wzL4

"Switch On: "
by Nick Seneca Jenkel
Find on Amazon at https://amzn.to/3KvlEfD

"Switch On Your Brain: The Key to Peak Happiness, Thinking, and Health"
by Dr. Caroline Leaf
Find on Amazon: https://amzn.to/4mPfrbN

"The Beauty Myth"
by Naomi Wolf
Find on Amazon: https://amzn.to/3IFbHM3

"The Big Leap: Conquer Your Hidden Fear and Take Life to the Next Level"
by Gay Hendricks
Find on Amazon: https://amzn.to/3IFbHM3

"The Body Keeps The Score: Brain, Mind and Body In The Healing of Trauma"
by Bessel Van Der Kolk, MD
Find on Amazon: https://amzn.to/4gUp3kd

"The Daily Stoic"
by Ryan Holiday
Find on Amazon: https://amzn.to/4o4vWSl

"The Four Agreements"
by Don Miguel Ruiz
Find on Amazon: https://amzn.to/3KzzhKD

"The Feminine Mystique"
by Betty Friedan
Find on Amazon: https://amzn.to/46yOFzw

"The Hundredth Monkey"
by Ken Keyes Jr.
Find on Amazon: https://amzn.to/4mPbsMe

"The Power of No: Because One Little Word Can Bring Health, Abundance, and Happiness"
by James Altucher
Find on Amazon: https://amzn.to/3Krx2cr

"The Spiritual Practice of Creating Income"
by Susan Lustenberger
Find on Amazon: https://amzn.to/4mJDfxP

"The State of Affairs: Rethinking Infidelity"
by Esther Perel
Find on Amazon: https://amzn.to/46SbVay

"The Truth"
by Neil Strauss
Find on Amazon: https://amzn.to/3IRwv2S

"Think and Grow Rich"
by Napoleon Hill
Find on Amazon: https://amzn.to/3WjIfOH

"Total Gut Reset: Optimize Your Health With Your Second Brain"
by Dr. Lauryn Lax
Find on Amazon: https://amzn.to/3WkgiGq

"You Are The Placebo"
by Joe Dispenza
Find on Amazon: https://amzn.to/3VOLpd5

LECTURES/ WEBINARS/ TALKS

"Understanding Women: Unlock the Mystery"
by Alison Armstrong
On Audible: https://amzn.to/4pZ5hZ4

"Rethinking Infidelity"
by Esther Perel
https://www.ted.com/talks/esther_perel_rethinking_infidelity_a_talk_for_anyone_who_has_ever_loved

"The Secret To Desire in A Long-term Relationship"
by Esther Perel:
https://www.ted.com/talks/esther_perel_the_secret_to_desire_in_a_long_term_relationship?language=en#t-358181

"Five Secrets from Psychology That make People Respect You"
by Tony Robbins
https://m.youtube.com/watch?v=Kb95t_v25Dw

"Your Body Language May Shape Who You Are"
by Amy Cuddy
https://m.youtube.com/watch?v=Ks-_Mh1QhMc

NOTES

Made in the USA
Coppell, TX
05 March 2026

72965010R00174